COOPERATIVES AT WORK

The Future of Work

The future of work is a vital contemporary area of debate both in business and management research, and in wider social, political and economic discourse. Globally relevant issues, including the aging workforce, rise of the gig economy, workplace automation and changing forms of business ownership, are all regularly the subject of discussion in both academic research and the mainstream media, having wider professional and public policy implications.

The Future of Work series features books examining key issues or challenges in the modern workplace, synthesizing prior developments in critical thinking, alongside current practical challenges in order to interrogate possible future developments in the world of work.

Offering future research agendas and suggesting practical outcomes for today's and tomorrow's businesses and workforce, the books in this series present a powerful, challenging and polemical analysis of a diverse range of subjects in their potential to address future challenges and possible new trajectories.

The series highlights what changes still need to be made to core areas of business practice and theory in order for them to be forward-facing, more representative and able to fulfill the industrial challenges of the future.

OTHER TITLES IN THE SERIES

HR Without People? Industrial Evolution in the Age of Automation, AI, and Machine Learning

Anthony R. Wheeler and Ronald M. Buckley

The Healthy Workforce: Enhancing Wellbeing and Productivity in the Workers of the Future

Stephen Bevan and Cary L. Cooper

FORTHCOMING TITLES

Spending Without Thinking: The Future of Consumption

Richard Whittle

The Cybersecurity Workforce of Tomorrow

Michael Nizich

COOPERATIVES AT WORK

BY

GEORGE CHENEY
University of Colorado, USA

MATT NOYES
*Solidarity Economy Educator and Organizer,
USA*

EMI DO
*Cooperative Educator and Organizer,
Canada*

MARCELO VIETA
University of Toronto, Canada

JOSEBA AZKARRAGA
University of the Basque Country, Spain

And

CHARLIE MICHEL
*Mission West Community Development
Partners, USA*

United Kingdom – North America – Japan – India
Malaysia – China

Emerald Publishing Limited
Howard House, Wagon Lane, Bingley BD16 1WA, UK

First edition 2023

British Library Cataloguing in Publication Data
A catalogue record for this book is available from the British Library

ISBN: 978-1-83867-828-9 (Print)
ISBN: 978-1-83867-825-8 (Online)
ISBN: 978-1-83867-827-2 (Epub)

ISOQAR certified
Management System,
awarded to Emerald
for adherence to
Environmental
standard
ISO 14001:2004.

Certificate Number 1985
ISO 14001

INVESTOR IN PEOPLE

CONTENTS

ABOUT THE AUTHORS

George Cheney (PhD, Purdue University, 1985) is Professor Emeritus in communication at the University of Colorado, Colorado Springs. He has published extensively on issues of identity, democracy, marketization, and ethics at work; also on economic justice, peace studies, and environmental issues. He has taught at and visited numerous universities in the United States, Western Europe, Latin America, and New Zealand. Currently, he is a facilitator and consultant, focused on equitable food systems, affordable housing/land access, and cooperative work solutions. He resides in Cortez, Colorado, in the Four Corners region of the US Southwest. He is a frequent contributor of op-eds and essays to newspapers and other outlets.

Matt Noyes (MA, Mondragon University, 2017) is a social movement educator and organizer living in Colorado Springs, Colorado, USA. He is a writer and translator of books and articles on solidarity economy, popular education, worker cooperatives, and union democracy and reform. He is a member of the Grassroots Economic Organizing Collective and several cooperatives, including Social.Coop, May-First.Coop, and the Colorado Solidarity Fund. Matt studied political economy at the New School for Social Research and cooperative organization and social economy at Mondragon

University, and has taught in unions, worker centers, and other movement organizations and universities in the United States and Japan.

Emi Do (PhD, Tokyo University of Agriculture, 2020) is a cooperative educator and organizer living in Vancouver, BC, Canada. Formerly an Assistant Professor in the Department of International Food and Agriculture Science at Tokyo University of Agriculture, she has taught and presented about agricultural cooperatives, cooperative education and governance. Her other areas of research include urban agriculture, local food systems, and food literacy initiatives. She is a member of unfiltered.coop and social.coop, and sits on the editorial board of the Asia Pacific Cooperative Research Partnership.

Marcelo Vieta (PhD, York University, Canada, 2012) is Associate Professor in the Adult Education and Community Development program and Director of the Centre for Learning, Social Economy & Work at the Ontario Institute for Studies in Education, University of Toronto. Marcelo has published on the social and solidarity economy, workplace democracy, and labor activism in the Global North and South, including *Workers' Self-Management in Argentina* (Brill/Haymarket, 2020) and *The Italian Road to Recuperating Enterprises and the Legge Marcora Framework* (EURICSE, 2017). Marcelo serves on the Canadian Association for Studies in Cooperation board and is an Americas representative on the International Cooperative Alliance's Committee on Cooperative Research.

Joseba Azkarraga, PhD in Sociology (University of the Basque Country, 2006) and in Psychology (Universitat Ramon Llull, Catalunya, 2021). He was a member of the cooperative movement of Mondragón for 15 years, as a professor and researcher at the University of Mondragon. Currently, he is Professor in sociology at the University of the Basque Country (Department of Sociology and Social Work, Education Faculty of Bilbao). He has published on issues of social economy, education, socioecological transition, food sovereignty, and postgrowth/degrowth. His focus is on the radical cultural change required for postgrowth societies. He resides in Durango (Basque Country, in Spain) and participates in the Basque ecological movement.

Charlie Michel (MS, Case Western Reserve University, 2017) is Regional Food Systems Program Coordinator for Mission West Community Development Partners (Ronan, Montana, USA). His background encompasses field work, advocacy, and education in agriculture, sustainability, and cooperatives. He is currently pursuing a Master of Management in Cooperatives and Credit Unions through Saint Mary's University (Halifax, Nova Scotia, Canada) using his work with the Northwest Food Hub Network as the focal point of his research. He currently resides in Spokane, Washington where he is active in the local food system and cooperative economy.

PREFACE

Worker cooperatives have held great promise since they first appeared on the economic scene almost two centuries ago. Interestingly, they have roots with *both* organized labor and social reformers at the end of the eighteenth century and the first half of the nineteenth century. Worker co-ops also stem from efforts by groups of people to control their own economic and social destinies in line with humanitarian, democratic, egalitarian, and sometimes revolutionary values. This vision has been made concrete in countless cases of people taking their work and social futures into their own hands, working against many obstacles and fashioning possibilities that many politicians and business leaders said were unrealistic or even impossible.

Worker co-ops represent one important way to address the multiple, interrelated crises of our times. Social, economic, political, health, and environmental crises have become even more apparent with the persistent pandemic of COVID-19 and its variants. For instance, the crisis of democracy today is bound up with economic inequality, racial injustice, and environmental degradation. The inadequacy of the coordinated global response to the pandemic is due to a variety of factors, but among those are inequitable distribution of resources as well as social and political divisions that undermine deep cooperation on public health, environmental stewardship, and the dignity of labor.

Worker co-ops have the capacity to maximize democratic practice and provide economic security for workers and their communities. Worker cooperatives at their best maximize shared ownership and self-governance. In places such as Emilia Romagna (Italy), The Basque Country (Spain), Québec (Canada), South Korea, Argentina, Brazil, and India, high concentrations of cooperatives, including worker co-ops, have made significant and well-documented contributions to the health and well-being of individuals, households, and communities.

Some of the most exciting experiments in worker cooperativism are embedded in larger projects and networks that involve community and movement organizing as well as focused development of an enterprise. These efforts are part of a much larger tapestry of initiatives and new organizational forms, including commoning, mutual aid, time banks, bartering, and informal neighborhood organizing. In recent years, many of these efforts have relied heavily on information and communication technology. Still, today, *worker-owned-and-managed* cooperatives remain a small segment of what can loosely be called "the cooperative economy," which is itself not yet the major force it could be. There is a remarkable array of organizations and initiatives that merge cooperation and work, mostly under the radar of mainstream media. Worker co-ops are thriving on every continent. In this book we step outside comfortable circles and familiar sources to open ourselves and our readers to the true diversity of cooperative enterprises, including related models that fall under different labels.

We have long been intrigued by worker co-ops as a space for robust workplace participation and the democratization of economic life. In the early 1990s, George Cheney decided to delve deeply into forms of workplace participation, ranging from historical labor movements to business models like quality circles and total quality management to European codetermination models to cooperatives at work. This path led George to the Mondragón cooperatives in the Basque Country, Spain and then back to cooperatives around the United States, then to international comparative studies of worker and other types of co-ops (including consumer, land, and housing). George is formally retired as an academic, but he continues to pursue applied research while also working on cooperative development; wider organizational consulting and community work; and communication about social, economic, and environmental justice.

Matt Noyes began to study worker cooperatives in 2010 – while living in Japan. After years of practical work in union democracy and worker education in the United States, it was the need to engage undergraduate students in a business administration program and a desire to open a dialogue with them on democracy and social transformation that led him to worker cooperatives. Like George, Matt ended up at Mondragón in the Basque Country, where he encountered the MTA and LEINN programs (which will be discussed later in this book), establishing relationships with young cooperative entrepreneurs. Platform cooperativism also became a focus for him that continues today, as does solidarity economy. After moving back to the United States in 2018, he was a caregiver for several years and is now pursuing solidarity economy education and organizing.

Emi Do came to cooperatives as a small-scale urban farmer trying to find a viable alternative to the dominant food distribution chain. The sense of empowerment, mutuality, and solidarity that the experience provided sparked an interest in the cooperative model as a means to democratize and transform relationships across different workplaces and contexts.

Through studying the largest agricultural cooperative federation in Japan for her PhD studies and incubating different worker cooperative enterprises under a new worker cooperative law there, Emi explored organizational practices that foster novel, collaborative ways for people to work together. Recently, she has returned to Canada. She continues to explore forms of solidarity in urban food systems and in environmental advocacy.

Marcelo Vieta arrived at worker cooperatives during his PhD studies. He was taken by the audaciousness of Argentines' taking over streets and companies, seizing plazas, and running entire neighborhoods via direct democracy during the crisis of its neoliberal economic system in 2001. Argentina's *empresas recuperadas por sus trabajadores* movement (ERTs) became the subject of his dissertation. Since then, he has researched all forms of cooperatives, especially worker co-ops; collaborated with the co-op sector in Canada, Argentina, and Italy; worked with community-based labor initiatives; studied other business conversions to cooperatives; and investigated avenues to scale up economic democracy and expand the solidarity economy. He now teaches and researches on these and other issues and the emancipative learning that takes place in participatory and solidarity-based organizations.

Joseba Azkarraga has been a member of the cooperative movement of Mondragón for 15 years, as a professor at Mondragon University. He focused on strengthening cooperative identity in a time of globalization (his doctoral dissertation received the Basque Government Research Award). In addition, he consulted for the Mondragon Corporation. Recently, he has explored socioecological resilience, analyzing social movements such as the Transition Movement. Along the same lines, he has been examining food sovereignty and agroecology, with a special emphasis on the pathbreaking work of young Basques immersed in agroecology. In general, his work addresses the fundamental cultural change required for postgrowth societies to emerge.

Charlie Michel found his way to cooperative studies via agriculture, volunteering through the Worldwide Opportunities on Organic Farms program and working a season in a peach orchard before stepping into a role as an educator and advocate with National Farmers Union. He is Regional Food Systems Program Coordinator for the Northwest Food Hub Network, a project in intercooperation among farmer-owned food hubs in the United States. He is also a master's student in the International Center for Cooperative Management at St. Mary's University, Halifax, Nova Scotia, Canada.

All of us find inspiration in cases such as: DisCOs, distributed cooperatives pursuing commons-based socioeconomic activity that incorporates feminist economic principles; *Unión Solidaria de Trabajadores* (UST), a construction and parks maintenance worker-recuperated co-op in Buenos Aires that redirects portions of surpluses to aiding surrounding communities; and recent efforts in the United States to bring together labor unions and cooperatives in fields like agriculture, energy, and social services. These initiatives show revolutionary approaches to work, governance, and communication that are not always aimed at a preset outcome but that have mutual support and the broader community at heart. We visit these, and many other organizations like them, throughout the book.

The multiple – and interconnected – global crises of the past few years are leading both to significant shifts in employment patterns and to a deeper rethinking of what jobs, careers, productivity, and organizations mean. COVID-19 brought our attention to other crises and their interrelationships such as the crucial role of "essential" care and service work marginalized by dominant discourses and the inability of the current market system to respond effectively to immediate local needs.

The COVID-19 pandemic has also called attention to the acceleration of climate change, mass extinctions, and associated disasters; the pressures and turbulence caused by severe economic inequality; and overdue reckoning and reparations for racial oppression. With these problems at the fore, accustomed socioeconomic and organizational structures are being challenged.

Many workers' and other cooperatives, especially in the Global North, have stepped up to these challenges, rewriting their policies and redirecting their practices in terms of stronger, more proactive principles of diversity, equity, and inclusion – far beyond accustomed public statements of values and principles.

The perspective for this book is multidisciplinary and multitheoretic, meaning that we draw upon a variety of traditions in the analysis of work, business, organizations, and broader institutions, especially when addressing umbrella concepts such as capitalism, democracy, and technology. We strive to be open to diverse viewpoints, frameworks, and types of evidence.

We have also tried to suspend our own biases, preferences, and expectations enough to see potential surprises, contradictions, and different ways of achieving the same goal, even where it concerns our primary focus on worker co-ops. Many of our interviews, for example, revealed long-standing cooperative cases that were new to us and uncovered the importance of cultural traditions that, while falling under many different names, manifest parallel cooperative principles. A few examples are the pre-Incan, Indigenous Andean notion of the *ayllu* (interfamily productive organizing and labor sharing); the Zapatistas' local self-managed councils and governance *caracoles* in Chiapas, México; cooperative health

and educational initiatives in North America; and cooperatives rooted in fair trade and fair work practices in South Asia.

Listening, understanding, and learning are key to a vibrant,
ongoing democratic process. In our engagements with the
many people and writings represented in this volume, we have
tried to exercise a provocative playfulness, especially with
terminology and labels. If a co-op board member or manager
claims that "the market is driving our decision," then we ask,
"Who or what is the market?" If certain forms of capitalism
are claimed to be kinder and gentler, if you will, then we ask,
"Specifically how is this being realized?" If a business –
whether incorporated as a worker cooperative or as some
other form – claims to be deeply democratic, then we ask, "By
what practices, what measures, and what outcomes?"

Our sources and methods are also pluralistic. We have
consulted many different resources, from academic research,
to reports by practitioners, to news and commentary, to
popular culture. When reflecting on the present and future it is
important to look for signs, trends, and conceivable options in
many different locations. Surveys and studies all around the
world testify to the persistence of workers' desires for
autonomy, or the ability to shape their own work situation to
a significant extent; and voice, or the capacity to contribute
not only to discussions about the firm's future but also to
actual decision-making.

For this book and related projects, we have conducted over
100 moderately structured interviews, mostly via telephone or
videoconferencing, and hundreds of email exchanges, to
ensure we are capturing a wide range of experiences and views
of worker co-ops on a global level. We do not pretend to be
comprehensive – there is much happening around the world
that cannot be easily uncovered – but we do our best to
represent diverse types of initiatives and trends. We term the
interviews "expert" in the sense of seeking people who are

well-positioned to speak about individual co-ops and communities as well as about wider trends. By following up on
referrals from interviewees about others to contact and tracing
posts and websites, we have encountered many co-ops and
initiatives around the world that have not been much publicized or examined. Still, there are many more conversations
that did not occur and cases of which we are still unaware.

There have been important lessons for us along the way of
creating this book. Although we began with a bias toward the
value of the worker–cooperative model, we sought to reopen a
wide investigation about the advantages, limits, and creative
possibilities for worker co-ops. We do not view them as
democratic and egalitarian business *islands*. In fact, as our
interviews have consistently shown, worker co-ops represent
an important path for labor, economic, and community justice
that are, more than ever, part of a web of formal and informal
initiatives all over the world. Thus, we widened our lens to
take in many other related business and organizational forms,
all in the interest of tracking what work, and the economy
would be like if both were profoundly cooperative.

It is impossible in a short book to do justice to our theme,
but shortcomings stand out. While we tried to include sources
from around the world, the cases we feature and the literature
on which we draw remain weighted toward the United States,
Europe, and Latin America. There are still too few cases from
Asia and the Pacific (only Japan, Korea, Australia, and New
Zealand), Africa (only Kenya and Rwanda), and especially,
South Asia (India). Most of the literature we cite is in English,
Spanish, or French. We are also aware that the Mondragón
cooperatives, in Euskadi, the Basque Country (Spain), loom
large. This is due to our familiarity with that experience, and
the major contributions to practice and theory they have made
over their 65 years of existence.

Feminist economics and organizational theory is important to our analysis, but we did not sufficiently address the specific challenge of organizing for women's liberation in the context of worker cooperativism. The same is true for the struggles of BIPOC, LGBTQ+ people, and others, which are important to so many of the people we were fortunate to interview. While we were not able to give many of the cases and interviews the in-depth treatment they deserve, we hope we have sparked curiosity in readers to pursue them and seek out others in their own communities and through their networks.

This volume is part of a series on the future of work, and that focus guides many of the questions that we address. How do worker co-ops figure into the future of work? What unique or at least distinctive benefits do they offer? How can they be part of a larger "eco-system" of cooperative and solidarity-based ventures? How can worker co-ops anticipate still other democratizing forces in the economy and society at large? What cultural, political, and economic conditions favor conversions of existing businesses to worker co-ops in addition to the establishment of wholly new enterprises in local and regional economies? These questions need thoughtful, informed, and timely responses, especially given the relative rarity of worker-owned-and-managed firms in today's economy.

ACKNOWLEDGMENTS

The direct contributions of coauthors and collaborators draw from the nourishment of communities of people who share interests, curiosity, hopes, and sometimes paths. We are deeply grateful to all the individuals and organizations that generously shared their time, reports, experiences, and insights for this project. All those conversations and exchanges have greatly enriched this book, even though many individuals and organizations are not mentioned in the text. The same is true for the groups and organizations to which we belong. We also wish to thank our families, friends, and colleagues who have offered crucial forms of support since this project began in January 2019. Ryan Wenzel generously assisted us with tracking down important references. Dean Ritz read the manuscript at the final stage and offered helpful suggestions. Sally Planalp did several rounds of careful proofreading and editing, offering sound advice. Thank you to the staff at Emerald Publishing for assistance and encouragement through every phase of this process.

1

CRISES AND OPPORTUNITIES

INTRODUCTION

We knew something was different about the workplace and
the organization just after we arrived at the Otalora Training
Center of the Mondragón Cooperative Corporation. George
Cheney and his wife Sally Planalp had the great fortune to
spend half of their sabbatical year of 1993–1994 working and
living among the Mondragón cooperatives. The director of the
center and another staff member introduced us to *all* of the
worker-owners or "socios" who were employed at Otalora,
including housekeeping and kitchen staff. While this episode
of recognition of each worker may seem trivial, it stands in
contrast to the ingrained hierarchies that characterize most
large businesses and how those show up in everyday
interactions.

Over the course of our 6 months working at the Center and
living in the nearby town of Aretzabaleta, we came to know
everyone in Otalora, often through discussions of their individual takes on the already famous worker cooperatives. The
Mondragón case looms large in the literature on
worker-owned and governed cooperatives, the cooperative

economy, and the larger landscape of efforts at economic and social equality. It is just one of many cases from around the world that we treat in this book, with idealism but also with a healthy pragmatism oriented toward new possibilities as well as lessons learned.

CRISES AND OPENINGS

COVID-19 had widespread and devastating effects around the world. Yet it became much more than a public health crisis because it also painfully exposed interrelated economic, political, social, and environmental problems, bringing existing divisions into sharper relief. None of the problems facing us are going away anytime soon: political, including threats to democratic institutions; social, especially racial and immigrant justice; economic inequality and disempowerment; public health and the critical need for coordinated community responses; and climate disruptions with desperately needed responses and changes in the way we do business.

The multidimensional crisis associated with climate change includes not just global warming, rising sea levels and ocean acidification, and increased severity of floods and droughts, but also exhaustion of nonrenewable resources; loss of habitat, species and biodiversity; food insecurity; starvation, war, and displacement of populations; and loss of linguistic and cultural diversity (Azkarraga et al., 2011).

It's easy to miss how these crises are interconnected, seeing them simply as happening at the same time, but the first two "pandemic years" of the twenty-first century (2020–2021) showed the world how the crises are interrelated (Gills, 2020). For instance, the likelihood of viral pandemics is increased because of human encroachment on wildlife habitats, allowing for more cross-species transmissions or "spillovers" (Quammen, 2013). In an intensely globalized world, the virus spread quickly. In addition, the persistence of the COVID-19 pandemic is clearly due in part to global inequities that impact both access to healthcare resources and vaccination opportunities within countries and between more and less affluent nations. Further, the erosion of a sense of the common good and social solidarity in a number of nations, especially more individualistic ones, makes confronting the pandemic and addressing inequities more challenging. Finally, the rise of autocratic nationalism and populist "strongmen" in many parts of the world in recent years set up obstacles to the kind of extensive global cooperation needed to address this pandemic.

The crises are unevenly presented and experienced with their epidemiological and socioeconomic impacts most felt by the working poor, women, children, and racial minorities, and other marginalized and dispossessed communities. Nationalist expressions and reactions against many immigrant groups have revealed widespread racism and xenophobia while many centrist or progressive political parties have failed to connect with the concerns of large swaths of working-class voters. Opportunities for "green jobs" within largely capitalistic economies have failed to materialize at the level that is needed to help both workers and the environment (ILO, 2018; McKibben, 2021).

Different ways of organizing the economy and society were already needed. These crises, taken individually and together, add new layers of necessity for change (CICOPA, n.d.). They also reveal opportunities for new ways of doing business. As famed journalist Naomi Klein put it early on in the pandemic: "Crisis blows open the sense of what is possible" (cited in Gaztambide-Fernández, 2020, para 28). Clearly, standard ways of doing business and chasing after consumer satisfaction are not working. We maintain that a new emphasis on values such as democracy, equity, solidarity, and sustainability can come not only with the advancement of worker cooperatives – our focus here – but also with a much wider web of creative and collaborative structures and processes, which are becoming stronger at this time of widening and deepening crises.

Within this global political environment, it is even more imperative that visions for acts of cooperation move into prominent places in collective consciousness and inspiration for action. Still, in the course of writing this book we have found many reasons to be hopeful – especially in the little-publicized, local grassroots initiatives for community empowerment. As the author of several books on co-ops around the world, E.G. Nadeau said in a published interview in 2021: "More than ever, I think the pandemic is telling us that we need a better way to organize the world economy right down to local community economies" (GEO Collective, 2021, para 5).

Rebecca Solnit (2009) describes so well the capacity of humans for cooperation in dire situations of natural and human-caused disasters in the powerful stories documented in her book *A Paradise Built in Hell*. Examples are myriad, including spontaneous neighborhood organizing during the financial crisis years of 2001–2002 in Argentina; the experimentations of Occupy Wall Street in the wake of the financial crisis of 2007–2008; many instances of cooperation and solidarity during and after Tropical Storm Sandy in New York City in 2012, Hurricane Katrina in New Orleans in 2005, and the Mexico City earthquake of 1985. Now in Ukraine we have reports of acts of resistance, courage and communal sacrifice as the Russian invasion unleashes untold suffering as we write these lines.

Solnit (2009), Klein (2007), Rutger Bregman (2017), Dean Spade (2020), and a growing group of commentators are explaining how, on the one hand, many of our systems – including capitalism, addiction to growth, and symbolically and often physically violent expressions of identity – make some kinds of disasters much more likely. On the other hand, we find that solidarity, mutual aid, and cooperation – rather than highly individualistic pursuits, unchecked greed, and bitter competition – provide what scholar Ana Maria Peredo calls "spaces of hope" amidst all the crises facing the world (Peredo, personal communication, 2021). Among those spaces and inspiring examples are networks of reciprocity and solidarity in the Andes, built on long-established indigenous traditions, allowing communities to better weather the pandemic period and support themselves economically (Córdoba et al., 2021). Worker cooperatives are also among those spaces, as we strive to demonstrate throughout this book.

To underscore the point, more grassroots efforts such as mutual aid, commoning, platform and distributed cooperativism, time banks, alternative trade networks, barter clubs, and related forms of horizontal organizing have been provoked directly or indirectly by the COVID-19 pandemic. A good example is work by the Kola Nut Collaborative in Chicago, Illinois, which is actively promoting the interconnections and synergies among diverse grassroots initiatives with a clear emphasis on collaborative relationships, grassroots democracy, and neighborhood empowerment (Strode, personal communication, 2022). Another timely work is *Pandemic Solidarity* (Sitrin & Sembrar, 2020), chronicling the rise of grassroots mutual aid and other efforts that foreshadowed recent political movements such as Occupy. Many of these movements leave their marks on society but often in non-obvious ways as participants move into other initiatives and organizations (Levitin, 2021).

Work and Labor Today

Today we find revived public interest in organized labor, as well as new organization drives in many countries (Azzellini, 2021). Illustrative cases of recent innovative labor-led initiatives include: efforts by Amazon.com employees to organize the first successful unionized warehouse on Staten Island in New York City (Lapavitsas et al., 2022); the wave of Starbucks unionizing (Molla, 2022); the McDonald's franchise in Marseille that was turned into a social hub and food distribution center for the local community by former employees (Noack & Mehl, 2021); and the rise of care workers, nurses, teachers, and contract faculty organizing throughout the world (Poydock et al., 2022). Although official statistics and reports cite a decline in labor actions such as official strikes in recent years, there has actually been a rise in workers' actions in the years just before and during the pandemic when one factors in multiple forms of workers resistances (Friedman, 2016; Moody, 2017).

During the time we were writing this book, many individuals, households, families, and occupational groups were questioning their jobs, occupations, careers, and even the role of work in their lives. What has come to be called in catchy but nebulous shorthand "The Great Resignation," refers to people quitting their jobs, taking a pause, retiring early, or changing occupations (Chugh, 2021; Parker & Horowitz, 2022).

Still, we are only beginning to understand the range of pressures and preferences that are part of the rethinking of work for many people around the world. This goes far beyond people in health and service professions finding the pressures of their work to be too great during the pandemic. The reasons are multiple, including pressures of responsibilities at home, fear of contracting COVID-19 at work, and the realization that, if one can manage without paid employment, it might be time to do so. Millions of workers who are able to do so are reevaluating their jobs, looking not only for more hospitable workplaces and organizations but also more fulfilling positions and even reconsidering what work itself means in their lives (Lepore, 2021).

The creative possibilities for survival and revival revealed by the multiple, global, and interconnected crises of our day are only just beginning to appear in academic journals as well as in news and commentary (e.g., Scott, 2021; Smit et al., 2021). It is clear, though, that this phase of reevaluation and rearrangement goes far beyond what was witnessed during the global economic crisis of 2007–2008 and the several years following. Interestingly, many recent publications on work have ventured into deep questioning about the roles and types of work in people's lives in the twenty-first century (Lucassen, 2021).

REIMAGINING WORK AND WORKING TOGETHER

Work is not something to be taken for granted as a concept or set of activities. As the history of work itself reminds us (Ciulla, 2000), changes in occupations occur for a number of reasons, including huge economic forces that have little connection with personal choices. Far too often, as the saying goes, workers have "checked their rights at the door," in the sense that democracy is not the norm in workplaces and work arrangements, whether those be factories, offices, or networked and technology-enabled businesses. This is true even in many avowedly democratic societies. Far too often, the individual and group rewards of work have been downplayed or even kept out of the design of workplaces and work organizations. Far too often, some types of work (e.g., the work of reproduction) have been degraded or pushed out of view. And far too often, the potential for collaboration and solidarity in labor processes has been left unrealized or, worse, not even imagined.

A great deal of work and the people who do it remain invisible in that economic and social hierarchies persist in devaluing many lines of work, many occupations. Accordingly, much of the work of "care" for others in industrial societies is neither featured when jobs and professions are discussed nor is it assigned worthwhile value in terms of compensation (Duffy, 2021). For example, Marilyn Waring's *If Women Counted* (1990) broke ground by detailing the many types of production, like a great deal of care work, that were excluded from measures like Gross Domestic Product. Furthermore, hierarchies by gender and race and education figure into both the visibility of work and the assignment of value to it, such as with doctors versus nurses and in the white male-dominated legal profession and business management.

How work is accomplished and how it is understood is greatly complicated by the roles and influences of technology. Work is already being drastically reconfigured through technological displacement, through freelancing and the celebrated "gig economy," and through virtual work in many industries. At the same time, concerns about the surveillance of work – in the office, on the shop floor, and at home – are growing (Hodder, 2020).

Precarity, referring to unstable or episodic employment and its effects, is "the condition of our time" as Ana Tsing observes (2015, p. 20). As systems of reliable, long-term employment diminish, most workers experience insecurity, little or no voice, unsatisfying work, and few avenues to enrich their experience. At the same time, there is evidence that many individuals not only accept but actually prefer the freelance or gig-organized labor market because of the variety of jobs and their own desire not to be wedded to a single organization or career (Standing, 2018).

Both the "gig economy" (Woodcock & Graham, 2019) and the role of technology in work are usually lauded in popular discourse as bringing about greater freedom for the individual, which is true in certain respects. However, ads for contract work from remote locations done by "digital nomads" are dreamy in tone and content while taken out of their social and economic contexts. Images of freedom in the marketing of such promotions seldom invite people to reflect on how their work is set within parameters of economic relations, shaped by organizations and managers, and too often treated as a wholly individual matter. It is as if "success" is about entrepreneurial individuals "making it" or not (Barrat et al., 2020).

Workers' needs and yearnings remain remarkably consistent, as shown empirically in surveys as well as through case-based evidence. They want dignified and meaningful work, in a climate of mutual respect; safe working conditions; equitable remuneration; some degree of autonomy at the job; and an opportunity for some degree of voice about the policies of an organization and workplace that define, constrain, and that also can enhance one's work experience (e.g., Freeman & Rogers, 1999; Hodson, 2001).

Indeed, we know there are many different values and meanings attached to work (Cheney et al., 2008), as well as long-standing analyses of how the value generated by human labor is used or abused (Marx, 1976). Perhaps the one insight from Marx on which the entire range of economists could agree is that workers, through their labor, create profit or surplus. Marx spotlighted the questions of *what happens with* the surplus value accrued by goods and services in the production process as well as the surplus value in the labor itself (as in the form of unpaid work). Workers' lived experiences, local knowledge, ability to resist, and capacity to mobilize with others to produce things make them more than wage labor. This is why workers can "take back" their creative and productive capacities for themselves, create worker co-ops, and engage in different forms of working collectively and cooperatively (Vieta, 2019).

Working people can practice different degrees of coopera- tion and self-determination in conventional workplaces. Worker- or management-led efforts to improve work oppor- tunities, conditions, and roles are numerous and diverse. As discussed further in Chapter 2, many of these fall under headings related to quality, efficiency and production, but also employee involvement and participation. Many others, notably labor organizing, have arisen as countervailing powers in the sense of responding to the frequently unchecked control exercised by owners and managers in businesses. Of course, individuals in such positions vary greatly in their personalities, values, and goals. Worker cooperatives provide an important avenue for organizing to achieve more inclusive, more just, and more humane workplaces.

Transformations in how tasks are done, in the needed skills, in what counts as work, in how workforces are struc- tured, and so on, are all part of the context in which coop- eratives develop and thrive. Creative, democratic, and responsive/responsible work arrangements are hidden in plain sight and hold tremendous potential for the future. There is no more important time to reimagine, recast, and reembody work in cooperative forms (Billiet, Dufays, Freidel, & Staessens, 2021). Because of their unique combination of characteristics as well as demonstrated resilience worker co-ops can lead the way.

International Cooperative Alliance's Definition of Co-ops

A good place to start in rethinking work and for understanding the "cooperative advantage" is with the well-accepted formal definition of a cooperative. The International Cooperative Alliance (ICA) defines a co-op as "an autonomous association of persons united voluntarily to meet their common economic, social and cultural needs and aspirations through a jointly-owned and democratically controlled enterprise" (ICA, n.d.). This language casts a broad net, but it expresses *the two main dimensions of co-ops as member-controlled businesses: member ownership and member governance.* These are sometimes called the economic and the social-structural sides of cooperatives. Ownership means literally that members share the equity or value of the firm, whether the co-op is consumer, producer, or employee-owned (or some combination or variation). Governance refers to the decision making around key policies and plans, understood to follow the core agreed-upon values of the firm. As part of governance, cooperatives have boards of directors drawn completely or largely from their membership. Specific arrangements vary, of course, depending on the type of business, how power is distributed, what kind of participation is expected of members, and how active members are. Among the many types of cooperatives, worker co-ops maximize the economic and sociopolitical dimensions of democracy at work by making shared ownership and decision making the twin pillars of worker empowerment and control.

THE COOPERATIVE SOLUTION: HIDDEN IN PLAIN SIGHT

So-called "alternatives" truly belong in the mainstream, especially at a time when creative solutions to problems are sorely needed. The ways alternatives are treated in popular discourse is itself interesting and important (Parker et al., 2014).

Cooperatives suffer from persistent stereotypes in the public mind, such as "It's unrealistic to have everyone share in decision making"; "there are no incentives for high-quality work or individual advancement in a relatively flat organization"; "idealistic cooperators know little about making a business run effectively and efficiently." Caricatures of cooperatives and any other institutions, of course, have their real-life instances; but they are employed as hammers to pound down possibilities for doing business and organizing human systems differently. This is a major reason for the limited media coverage of co-ops (see, e.g., Mangan & Byrne, 2018 on content analyses of media coverage of co-ops).

Every one of us, in giving public talks or facilitating community discussions, has encountered entrenched stereotypes of cooperatives, and even more so for worker cooperatives. Often the caricatures are held even by persons sympathetic with grassroots economic and political democracy. The views often echo what's depicted in a *New Yorker* magazine cartoon, where a group of mechanics struggles to decide how best to fix a car. The caption reads: "We can't come to an agreement about how to fix your car, Mr. Simons. Sometimes that's the way things happen in a democracy" (Handelsman, 1987). Of course, that is the way things *sometimes* happen, but it doesn't prove that democratic decision making is inherently flawed.

As psychologist Alfie Kohn (1992) explains so clearly: if competition is *the* natural order of human affairs, why does it require such aggressive and ongoing promotion? By contrast, cooperation is often framed in popular culture as weak and ineffective, even though it can be argued just as persuasively that cooperation, or what Razeto (2019) calls "the C factor," is a key dimension of human existence – and continuance.

It is important to distinguish between the history of cooperatives as distinctive organizations, often incorporated under legal systems, and the much longer and wider history of cooperation in the human experience. From his several decades of field work in a variety of businesses, Sennett (2012) chronicles a variety of forms of cooperation at work, many of them informal: within neighborhoods, in small businesses, in public parks, and among workers on Wall Street struggling with extreme time pressures.

Myths About Cooperatives

Several of us have found that when students and participants in community workshops are asked to create a new, desired, perhaps ideal organization on paper, they simply reproduce the familiar pyramidal arrangements. But when they learn about cooperative ways of organizing and that democratically co-owned business models exist students are quickly taken by and intuitively understand the co-op model. This is why vivid examples of doing business otherwise – by different assumptions and with different outcomes – are so important. *Take Back the Economy* (2013), by Katherine Gibson-Graham, Jenny Cameron and Stephen Healy is a wonderfully practical guide to alternative economic practices from around the world, including worker cooperatives.

It is interesting that when any cooperative – but especially a worker co-op – goes out of business or has financial difficulties, proponents of business as usual often jump on such a report to say, "See, that kind of business organization is unrealistic." But this strategic dismissal diverts attention from the fact that business failure is the norm. This type of argument is also used, usually without evidence, to suggest that "good business sense" is incompatible with the democratic governance and social goals of cooperatives. But evidence for the viability of worker co-ops, actually, shows otherwise:

Empirical research shows that worker owned and governed co-ops, especially ones that have converted from another business model to a co-operative, fail less than and outlast conventional firms (Deller et al., 2009; Vieta et al., 2017; Zevi et al., 2011).

To be sure, the stereotypes of co-ops are not entirely without basis. For example, the Burley Design Worker Cooperative in Eugene, Oregon, US, existed for three decades until it was bought out by a single private entrepreneur in 2006 (Schoening, 2010). In its early years, this cooperative manufacturer of colorful carts to attach to bicycles for carrying groceries or kids, was deeply committed to democratic decision-making; in fact, to consensus. One story from a founder revealed how far this commitment can be taken. There was a time when nearly all decisions were discussed and made by the committee of all worker-owners. One time, everyone got involved in a decision about a new dumpster to place behind the building, and discussion was protracted. Fortunately, the co-op learned that consensus could be modified – not diluted – and that the workforce could come to consensus around the most important values, principles and policies while at the same time delegating some decisions to committees and individuals. This latter solution is the way that decision-making works at most of Argentina's worker-recuperated companies (Vieta, 2020), and at the Mondragón co-ops (Cheney, 2002), two worker co-op movements that will make recurring appearances in the following pages.

There is a broader point about organizational learning here: about "the tyranny of structurelessness," a term coined in an analysis of some parts of the feminist movement (Freeman, 1972). Although the use of the term is contested, we can say that in their exuberant beginnings some groups of cooperators assume that they can completely transcend power dynamics among people or achieve a kind of perfect post-bureaucratic democracy that will stand as a completed project not requiring nurturing, internal conflict management, and revision. The counterpoint is that in not maintaining a commitment to cooperative values, and especially a broad and deep role for participation, a worker co-op or similarly structured business can lose cohesion, energy, and ultimately its organizational independence. Indeed, it was this kind of deterioration and not excessive adherence to consensus that is understood to have brought about Burley's end as a worker co-op, or what is generally called "de-mutualization" meaning conversion to a privately owned and managed firm (Battilani & Schröter, 2012; Fulton & Girard, 2015).

In much the same way, there are common "stylized facts" about worker and other cooperatives which do not stand up under the scrutiny of the empirical data along with many case studies. Virginie Pérotin (2016) calls upon both applied researchers and analysts of economic and social trends to look more closely at the data on individual worker co-ops and networks of them, finding that they are more widely distributed across industries, larger, and often more successful and resilient than many commentators would suggest (see Birchall & Ketilson, 2009).

ORIGINS AND RANGE OF WORKER CO-OPS

There is not just one history of worker cooperatives but many. We can't pretend to offer a comprehensive history of worker cooperatives or the larger cooperative economy here but a representative account based on our own views, research, and experiences. There are numerous histories of the cooperative movement and of worker co-ops (e.g., Cole, 1944; Gordon Nembhard, 2014; Patmore & Balknave, 2018; Potter, 1893;

Thompson, 2012; Wright, 2014). These are not static or completed stories. Histories of cooperatives and cooperation around the world are still being uncovered, developed, and expressed. For example, the experiences with co-ops in Africa are only just now gaining broad recognition in the wider international cooperative community.

To present any single, unbroken historical story line of cooperatives and cooperation would be misleading. For example, there can be no certainty about the first worker co-op. Scotland's Fenwick Weavers' Society, formed in the early 1760s, is recognized as one of the first formal cooperatives of the modern era, and workers in the same or related professions were already organizing cooperatively by the 1820s in England and a few decades later in France. Yet it is impossible to know how many cooperative efforts related to shared work took place in prior centuries but under different labels. For instance, professional guilds came to their own throughout Europe during the medieval period, with roots in ancient Babylon, Egypt, Greece, and Rome (Azzellini, 2021). Russian *artels* (crafts and artisans associations) and *mir* (communities of peasant households) date back centuries (Vieta, 2020). The *quilombos* created by escaped slaves and free blacks and Indigenous people in Brazil and other countries from the 1600s to the 1800s are remarkable examples of self-determined communities (Gomes & Reis, 2016). Many forms of communal work such as barn-raisings, "work bees," the Andean pre-Incan *ayllu*, the Mapuche *minga*, the Filipino *bayanihan*, Tanzania's *ujamaa* cooperative villages, and Sub-Saharan Africa's social philosophy and practices of community sharing and mutual aid called *ubuntu* all have ancient origins and are still present in these and other communities worldwide (Paterson, 2010; Visser & Tolhurst, 2017).

What we underscore here is that today's worker cooperatives have their roots in millennia-old practices of community economies, mutual aid, shared labor, and, more recently, inspired and socially focused economic efforts. Indeed, businesses centered on community wellbeing – rather than just profit – were widely discussed in the UK and the US from the late 1700s to the mid-1800s. Interestingly, that's also a period when communities took seriously their roles in chartering corporations and keeping them from concentrating monopolistic control of economic sectors. Thus, it was a period when corporate power was not as overwhelming in its societal roles as it became by the late 1800s and, of course, that we still see today.

Types and Prevalence of Cooperatives

- Community: Where members come from various stakeholder groups of the community are the members, such as when a neighborhood collectively owns a common service for food, transportation, or childcare. In some jurisdictions, these are multi-stakeholder and nonprofit co-ops.

- Consumer: Sometimes called community-owned, where the consumers are the members.

- Financial/Mutual: A form of cooperative, usually in the insurance or banking sectors, where customers or policyholders are its members and share in the profits. Credit unions or cooperative banks can be said to be a form of a mutual because savers and borrowers are its members.

- Housing, including the co-housing model: Owners or renters are the members.

- Hybrid: Can be a type of multi-stakeholder co-op, usually with significant investor involvement and/or different forms of business activity.

- Multi-stakeholder: Co-ops with multiple member types such as consumers and producers, or consumers and workers.

- Next (New) Generation: A type of multi-stakeholder or hybrid co-op found in the agricultural sector in North America. In new-gen co-ops, different investor types are allowed in order to better fund complex value-added agricultural processing in the production and distribution of foods.

- Platform: This is not exactly a *type* of cooperative in the same sense, but it features collaborative development and shared ownership of technology.

- Producer: For marketing purposes or bulk purchasing, among other activities and shared resources. Producers (usually of agricultural goods) or farmers are the members.

- Social: Started in Italy and common throughout Europe, a type of multi-stakeholder or community co-op formed by residents to deliver social services or offer work-integration support for marginalized groups where the beneficiaries are

Crises and Opportunities 19

also members, together with other community stakeholders.

- Union–worker co-ops: Worker co-ops where organized labor performs specific functions within the co-op and helps define and regulate the conditions of work.

- Utilities: Rural electric and other. A type of consumer co-op where the utility consumers are the members.

- Worker or Worker-Owned and Governed (or employee-owned): Workers or employees are the members, and where "labor hires capital" rather than the reverse as in conventional firms. Work is the common contribution of each member; control is linked to work rather than financial investment; and revenues are the common property of the cooperative's members.

- Co-op clusters or federations: Formal or informal associations of co-ops organized for collaboration and concentration in different parts of the same industry.

- Second- and third-tier cooperatives: Usually co-op federations, associations, or networks comprised members that are themselves cooperatives.

Related Organizational Forms

- Employee Stock Ownership Plans (ESOPs): Where employees are given partial share-ownership of the firm via stock options but where they do not usually enjoy decision-making rights. An Employee Ownership Trust is similar, but the employee shares are kept in trust on behalf of the workers. In both models, the employees can cash out their share capital upon exiting the firm or upon retirement, or use the funds collectively for a collective buyout of the firm.

- Uses of LLCs (limited liability corporations) or various non-profit models for incorporation of businesses operating cooperatively or for associations supporting cooperatives. The form depends either on the will of members, and/or regional or national legislation pertaining to co-ops.

- *Sociedades anónimas laborales* (SALs) (Spain), worker-shareholder cooperatives (WSCs) (Quebec), and other similar models: hybrid organizational models where the majority of employees co-own the firm while sharing ownership with conventional investors. Usually, SAL or WSC members have some decision-making rights and the majority of employee work hours of the firm must be allocated to the SAL or WSC members.

Despite pockets of concentration, worker cooperatives represent a comparatively small portion of the cooperative sector overall (Kremer, 1997). Reliable statistics are hard to come by, due to incomplete reporting and inconsistent measures (Reuten, 2021). Still, the following figures should provide some sense of the relative size of the worker cooperative portion of the global cooperative sector.

It is estimated that there are 85,000 worker cooperatives (WCs) in the world:

- WCs comprise 3% of all cooperatives in the world (Dave Grace and Associates, 2014);

- WCs employ 12 million people, or 4% of total cooperative employment (Eum, 2017);

- WCs own 0.02% of all cooperative assets (excluding cooperative banks and credit unions) (Dave Grace and Associates, 2014); and

- Five WCs are listed among the top 300 global cooperatives (by annual turnover of assets ratios) (Carini et al., 2020).

Worker co-ops are grounded in core social values of participation, equality, and solidarity in the workplace and organization. Worker co-ops are fundamentally about giving working people a say in and control over how they work, what they work on, and how they get remunerated rather than having workers relegate these core dimensions to the decisions of bosses, managers, or owners. Worker co-ops democratically (re)organize work and, as organizations where "membership" of the organization is linked directly to work, have the capacity to maximize economic (equity) and sociopolitical (governance) dimensions of member participation (Dahl, 1985). In a healthy worker co-op, democracy itself is part of ongoing education and discussion, and that includes financial literacy as well as vibrant forms of collaboration and governance (Cheney, 2002).

As illustrated in the chapters that follow, focusing on worker cooperatives allows for the reframing of work, relationships, and power, "produc[ing] very different understandings that can lead to previously unthinkable actions" (Gibson-Graham et al., 2013, p. 7).

Today we find worker co-ops in a wide array of fields and industries, from crafts to high-tech, from food systems to renewable energy, from coffee shops to heavy industry, from marketing to home health care (Kerswell & Pratap, 2019; Zamagni & Zamagni, 2010). Worker co-ops are in urban, suburban, and rural areas. Some worker co-ops include unions in significant check-and-balance roles (Witherell et al., 2012); others have strong partnerships with local business coalitions and entrepreneurship centers; still others are on the cutting edge of democratic revival and ecological action. The worker-cooperative model is not one-size-fits-all but rather one that can be adapted to specific business, sector, and community needs.

COOPERATIVE PRINCIPLES

What do such a wide variety of enterprises spread across all sectors of the economy have in common? How do cooperatives differ in practice and principle from other socially responsible, sustainable, or progressive businesses? To differentiate themselves and to orient their work, worker cooperatives often draw up a list of basic values or principles. Most worker cooperatives adhere to the Seven Cooperative Principles of the International Cooperative Alliance (ICA), which trace their roots to the Rochdale Pioneers in England in 1844. The principles have been modified, augmented, and applied in various ways since that time.

International Cooperative Alliance's Seven Principles

1. *Voluntary and Open Membership*: This means openness to all people who use a co-op's services, contribute to the whole, and are willing to accept other responsibilities. One implication is that co-ops have a responsibility to reach out beyond their familiar networks in terms of recruiting members.

2. *Democratic Member Control*: This is usually operationalized as "one-member, one-vote": for example, in the committee of the whole as the chief governing body of the co-op, and in the (usually annual) general assembly of members.

3. *Member Economic Participation*: Members contribute equally upon entry to the value of the cooperative. This initial contribution – called a "membership fee" or something similar – can be a modest sum of money, a certain number of hours of work, or equipment and other resources. Members receive benefits in accord with their work or other offerings to the business. In a worker co-op, members' benefits are linked to their work in the co-op.

4. *Autonomy and Independence*: Cooperatives are independent, self-help organizations. A good example of this principle in action is when a co-op enters into a partnership agreement of some type. Member control of decision-making

is a key part of this process and for any other major policies or actions by the co-op.

5. *Education, Training and Information*: This principle has two domains of application: internal and external. Co-ops have a stated responsibility to provide necessary training and education to members; at the same time, co-ops pursue a commitment to inform the public about cooperatives and their advantages.

6. *Cooperation Among Cooperatives*: This is yet another principle that distinguishes true co-ops from conventional businesses: co-ops understand that their success is intertwined with that of other cooperatives and that together they can work most effectively through not just ad hoc collaborations but also through participation in local, regional, national and international associations.

7. *Concern for Community*: Although the term "concern" doesn't necessarily imply action, co-ops show their commitment to community through a range of types of contributions, both monetary and in-kind. Many co-ops pride themselves on being intimately involved in supporting the activities and well-being of their communities; others will take up specific causes as decided by their membership; and still others are intimately connected to the sustenance and development of their communities.

Because worker cooperativism is pluralistic and evolving – more an experience, to use Arizmendiarrieta's term, than a model – cooperative principles are always open to reform and reinvention (Noyes, 2017). In 1987, members of the newly formed Mondragón Cooperative Group, now the largest single worker-owned-and-governed business in the world, adopted a list of 10 basic values, based on the ICA principles. After extensive debate, members came to agreement on three new principles (Mondragón, 1987):

1. Sovereignty of labor, in the workplace and in relation to capital.

2. The subordinate and instrumental character of capital, that is, that capital is subordinated to labor and remunerated fairly like any other external resource.

3. Wage solidarity, an explicit commitment to maintain a narrow ratio of lowest to highest paid worker-owners and to maintain wages rates in line those paid to workers in the region so that all rise together;

They also replaced ICA principle #7, Concern for Community, with "Social Transformation," explicitly committing the cooperative group to a more just and inclusive economy.

The Mondragón principles, which some considered unorthodox or even heretical, reflected their commitment to "find the best formula for social development and transformation, consistent with an unwavering social commitment" to the primacy and dignity of labor (Azurmendi, 1992, p. 459). Sovereignty of Labor is an unusual expression that captures both the ultimate authority and power of workers in their workplace and the centrality of work in society. A sovereign is one who has the power to create, enforce, and even suspend the law (Derrida, 2011). If labor is sovereign, who or what is its subject? Capital. In a worker cooperative, capital has the status of any other input: when needed, it is borrowed on the market, at a fair price, and its owners are not accorded any control or authority in the cooperative.

Labor sovereignty is not just a matter of governance and ownership. It also implies the transformation of the most basic relations of work and production: either directly or through elected representatives: worker-members choose and monitor management, make strategic decisions, decide how to reinvest revenues back into the firm, determine how much to allocate revenues to worker-members, and whether or not to raise salaries. Worker-members can "fire" management or recall their elected officials. In economic downturns, worker co-ops tend to adjust salaries and hours, rather than laying off workers or, in the case of Mondragón, shift members to other co-ops in the network.

They also play a different role in their communities, creating cooperative employment in businesses that are unlikely to relocate in search, of "cheaper" labor because members are also residents of local communities. The commitment to wage solidarity with workers outside the cooperative reflects the commitment to raise the standards for all workers. These are not the common practices of conventional, for-profit, shareholder-owned firms.

Values Change

Ana Aguirre, a committed worker-owner and co-op developer, explains the importance of core values, as opposed to policies, in terms of reversibility or degeneration. If a company like Patagonia has progressive policies, that is laudable; but the fact remains that under a new owner, those policies could change or even be dissolved altogether. In a worker cooperative, the key values are "baked into" the structure of the organization, its statutes, and its formal legal status (Aguirre, personal communication, 2020). Still, values change over time, or fall out of sync with the realities of practice, requiring reconsideration and renewal.

Aguirre is not afraid to use humor yet be direct. She tells the story of leading tours at Mondragón:

> *I started asking people, "so you work in a co-op, are you a worker-owner?" And they are like "no, no, my cooperative is a credit cooperative or it's a medical cooperative." So I say, "so really, why do you work in a coop?" And they were like, "because [of] the mission and..." And I am like, "this is cheating, no? You work in a co-op but you don't own it, so for you, you are like an employee and if they don't need you, they kick you out." And they are like, "no, no, but the mission, the philosophy..." And I'm like, "meh, it's a little cheating..."*
>
> (Aguirre, personal communication, 2021)

In the 1990s George questioned management at Mondragón about their ceasing to push their cooperative identity in marketing messages around Spain. They blamed "the market," treating it as a kind of super-agent, as if it required no further explanation. But, when asked to cite evidence of "market pressure," they often came up short. Such conversations show how market pressure becomes a kind of unexamined premise, a refrain, in the context of global market

capitalism (Goll, 1991). Market pressures are certainly very
real at times. Responding to them as they are encountered or
perceived has led many co-ops to suppress value-based concerns in efforts to be more competitive. This may involve
pushing workers to devote extra time "for the good of the
team" or even selling off the firm. Vieta (2020) found evidence
of this, in his study of Argentina's worker-recuperated firms.
In some worker co-ops, the seductions of market value have
led to de-mutualization (OpenMinds, 2019).

Expanded Principles

Cooperative principles have important parallels with other
value-based approaches to our economy. For example, the
principles of Kwanzaa, the African-American year-end holi-
day, includes an express commitment to cooperative economics, defined as an economic system that is both governed
by and in the service of all. Cities and regions around the
world are innovating for economic and environmental justice.
Some identify with the Transition Town movement; some are
taking up cooperative principles and extending them to help
bring into being a wider solidarity-based and ecologically
attuned system. Amsterdam, for instance, has recently
embraced the Doughnut Economy approach to city planning
which takes into account planetary limits and social needs
(Doughnut Economics Action Lab, 2020).

The city of Preston in the UK, has adopted "the principles
of Community Wealth Building" for its city council and the
wider Lancashire area, merging these principles with the traditions of nearby Rochdale, where the modern co-op movement was born, by including in its local governance and
economic   development: new   co-operatives   (including

converting local businesses to worker co-ops and creating new co-ops), participatory budgeting and policy making, public procurement and social contracting with local community businesses, and encouraging fair and decent living wages (Preston City Council, n.d.). Jackson, Mississippi is home to a similar yet still emerging initiative, called Cooperation Jackson, which has adapted the Mondragón principles to fit their unique context and history of struggle.

Cooperation Jackson

In Jackson, Mississippi, a group of activists and cooperators are attempting to work with and beyond the city government in order to develop an inclusive, democratic, fair and just social and solidarity economy as a basis for systemic transformation and community wealth building. Its aim is to fundamentally and positively transform the lives of its historically marginalized groups, including the Black and Latino/a/x communities. Co-founded by Kali Akuno and other community organizers, Cooperation Jackson includes the development of new community and worker cooperatives, a community land trust, and mutual aid organizations, all working toward essentially creating a cooperative and networked economy. Inspired by the philosophy of W.E.B. Dubois and other Black leaders, Jessica Gordon Nembhard's book, *Collective Courage*, articulating the history of Black cooperation in the US, and the governance structure of the Mondragón co-ops, the initiative has also been advocating for participatory budgeting and policies, social procurement and contracting, and has worked extensively throughout the pandemic with at-risk people in Jackson.

Cooperation Jackson's principles reflect the group's long-term engagement with Black liberation movements, as seen especially in their version of Social Transformation (Cooperation Jackson, 2022):

Social Transformation: *Cooperation in the Cooperation Jackson system is an instrument for social transformation. Its cooperatives will reinvest the major portion of their surpluses in Jackson and Kush District, the contiguously Afrikan counties of western Mississippi, and a significant remaining portion will go towards cooperation with other institutions advancing the cause of workers and developing a transformative culture in Mississippi.*

In recent years, there has been serious discussion in many circles about adding two other principles to the ICA's seven. At the "Imagine 2012" international cooperative conference in Quebec, a proposal was approved by the assembly to add a clear statement of commitment to ecological values to the list. The intent is that the environment would be a guiding concern in both internal affairs of co-ops such as energy use and to external relationships such as overall environmental impact.

Another principle receiving a great deal of attention now is one that would put a spotlight on efforts toward greater diversity, equity, and inclusion. A new principle along these lines would go beyond open membership – the first principle – to stress proactive outreach to communities that have not been well represented in the cooperative world or even sometimes ignored.

Cooperative principles find an echo in principles of what is termed "the solidarity economy," which are also subject to frequent re-consideration and revision (Noyes, 2017, p. 23). For example, in 2021, a large group of US cooperative and other practitioners conducted a series of discussions about Solidarity Economy Principles (https://solidarityeconomyprinciples.org/about/)

WORKER CO-OPS EMBEDDED IN NETWORKS

Finally, it is important to underscore that cooperatives and other forms of work-centered and collectively self-determined organizations are embedded in larger networks. The density, dispersion, and diversity of membership in these networks, along with the nature of linkages between co-ops and other organizations are all important factors (see Yang et al., 2017). Around the world, in Italy's Emilia Romagna region, the Basque Country in Spain, and the state of Kerala in India, we find a combination of enabling factors:

- a variety of strong and "weak" ties (Granovetter, 1973) in social, familial, and community networks;

- special business districts of interlocking production and a plurality of small- and medium-sized enterprise types;

- strong links between traditional unions and new forms of community organizing like online social networking and immigrant workers' centers;

- accessible and robust financing and funding mechanisms for local economic development that come from multiple sources;

- supportive legislation and policies sensitive to the socio-economic characteristics of the region; and

- numerous locally driven and movement-led initiatives such as struggles to preserve commons-type resources, to effectively provision social services outside of dwindling state programs, and various initiatives for equitable community wealth creation.

Not coincidentally, they all have strong co-operative – and particularly worker and community co-op – sectors, suggestive of what it takes to foster and nourish a cooperative economy. The Bay Area of the US, New York City, and to lesser extents the states of Vermont, Colorado, and Minnesota offer similar, if still emergent, "ecosystems" for co-op development. For example, NoBAWC, the Network of Bay Area Worker Cooperatives (USA) that was founded in 1994, now consists of 36 democratic workplaces that are all part of resource sharing and mutual support (NoBAWC, n.d.). As Aaron Dawson from Industrial Commons, a network of worker and other co-ops in North Carolina, USA, underscores:

> *The greatest advantage to networking across diverse organizations and multiple sectors is the ability to share resources, learnings and skills. A resource or learning developed in one organization, shared out to the greater whole, allows for the entire ecosystem to grow together. But what is important about the networking is that it must all be underpinned by common need. If common need is not the focus, the connection will be superficial, and ultimately fade away.*

(Dawson, personal communication, 2022)

In sum, worker cooperatives are one vehicle – they are not the goal or destination. We believe that they offer workers and communities a better chance of staying on an ethical course than many other business forms. The fact that any organization can "take on a life of its own" and come to be untethered to its founding values is always a concern (Weber, 1978). However, an interesting thought experiment is to imagine a world where cooperatives, including worker co-ops, would be the rule rather than exception. Carrying that idea a bit further, we ask how co-ops would behave if they were the mainstream.

We raise this question to acknowledge that we are not presenting worker co-ops and related organizations as a kind of panacea but rather an inspiring and realistic set of possibilities.

There are some tried and tested cases from which we can learn a lot, notably about employee ownership and democratic governance and which we can extend to still other forms and collaborations. Business as usual – in any sector – is not the way to go, even for worker cooperatives. Hitting the pause button, then, to reflect on what we all are doing and to look for better ways is crucial. Worker co-ops can be an important part of that reflection, subsequent conversation, and much-needed process of restoration by really grappling with the challenges before us and how best to address them creatively and proactively.

OVERVIEW OF THE BOOK

Each chapter that follows posits cooperation at work around a key term: Democracy, Innovation, Community, Environment, and Education.

To help to capture trends and stimulate the organizational imagination about the future, at the end of each chapter we offer a sketch of emergent and conceivable initiatives. Each chapter is designed to incorporate more than one "story line" and to be open to alternative futures.

In Chapter 2, we probe different meanings of democracy at the same time we celebrate democratic models. We do so by considering limitations to certain democratic practices and ways they need to be adapted over time because of developments in organizations and communities, but also because of changing perspectives of successive generations of participants.

We also consider what equity means in terms of both financial stake and economic justice.

In Chapter 3, treating social innovation and entrepreneurship, we push the boundaries of contemporary discussions toward a broader reevaluation of work and economy. Beyond isolated technical or innovations, important as some may be, we and many of our interviewees question received views about pursuing change within largely capitalist frameworks, looking toward broader transformation.

In Chapter 4, we explore traditional, popular, and recent notions of community, advocating a shift toward solidarity as a key term and set of principles. This leads us to apply solidarity to work and community, with examples of worker co-ops and related initiatives from around the world.

Chapter 5, on ecology, questions the paradigm of growth and explains how denial as well as greed operate from systemic levels to the domain of individual choices. We challenge worker co-ops and other types of organizations to deepen commitments to sustainability, integrating them into internal and external practices.

We reconsider education in Chapter 6, particularly in an age of where dialogue, justice, and inclusion must be part of a vision of democratic participation. There are many types of educational and communication initiatives that reach groups small and large, encouraging them to design their own projects and pursue their own dreams.

In the pages that follow, we invite you to revisit familiar assumptions about these topics, to discover more about the potential for worker co-ops and the wider cooperative economy, and to see through the eyes of many people who are working in and building an economy that truly fits our democratic ideals.

2

DEMOCRACY, EQUITY, AND JUSTICE

INTRODUCTION

Molly Kendall was attracted to work at RESOURCE, in Tasmania, Australia, because the people working there looked happy. There was a positive vibe about this worker cooperative that promotes waste minimization by selling salvaged items from the landfill in a "tip shop" (shops located at landfills that sell salvaged objects), operates an arts supply store of recovered art parts and a sustainability focused deconstruction (demolition with an eye for reclamation of materials) service. The slogan emblazoned across the bottom of their website, "Reduce → Reuse → Recycle → Resource," speaks to their vision for the community; but their first objective, as a worker cooperative, is to create just employment. It is this commitment that has spurred the cooperative to expand activities beyond the tip shop, adding projects and offering educational workshops, starting their deconstruction service and opening an arts supply shop. The cooperative also funds an Art from Trash exhibition and donates to various charities that are mission aligned.

Operational decisions are made by the active worker-members of the co-op. The decision to limit participation to active status – determined by a minimum threshold of working hours and attendance at meetings – ensures that those workers who are impacted by the operational decisions participate in making those decisions. In this way, democratic practices play a critical role in the experience of what it means to work at RESOURCE and perhaps explain the joyful culture that attracted Molly to work there in the first place.

In this chapter, we discuss a range of meanings and applications of the important term "democracy." We then demonstrate that worker co-ops and related organizations have the structure and capacity to maximize the economic sharing and collective decision making which together make work more democratic.

WHAT IS DEMOCRACY, AND WHY DOES IT MATTER?

Democracy, literally "rule by the people," remains one of the most important yet contested terms today. The terminology itself matters, not only because of confusion and contention over what democracy *is* but also because we can think of democracy as part of a larger constellation of concepts including cooperation, collaboration, governance, voting, majority rule, consensus, commoning, sharing, horizontal organizational structure, and, of course, participation.

Today, democracy may be imperfect in any of its expressions, yet it remains a beacon for many societies in their strivings toward a future with greater justice for all (Taylor, 2019). A majority of contemporary nations will assert a commitment to democracy, yet many people harbor doubts about how democracy can be maintained (Rancière, 2006).

Democracy is asserted cynically by many leaders as well, including in authoritarian regimes claiming to represent or speak for "the people." It has become common in recent years to speak of a crisis of democracy in a way that was not as prevalent before the 2010s.

Modern democracy, as a commitment to the will and participation of the people, is often seen as progressive realization of a liberal social and political order in which rights are gradually expanded – both in the constellation of rights and in the inclusion of more people and even non-humans such as chimpanzees and rivers (compare Benhabib, 2004; Ishay, 2004). The Universal Declaration of Human Rights (1948), albeit formulated largely within Euro-American traditions by the Allied powers in the ashes of World War II, was nevertheless revolutionary in according to all people a long list of rights, including "positive" economic, social and cultural rights, and "negative" freedoms, such as freedom from coercion and torture. Today we find opposition to political democracy – understood as a form of direct or representative governance or some mix of the two – to be significant across many nations of the world, including within the largely capitalist democratic powers. Across a clear majority of nations, still, we find a commonality with respect to the world of work: most workers are required to leave many of their rights behind as they go to work.

Many versions of democracy spring from grassroots efforts all over the world, especially in response to local needs and often outside the reach of large corporations and without the help of government. Worker cooperatives are part of local webs, as shown in Indian villages such as Menda, Maharashtra, where villagers have not only organized themselves ownership of many small businesses but also agreed on their own set of principles that include disaster preparedness, management of natural resources, and mobilization in times of crisis (Kerswell & Pratap, 2019).

The history of democracy and democratic yearnings is tightly intertwined with the history of power, another concept with great resonance in vernacular as well as academic discourses. Power is an equally contested and ambiguous term; still, no one doubts its significance as a key dimension of human experience, often defined as one's or a group's ability to do something, even against the will of others (Weber, 1978; compare Foucault, 1984; and Habermas, 1979). In the intellectual and practical history of power, the notion of "power over" (i.e., *potere*) is the accustomed sense of the term, much more than is "power with" (i.e., *potenza*) (e.g., Lukes, 1974). This dual understanding of power is instructive in that it crystallizes common doubts about the prospects for collective empowerment, horizontal cooperation, and something even beginning to approach universal participation.

Beginning in the 2010s, at the same time that prevailing Euro-American plans for economic globalization were being further disrupted, there was a significant rise in authoritarian political parties and governments in many countries from Hungary to the Philippines (Bloom, 2016). Importantly, many observers do not see large-scale democratic governance as even viable, while others offer specific solutions including elevating the role of *mediating organizations* at the levels of communities and regions to bridge some of the structural distance between members of society and their national or federal government in large countries. Discussions range from announcements of the coming collapse of democratic institutions (e.g., Levitsky & Ziblatt, 2018) to how best to regain democracy in unexpected, open, grassroots, and proliferating forms (Landemore, 2020).

Worker Cooperatives, Politics, and the State

Worker cooperativism has always been, in certain ways, political. As Jessica Gordon Nembhard reminds us in *Collective Courage* (2016), the mere existence of cooperation in Black communities in the US was seen as such a threat to the white power structure that it was repressed, often with violence and terror. In various historical contexts, trade unionism, cooperativism, and commoning have coincided in visions of a true *commonwealth*. The overtly political cooperatives supported by the Zapatista movement in Chiapas, Mexico and the women's and social ecology cooperatives of Rojava in northeastern Syria are important examples. But the political role of cooperatives has spanned the political spectrum. In former colonies like Kenya, South Africa, and Sri Lanka, cooperatives were integrated into the politics of colonial domination and imperialism, only to become important players in more democratic newly established states (Patmore & Balnave, 2018; Rhodes, 2012).

Certainly, cooperatives have not ignored the state. In Emilia-Romagna, Catalunya, Venezuela, South Korea, and Ghana, for example, cooperatives and their supporters have lobbied municipal and national governments to take steps to encourage the formation of cooperatives. The results have been remarkable and not limited to the best-known examples in Emilia Romagna and the Basque Country. Other examples are found in Kerala, India where cooperatives like the Uralungal Labour Contract Co-operative Society (ULCCS) benefit from exclusive government contracts and Japan, where the Japan Worker Cooperative Union (JWCU), which started as a labor union, transformed itself into a worker cooperative group that contracts with the state, providing social services. The initial wave of cooperative development in South Korea yielded 25,000 cooperatives, approximately 400 of them worker cooperatives, with government financial support rising from $25 million in 2012 to $560 million in 2020 (Ji, personal communication, 2021).

One lesson of these examples has been that the development of successful worker cooperatives depends on worker self-organization for which even the best-intentioned government support is no substitute (Razeto, 2019). In Chiapas,

Mexico, for instance, most worker cooperatives are deeply rooted in communities which are organized to operate mostly autonomously from the Mexican government (Irezabal, personal communication, 2022; Zentle Colotl, personal communication, 2021). The Rojava Cooperatives were organized in the context of a military struggle for autonomy against multiple states, integrating feminist principles and practice in a context of economic crisis, corporate failure, and government austerity. In the recuperated factories in Argentina, abandoned by their owners, resources were seized and placed at the service of communities (Ranis, 2016; Vieta, 2020).

DEMOCRACY AT WORK AND BEYOND

Many of the issues concerning political democracy are also relevant to organizations, work, and work arrangements. This is a central point of Pateman's (1970) now-classic book about democracy and participation in workplaces, cooperatives, and in societies. She examined a range of cases from the first two thirds of the twentieth century, ranging from the implementation of socio-technical systems in coal mines in the UK to self-management by workers' councils in the former Yugoslavia. In these and many other cases, a broad-scale analysis of participation at work necessarily brings in the life of the larger polity (Cheney, 1998).

If democratic ideals and practices are to be taken seriously and applied deeply, then the realm of work cannot be cordoned off from social and political life – especially in terms of the freedoms of workers – regardless of whether an employer is private, public or nonprofit (Ezorsky, 2007). Carrying this point even further, Ellerman (2021) presents a case for "the abolition of all human rentals," referring to any employment situation where wages or salaries compensate workers but where they do not control the equity and decision-making of the firm. While obviously a radical proposition in certain respects, Ellerman ultimately argues that a two-pronged workplace democracy – workers' co-ownership and democratic governance – actually transcends the usual bifurcation between capitalism and socialism.

Types and Levels of Participation at Work

Because power and democracy are closely intertwined, it is important for analysts of organizations as well as cooperative members to make distinctions among levels and impacts of participation by workers or employees. Based on his studies of many different types of organizations, Paul Bernstein (1982, 2012) calls attention to three factors with respect to participation in decision-making: (1) *the degree* of control employees exert in decision making by the firm; (2) *the issues* over which workers can have influence; and (3) *the level* of the hierarchy that can be "reached" by employees. Each of these criteria invites practical questions in organizational design and, above all, about the potential for worker control. For Bernstein, worker participation is a spectrum – from less consequential "comments box" schemes on one end, to full decision-making power on the other. Thus, a meeting may be an opportunity for full participation on key decisions or it may consist largely of one-way messages from managers. Employees may participate in self-directed work teams, but are their recommendations about improving products, services, working conditions, or major policies taken seriously by upper levels of the organization?

From a different angle, relying on feminist organizational theory, Iannello (2013) directs our attention to "the starting point" in any organizational analysis. If the starting point is a hierarchical bureaucracy, then the analysis of power and participation is already in a "subordinate" position, if you will, in terms of arguing for democratization, consensus, and more relational approaches to work and organizational structure.

42   Cooperatives at Work

> This makes it even more important to consider what anybody
> takes for granted in terms of organizational structure: as
> George has found in the classroom, it is often difficult for
> students to consider concentric circles as an alternative to the
> familiar pyramidal form.

Governance is another term with many meanings. Its practical applications include contexts such as the composition of corporate boards, the system by which decisions are made in any organization, and national or international governmental structures. Treating businesses and other organizations as political entities, in the sense of their being seats of power and decision making, Ferreras (2017) argues strongly for "bicameralism," by which she refers to balances of power that are structurally built into a worker co-op or similar enterprise through checks and balances between at least two main bodies. In fact, this structure is a chief feature of the Mondragón cooperatives, where selected managers have a specified domain of concern with the day-to-day operations of the firm whereas the general assembly and elected councils (or committees) are intended to be the chief policy-making organs of the business (Whyte & Whyte, 1991).

There are also meaningful interactions between work-based participation and participation in the wider community (Bianchi & Vieta, 2020). For example, equitable and informed participation is considered essential to the integrity and success of both cooperative businesses and their wider communities. Issues related to power, hierarchy, and conflict also must be confronted in cooperative structure, development and day-to-day operations, just as they are in communities (Tompkins, 1962). For instance, "creeping hierarchical distance" can develop over time between those who hold positions of authority and those who do not in co-ops as well as in communities. Such problems can lead to the atrophy of participation as well as widespread cynicism about adherence to core values (Cheney, 2002; Rothschild & Whitt, 1986).

Today, a great deal of research is devoted to participatory "spillover effects," referring to how co-op level, workplace, and organizational participation can inspire and engender more active community and political participation (DuFays et al., 2020; Pateman, 1970). We see these dynamics in and around the Mondragón cooperatives, for example, in programs that have emerged around the co-ops to revive community participation and neighborhood control over issues that matter in the lives of the people outside of work.

The question of the effects of participation in worker co-ops on political life more broadly is far from new. For example, Greenberg (1986) looked closely at the data for the plywood cooperatives of the Pacific Northwest of the United States during their heyday in the 1940s and 1950s, and those of other cooperative institutions including Israeli kibbutzim. He concluded that the level of engagement of worker-owners in wider political life was highly variable by context but also that education about democracy was key to overcoming political alienation in the public sphere and encouraging cooperative practices.

Spillover can also work in the other direction. Political participation in the wider community can stimulate or even initiate forms of workplace participation, social entrepreneurship, and formation of cooperatives (Spear, 2019). Workers or other community stakeholders can import expectations for participation from the political sphere to work, even if they are not formally organized in unions, committees, or any other structure. Some accounts of the Occupy movement, at its height in 2011–2012, trace the development of new worker co-ops 10 years later to the legacy of activism in that broad-based, decentralized democratic

movement (Gitlin, 2012), which had as a core principle
challenging centralized corporate power (Kelly, personal
communication, 2020).

In his work with Argentina's *empresas recuperadas* co-ops,
Marcelo found positive impacts on worker attitudes toward
both democracy at work and involvement in the community.
Specifically, because of their shared workplace struggles and
engagement in co-operative projects, most of the workers he
interviewed experienced "some degree of positive transformations in their knowledge, skills, attitudes, or values" in
six key areas of participatory life:

> *(1) in their democratic and cooperative practices at*
> *work...; (2) in their personal behaviours towards*
> *and interactions with others...; (3) in their ability to*
> *influence political decisions both inside and outside*
> *of the [cooperative]; (4) in their concern and interest*
> *in community affairs beyond the [co-op]; (5) in how*
> *connected they feel to the broader community; and*
> *(6) in their actual participation in community within*
> *and outside of the [co-op].*
>
>   (Vieta, 2020, p. 492)

Democratic influences can also be historically and culturally embedded. For the Basque Country, it has been observed
that democratic territorial practices preexisted modern institutions. Among them were laws that protected collective
forms of property, enduring norms of reciprocity typical of
rural society, and the existence of numerous local social clubs
at the beginning of industrialization. These are among the
cultural institutions by which social capital was established
and sustained in the Basque territory, creating fertile soil for
cooperative development (Azkarraga, 2018).

It has been observed that the "*fueros*," or democratic territorial charters that preexisted the incorporation of the Basque Country into the monarchy, and now federation, of

modern Spain, are far more than historical footnotes. The *fueros* left important legacies that manifest still in the popularity of open debate in public places about political issues, in the creation of numerous local social clubs, and in the insistence that the highest political body is the general assembly representing the people. This is one of cultural traditions that made fertile soil for cooperative development (Azkarraga, 2018). Similarly, many of the workplaces that would be converted to cooperatives in Argentina had long traditions of working-class democratic organs on shop floors, including shop stewards' committees and union-based workers' assemblies (Vieta, 2020).

In short, long-standing cultural commitments to democratic practice can provide fertile cultural soil for cooperatives; at the same time, cultural leanings toward individualism, short-term perspectives, and immediate consumer demands, can create headwinds even for existing cooperative systems like Mondragón (Freundlich, personal communication, 2022), as we discuss further in Chapters 4 and 5.

The consequences of creating more democratic workplaces can extend beyond social and cultural practices and stimulate bottom-up responses to rising wealth inequalities. Indeed, the wealth gap is one of the motivators for the development of worker co-ops. As Camille Kerr (personal communication, 2021), co-op developer who helped found ChiFresh and Principal at Upside Down Consulting, in Chicago, puts it: "Worker co-ops open the door for people's imagination for what our economy could look like if our priorities are different from those of the elite, and instead reflect our values [when] our values are around people."

The concentration of wealth and the favor given to transnational corporate enterprises, nevertheless, make democratic experimentation at the grassroots level extremely challenging. Understanding both political participation and economic stakes is crucial for analyzing any large-scale democracy but also for realizing the full potential of the worker-cooperative and other related models locally.

In addition, worker cooperatives that are exclusive in terms of membership, risk maintaining racial and cultural privilege because of a conscious or partially conscious leaning toward homogeneity. As network research demonstrates, such in-group "closure" also limits the input of new information and new ideas, including perspective-taking on the organization's own practices (Granovetter, 1973). As has been documented, some co-ops have fallen into this trap when people of similar backgrounds and overlapping identities come together to create a cooperative (Rothschild & Whitt, 1986).

Diversity, Inclusion, and Power in Co-ops

In 2020, #blacklivesmatter protesters took to the streets in countries around the world. Like the #MeToo movement of the several previous years, these protests caused many organizations, including cooperatives and other values-driven businesses, to look inwardly at their own practices and to consider whether they were truly reflective of the inclusiveness they espoused.

Jessica Gordon Nembhard reflects that since the publication of *Collective Courage* (Gordon Nembhard, 2014) she is often asked to speak to groups that have come to feel that they have missed opportunities to connect with Black and Brown communities in particular. Her recommendations include the following:

- Make sure to connect with people's histories and that you recognize what kinds of cooperative initiatives that people are already active in, even if informal.

- Diversity is not just one-stop thinking about individuals and more about inclusion of groups of people. Don't ask one person to be the spokesperson for a group of people or a token participant.

- Recently, Gordon Nembhard and others have adopted the acronym DIEJ, for Diversity, Inclusion, Equity, and Justice. Gordon-Nembhard explains DIEJ this way: "Diversity means you are invited to the dance. Inclusion means you are asked to dance, you actually dance, and are talked to at the dance. Equity [means]... not just dancing but participating in planning the dance and helping make decisions about food, music, invitation list, etc... Justice means power is shared and there is... democratic ownership and control. Unlike diversity and inclusion, which are low level and low stakes activities, equity and actual justice... are more difficult. Achieving justice is a continuous process – to achieve it we must continuously address power inequities and inequalities" (Gordon Nembhard, personal communication, 2022).

Some worker cooperatives such as the US-based AORTA (Anti-Oppression Resource and Training Alliance), offer consulting, facilitating, education and training for businesses, institutions, and other cooperatives to overcome existing power structures that reinforce historically discriminatory practices. In particular, AORTA identified effective conflict resolution processes as being core to an organization's being able to disrupt harmful power dynamics when under stress. ACE, the Association of Cooperative Educators (https://ed.coop/learning-path/inclusion/), is notable among co-op associations for having compiled many DEI (Diversity-Equity-Inclusion) materials on their website for all individuals and organizations to share. The University of Wisconsin Center for Cooperatives, with a long-standing research arm, has recently found that a much larger number of worker and other co-ops in North America consist of Latinx worker-owners than was previously on the cooperative radar (West & Gordon Nembhard, 2020).

Tim Huet, co-founder and co-op developer with Arizmendi Association of Cooperatives in California agrees that a clear conflict management process needs to be part of every worker-member's co-operative training (Huet, personal communication, 2022). In the chain of Arizmendi bakeries in the Bay Area, each co-op has a conflict resolution team that can be called upon if there is uncertainty in how to deal with an issue, in addition to all member-owners agreeing on a set of guidelines of dealing with problems as they arise. In preparing for moments when entrenched patterns of power dynamics can arise, cooperatives can deal with all sorts of differences and misunderstandings effectively.

The trends discussed in the previous paragraphs, if anything, underscore the importance of diversity, inclusion, equity and justice. Worker cooperatives are unique among the range of cooperative models because of their twin pillars of shared financial equity and participation in decision making (Pencavel, 2013). This is not to dismiss other forms of businesses that allow for degrees of participation, such as ESOPs or non-cooperative or social enterprises, but it is to say that worker co-ops by design and function aim to maximize both dimensions.

The expansion of democracy to workplaces is not only about political rights but also about economic share and common ownership. Shared ownership can take many forms, from certain types of profit sharing with employees, to employee stock ownership plans (or ESOPs), to solidarity-based investment clubs, to worker cooperatives of employees co-sharing ownership with more traditional shareholders (as in with Quebec's worker-shareholder co-ops), to large-scale networks of worker-owned and social enterprises called "Fair Shares" (Ridley-Duff, 2015). Here, we focus on worker cooperatives where the overwhelming bulk of equity value of the firm is literally co-owned by members, even if some non-voting stock is held by supporting investors.

ESOPs and their equivalents, while having impressive track records in a number of countries, focus on one of these dimensions: employee ownership, which involves a percentage of the equity or monetary value of the firm that can reach 100%. They vary in terms of worker input into and control of decisions, which in most cases remains with managers or conventional owners. Moreover, most ESOPs are incentivized by offering tax credits to the firms' original owners and access to equity is normally concentrated in retirement earnings, including the accrual of interest (Vieta et al., 2016). It is true that ESOPs offer employees intrinsic (i.e., social, psychological) and extrinsic (i.e., monetary) benefits (Blasi et al., 2017). Recent empirical evidence shows that for US-based ESOPs, as compared with firms where there is no significant collective ownership, turnover is less, median income is higher, and job satisfaction is greater (Marks, 2022). Still, democratic decision making is not inherent or maximized in the ESOP structure, and therefore must be assessed in specific cases.

Some cooperative development centers and employee ownership centers deal with both worker co-ops and ESOPs. They focus on increasing public and, in particular, business owner awareness of the possibilities of converting private firms to worker co-ops or ESOPs. This is occurring in a variety of industries from farms to factories to childcare centers. The argument often made is that if the existing owners want to preserve their companies' core activities and social values, they can effectively do so by converting to worker-owned businesses of one type or another (for more on this, see Co-opConvert https://www.coopconvert.ca/). The Ohio Employee Ownership Center and the Vermont Employee

Ownership Center's (VEOC) projects are predominantly conversions. These centers speak about the "silver tsunami" of retiring Baby Boomer business owners who may not have plans for succession. Matt Cropp, Director of VEOC, emphasizes different "perks" such as job retention, career goals, or legacy for business owners, depending on whether he's addressing those in their early careers versus those who are semi-retired (Cropp, personal communication, 2022). At the same time, publications by these and other similar centers stress growing economic inequality in the US and other countries and the advantages of employee ownership for creating stable employment in communities (Palmieri & Cooper, 2021).

UNION DEMOCRACY AND WORKER CO-OP DEMOCRACY

Democracy in the workplace and in work arrangements has had a shaky standing, even in many avowedly democratic countries. Of course, one of the major thrusts of the organized labor movement since the early nineteenth century has been an effort to strengthen workers relative to corporate owners and top-level managers, often at great struggle and sacrifice, and with significant backsliding in Labor power at times, including the past 40-plus years (Lichtenstein, 2013).

From the standpoint of theories of power, labor unions are typically positioned as "countervailing" forces that both help set limits on corporate and managerial power and promote workers' rights – understood first in collective terms and then by offering security and recourse for individual workers. The labor movement's achievements are many, although they are often subsumed or marginalized in historical accounts of modern business (Greenhouse, 2019). That has been even truer during the period of labor's diminished power under the dominance of neoliberal economic policies that include, for instance, a comparatively greater emphasis on taming inflation than on guaranteeing full or stable employment. The uneasy compromise with organized labor during the post-war period was followed by many employer strategies that undermined, co-opted, and in some cases attacked union power.

For the past two centuries, the labor movement and the cooperative movement have not always been tightly intertwined. In fact, there has often been tension between the two despite the fact that some of the very first cooperatives in the United States in the late 1700s and early 1800s were themselves sponsored by labor organizations. One exceptional example of union collaboration with co-ops was the endorsement and promotion of worker cooperatives by the Knights of Labor in the late-nineteenth and early-twentieth centuries (Curl, 2012). The overall lack of historical relationship between these two movements, however, is due to misunderstanding as well as struggles over influence. There have been important philosophical and practical differences as well. In a worker cooperative a key premise is that labor is considered to "hire" capital, rather than the reverse as in conventional capitalist firms. That is, there is not an obvious need for a union to mediate the capital–labor relationship when it is labor that effectively controls capital.

It was on this basis, for example, that the Mondragón cooperatives actually fired labor organizers in 1974. At the same time, some commentators in recent decades have been observing the continued need for unions in worker co-op workplaces since the organizational evolution of any particular cooperative (and union) may lead to significant hierarchical distance between the rank-and-file members and individuals in what we would generally call managerial roles (Basterretxea et al., 2022; Clay, 2013). This is often part of the dynamic of organizational growth, the concentration of power, and the temptation toward excessive bureaucratization that were understood so well by sociologist Max Weber (1978) in the first two decades of the twentieth century (see also Michels et al., 2017).

In principle, worker cooperatives, like labor unions, are democratic, member-controlled worker organizations. Both are owned by their members and operate with by-laws that establish the democratic rights of members. The existence of legal rights by itself of course does not guarantee that organizations will operate democratically. The enforcement mechanisms are in many ways insufficient, and undemocratic and corrupt practices persist (Benson, 2004). But union members continue in their efforts to make their organizations more democratic and effective, as seen in the decades-long organizing of the Teamsters for a Democratic Union, for example.

Worker cooperatives benefit from a more comprehensive and coherent legal framework at the start: the business itself is a statute-based democracy. Because worker cooperatives are still businesses operating in a capitalist market, there are tendencies to adopt structures and practices that are well suited to the business environment but ill-suited to the development and renewal of grassroots democracy. Interestingly, where union democracy and cooperative democracy overlap, we see how bottom-up worker organization can flourish.

> *In the worker-owned cooperative if these two interests can come together, the likelihood for high productivity, worker loyalty and other material benefits for the firm is high. Further, the two can be partners supporting unions in non-cooperative*

> *enterprises in the area and more broadly. In the case*
> *of Mondragón, for example, its worker-members*
> *support the unionization of and collective bargaining*
> *in surrounding non-cooperative firms.*
>
> (Miller, personal communication, 2022)

The series of factory occupations at Republic Windows and Doors in Chicago in 2008–2011 that led to the recuperation of the plant as a worker cooperative called New Era Windows gained public attention, in part, because the workers revived an old labor tactic, emulating what the workers of the *empresas recuperadas por sus trabajadores* (worker-recuperated companies) of Argentina did: the factory occupation. Less known is the struggle for union democracy that laid the foundation of grassroots democratic organization with the workers of Republic Windows and Doors. When the previous company union failed to defend the Republic workers' rights, the workers organized a decertification campaign and created a new local of the United Electrical (UE) union, a union well-known for its internal democracy (Lyderson, 2009; Mulder, 2015). In this now-famous case, democratic self-organizing was the thread running from the fight for union democracy through the factory occupations and resulting in the successful conversion of the company to a worker-owned and -governed cooperative.

Argentina's Empresas Recuperadas por sus Trabajadores (Worker-Recuperated Companies)

Argentina's *empresas recuperadas por sus trabajadores* (ERTs, or worker-recuperated companies) began to emerge in the 1990s and early 2000s as workers' responses to neoliberal structural adjustments by multilateral institutions such as the World Bank and the International Monetary Fund, business restructurings, and the ultimate (if temporary) failure of the country's neoliberal political economy at the turn of the millennium. The ensuing socioeconomic crisis caused thousands of business closures. Many of the closures were caused by business owners themselves taking advantage of the crisis. For example, owners would declare bankruptcy and then take assets such as machines – which should have gone to pay for the bankruptcy – in order to sell them privately or use them to restart a business in another locale. Together with an increasingly unresponsive state that had become overwhelmed by growing life precariousness and its eventual loss of legitimacy, more and more workers in insolvent capitalist firms were thus compelled to take matters into their own hands by occupying and ultimately converting them into worker cooperatives. Continuing to emerge to this day, ERTs have become bottom-up initiatives spearheaded by workers themselves for saving jobs and businesses. They have also proven to be a new form of labor organizing linked to the country's newest grassroots social movements that arose during the neoliberal crisis years (Ranis, 2016; Vieta, 2019, 2020).

ERTs are a form of "labor-conflict" conversion to a co-operative, as differentiated from "negotiated" worker buyouts or succession conversions, such as many planned conversions assisted by employee ownership and cooperative development centers. ERTs are also to be found in other jurisdictions with a rich labor or worker cooperative tradition, deep-rooted social movement activity, and that have experienced neoliberal crises in recent years, such as in Brazil and Uruguay, and with smaller pockets in Mexico, Paraguay, Colombia, Peru, Greece, Turkey, Tunisia, Egypt, Italy, France, and Spain. Argentina's ERT movement remains the world's largest. As of this writing, around 16,000 workers were self-managing more than 400 ERTs throughout Argentina's urban economy in sectors as diverse as printing and publishing, media, metallurgy, foodstuffs, construction, textiles, tourism, education, health care, and shipbuilding (Ruggeri, personal communication, 2021).

Indeed, unions have been involved in creating and converting to co-ops in varying degrees in different national contexts in recent years. In Quebec, for instance, union assistance in workplace conversions and co-operative start-ups occurs with the backing of Quebec's Confédération des Sindicats Nationaux (CSN, National Confederation of Unions), union and social economy consulting entities, and the use of labor-run solidarity funds (see the case studies on Quebec in Co-opConvert, 2022). Facilitated by Italy's Macora Law provisions (see Chapter 3), many of Italy's unions work with the country's cooperative federations and other support organizations to create new co-ops via worker buyouts or by converting former mafia-owned businesses to cooperatives (Vieta et al., 2017). Argentina's more historically militant unions, such as the steelworkers and printing and graphics unions, have also played central roles in supporting worker-recuperated companies. In Uruguay, 50 or so *empresas recuperadas* have been supported by the country's apex union federation, the PIT–CNT, working with its traditional cooperative sector's apex organization, the FCPU (Federation of Producer Cooperatives of Uruguay) (Vieta, 2020).

Because worker cooperatives have, in principle, resolved the fundamental contradiction between wage-labor and capital by sharing ownership and democratizing governance its worker-members are less likely to outwardly seek out or think they need organized labor's support compared to workers employed by an owner or manager in a conventional capitalist business. On the other hand, this localized resolution of class conflict in favor of a type of unitary democracy (Mansbridge, 1983) in worker co-ops can still lead to "movement degeneration," the loss of solidarity with workers within the co-op and with workers in other companies, industries, regions, and nations.

Union Worker Co-Ops

We have spoken about parallels and differences between labor union-based democracy and democracy in a worker co-op. An important development since 2012 is the emergence of explicit joint relationships between labor unions and worker co-ops. This is an important trend for several reasons, not the least being that they have often operated in different spheres, with limited collaboration, and with occasional tensions.

The joining of labor unions and worker co-ops in certain ventures, such as in start-ups in the US, Italy, Quebec, Uruguay, Argentina, and elsewhere is in part a recognition of the need for broader coalitions and the pooling of resources, including for frequently under-funded worker co-op start-ups. It also represents an opening to new forms of cooperative structure. In a foundational white paper (Witherell et al., 2012), possible arrangements between a formal union (whether industrial, service, communication, or some other type) and co-ops are articulated. The union worker co-op has typical by-laws spelling out roles, governance, and patronage (or owner) dividends. Alongside such a document is also a collective bargaining agreement for those worker-owners who are members of the union. That agreement would typically cover such policies as: relations with management, wages, sick days, vacations, discipline, and dispute resolution.

Importantly, the role of what is called the social council in the Mondragón system, a key union-like organ that represents workers from across the co-op to preserve and advocate their interests, is replicated by the labor union in the model which has been tested in the large co-op network Co-op Cincy (Ohio), Cooperation Jackson (Mississippi), and similar initiatives in Seattle, Pittsburgh, and Denver – all in the US. These union-co-op initiatives give a specific, additional collective voice to worker-owners, in the interest of checks and balances with both elected leaders and appointed managers (in cases where there are both). To date, union worker co-ops have been developed in a wide range of fields or industries: care work, alternative energy, bakeries, grocery stores, taxi services, and greenhouses. Baldemar Velasquez, president of the Farm Labor Organizing Committee, based in North Carolina but extending across many US states, sees great promise for union-worker co-ops in agriculture as well, especially to give bargaining power to farm laborers and at the same time offer them a route to accruing equity for themselves (Velasquez, 2021).

As Kristen Barker, Executive Director of Co-op Cincy, observes about this type of coalition:

> *The union co-op model joins the best tenets of the labor movement with opportunities for sustainable wealth-building and self-determination. We love it because it creates a reinforcing structure within a co-op that helps a co-op to scale with its values intact, maintaining worker voice and input as the co-op grows. Just as importantly, the model connects co-op workers to the larger labor movement, a key platform for acting in solidarity with other workers and improving conditions for all.*
>
> (Barker, personal communication, 2022)

DEMOCRACY AT WORK AS AN ONGOING PROCESS

One of the most challenging aspects of a commitment to democratic practice is the acceptance of change in democratic structures themselves. This is the "reflexive" dimension of democracy; that is, to be true to democratic ideals, the system itself cannot be static. At the national level, the dilemma arises over successive interpretations of a constitution. At the organizational level, it means that designs themselves must be subject

to review and change – with democracy itself subject to reinvention. At the level of a meeting, a facilitator or team leader
confronts the ethical challenge when they allow for a democratic
process to unfold even while fearing – perhaps for what they feel
is a very good reason – the specific decisional outcome.

Democracy and ethics have a complex relationship. To raise
democracy to the level of a core principle is to affirm it as a virtue
at the collective level (see Appiah, 2008). This is true in contexts
from small groups to global systems. Yet, the primacy of
democracy is challenged not only because of genuine disagree-
ments over its status as a primary goal but also because of certain
leaders' fear of losing control.

At the same time, the path for any avowedly democratic
arrangement – including at work – involves confronting ethical
as well as practical tensions. In ethical theory, a major distinction is between "consequentialist" approaches that emphasize
the outcome of a decision and a "deontological" position that
stresses duty to uphold certain principles (Frankena, 1973). This
difference heightens awareness that a democratic (including
consensus-based) decision-making method can still yield an
undesirable outcome. Conversely, a non- or partially democratic method can result in an ultimately desirable outcome.
How this tension is managed in practice requires self-reflection
for any group (Cheney et al., 2010).

Institutionalizing democracy, as planned by a worker cooperative, should be pursued with awareness of the need to modify
the system itself. Commitment to democracy together with
adaptability become essential for the vibrancy of a democratic
system. Ongoing attention to governance and participation are
in these ways key to a co-op's longevity as well as success
(Cornforth, 2004; Cornforth et al., 1988).

A closely related issue for democratic organizations is what
Weber (1978) understood very well: how does the organization preserve the spirit and energy of the founders? In his view,

this is the predicament of trying to "routinize charisma" in an organization, which is especially important for businesses and other enterprises that are value-driven. For a worker cooperative, as with many other value-based organizations, allowing for new perspectives on the principles and practices to emerge with subsequent waves of workers is a major challenge. Democracy itself, if its principles are taken seriously, must be subject to revisions over time. At Mondragón or any other long-standing cooperative or cooperative network allowing for new inputs and even new interpretations of fundamental values is crucial.

At the same time a worker co-op, like most other groups or organizations, will itself go through certain phases. Whitman (2011) uses the term "life cycle," a common metaphor in research on groups and organizations. In practice this means that certain kinds of functions and roles will be more important at different times in the life of a cooperative. The documentary *Food for Change* (Alves, 2014) portrays this very well through interviews with founding members and later joiners of a food cooperative. For example, there are roles for people who are visionaries, especially in the early stages of the development of a co-op. But other functions are needed as the co-op gets established, standardizes its operations, and solidifies its identity in its community and its industry. It may be more appropriate, though, to speak of cycles rather than a single lifecycle, simply because a vibrant democratic workplace can and should reinvent itself.

Indeed, reflecting deeply on the role of democracy and participation in the firm, and perhaps reinventing democracy itself, may be so much a part of the make-up of a democratic organization that relationships and structures become more fluid than solidified. This is a case of "strength in diversity" advantage of the multi-stakeholder or inclusive cooperative (Miner & Novkovic, 2020). For example, rotating savings and credit associations (ROSCAs) organized by Black women throughout the Caribbean and in other parts of the world, are co-operative and community-driven MSC self-help banks that directly address the marginalization of these communities by mainstream banks. They do so by being "embedded in social relationships" of mutual support, including family and wider social networks (Hossein, 2015, p. 7). Cuba's *organopónico* urban farms also bring a wide cross-section of stakeholders from the neighborhood to ensure the steady cultivation, harvesting, and distribution of produce to local people (Koont, 2011).

Voting and Democracy at Mondragón

Joxe Azurmendi (1992) tells the story of how Mondragón founder José María Arizmendiarrieta once intervened in a unique way in a debate about democracy taking place in the industrial cooperatives: should they introduce a system of "qualified" voting in which the votes cast by members with more skill or experience would be given extra weight? (p. 593–596).

In the August 1963 issue of the Mondragón newsletter *Cooperación*, which he edited and largely wrote, Arizmendiarrieta published two letters to the editor taking opposing positions (Arizmendiarrieta, 1963). The first, presented as coming from "a group of cooperativists," argued that the vote of the "most qualified" members should count for more, with a maximum limit of 3:1. They argued:

- Cooperatives are in a war, fighting for a new social order, and have to wage that war in an economy undergoing constant technological change.

- Any social movement needs leaders who are tested and supported by the members. In return, the leaders have a great burden of solidarity to their fellow members.

- People are different and have different skills and capabilities. It is dehumanizing to treat human beings as if they were abstract units, as in "One member equals one vote."

- The qualification is not arbitrary. Technical, personal, leadership skills, as well as experience and commitment should all be taken into account. Not everyone is suited to leadership.

- It is not unfair. The constant education of cooperative members would enable any worker to obtain these qualifications over time.

- In the necessary search for effective and bold management, democracy should not be treated as a dogma, but as a practical solution. Voting is a tool not a dogma.

The second letter, from "a visitor to Mondragón," argued that the "qualified" vote was simply a fraud, a kind of "aristo-democracy" that reflected the corrupting influence of the capitalist society on cooperatives, which, voluntarily or involuntarily begin to incorporate its elements.

- Qualified voting is reactionary. It favors those already in control and weakens those who are already weak. The holders of the more qualified votes already exercise disproportionate influence in the organization due to their socioeconomic position.

- The qualified vote rests on a false premise: that all members have the same consciousness and only differ in their technical capacity and that when making decisions, those with higher qualifications will be

motivated purely by technical considerations. In reality
purely technical decisions rarely if ever occur.

- Our ideologies are shaped by our socio-economic
  positions. Not all members share the same interests
  and ideology, consequently the weighted vote is really
  just a way to reinforce the domination of one group of
  interests and ideology – those of the people already in
  control.

- Not only does qualified voting "give weapons to those
  who are already best armed," the idea that the qualified voters will use those "weapons" to make good
  decisions on behalf of the others is just vulgar
  paternalism.

In fact, both letters were secretly written by Arizmendiarrieta, a tactic that enabled Arizmendiarrieta to sharpen and
deepen the debate without using his authority to sway the
reader. It also reflected his faith in dialogue as the fundamental
condition of learning and cooperation, and his unwillingness
to try to resolve even fundamental questions on the basis of
dogma.

Who won the debate? Azurmendi does not say in his book,
although he mentions that Arizmendiarrieta supported
weighted voting on a number of occasions. "One member, one
vote" remains a key principle for the Mondragón cooperatives,
though it continues to be debated to this day (see, e.g.,
Santos-Larrazabal & Basterretxea, 2021).

CECOSESOLA, founded in the 1960s, is a cooperative of
80 community organizations with more than 20,000 members
based in Barquisimeto, Venezuela (Fox, 2006). The activities
they are engaged in are varied, including agricultural

production, funerary services, health care, transportation and mutual support funds. Their approach is creative and radical; everything is subject to reexamination, even trust:

> *A couple of years ago we spoke about "trust" as a fundamental part of our organization. Today, ... we say, it's not like that. Because trust is not something we can decree. [Now] we give ourselves the freedom to build trust. It's a much more profound process in which you have to take responsibility, you have to demonstrate sincerity, honesty, good work, so that I can trust you. If I say "I trust you" it's because I know you, how you relate to people, how you act, right? Currently, we are working on "empathy" and "compassion." We are now in the 38th week of a year-long series of conversations on compassion. This is another example of a value or principle that we are collectivizing. Of course, it is a process.*
> (CECOSESOLA, personal communication, 2021)

The democratic decision-making process can be slow: a critique often leveled against co-ops by orthodox economists and skeptics. However, this more reflective pace secures the long-term viability – and underscores the strengths – of more horizontal and network-based organizations.

MAXIMIZING PARTICIPATION AT WORK BY DESIGN

The design of an organization for specific purposes and functions is not new. In fact, as Weber (1978) revealed in his comparative historical analyses of the world's organizations, the seeds of bureaucratic form can be traced to ancient China about 5,000 years ago. Bureaucracy, contrary to the negative popular image, has many merits that are often overlooked. Bureaucratic designs of organizations became common in the late nineteenth and twentieth centuries in order to regularize activities and achieve fairness by eliminating personal preferences in hiring and promotions. An important advantage of bureaucracy is that when instituted well, it has opened doors for women and minorities to attain positions based on bona fide occupational qualifications. In this sense, bureaucracy is democratic, although at the same time it can limit creativity, individual expression, and the shaping of organizational roles.

The diagram below (Fig. 2.1) depicts a range of organizational structures from a pyramidal bureaucratic form through team-based structures to what the Morgan calls "a loosely coupled organic network" (1988, p. 66). The term "network" is now widely used to apply to many different kinds of organizations and relationships between organizations, as we discuss this in depth in Chapter 3.

In designing organizations with workplace participation as an objective, there is a long record of many different types of interventions (Jacques, 1996). In Fig. 2.2 an array of participatory work-design programs introduced over the course of the twentieth century, from managerially-driven to more worker-driven ones, are displayed along a continuum, moving from less to more worker control. While we do not have the space to discuss each of these programs, we offer summarizing points: (1) Initiatives vary extensively in terms of motivation, structure, implementation and outcomes (Dachler & Wilpert, 1978). (2) Frequently, these programs are used as either a pale substitute for or as a way of undermining workers' control (Parker & Slaughter, 1988). (3) From these programs, as well as experiences with unionized workplaces and worker coops, we can derive many lessons about the implementation of democratic policies (Heller et al., 1998). Among these findings are tensions and even paradoxes to the implementation of

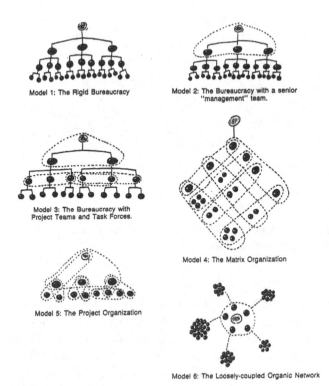

Model 1: The Rigid Bureaucracy

Model 2: The Bureaucracy with a senior "management" team.

Model 3: The Bureaucracy with Project Teams and Task Forces.

Model 4: The Matrix Organization

Model 5: The Project Organization

Model 6: The Loosely-coupled Organic Network

Source: Morgan (1988, p. 66).

Fig. 2.1. Morgan's Organizational Models.

democratic practices (Stohl & Cheney, 2001). For example, implementing democratic practices itself in any kind of top-down manner, whether by management of a worker co-op or a conventional business, entails a tension that cannot be ignored. Also is the often-overlooked fact that many people, even in a democratic workplace, do not wish to participate actively while still enjoying the benefits that the worker co-op has to offer. They may well feel that "extra" participation encroaches on other parts of their lives and negatively affects their well-being.

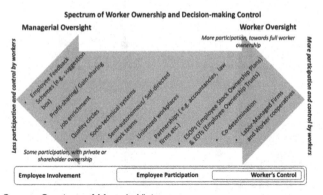

Source: Courtesy of Marcelo Vieta.

Fig. 2.2. Spectrum of Worker Ownership and Decision-Making Control.

Democratic practice inevitably involves tensions and surprises. In 2005, German multinational Continental Tire sold a majority stake in its factory in El Salto, México, to a new worker cooperative TRADOC. The sale settled a three-year strike by the National Revolutionary Union of Euzkadi Workers (SNRTE) which included an international solidarity campaign and a very effective blockade of the factory (to prevent the company from removing machinery). Journalist Jane Slaughter, author of several books critical of the labor-management cooperation programs that swept US industry from the 1970s to the 1990s, was stunned to find the militant workers' cooperative using the same methods and slogans as their capitalist counterparts. It was jarring, she wrote, to see "Team Concept" resurrected under a different ownership structure. "The hallmarks of the team concept are workers monitoring each other and competing to come up with labor-saving suggestions. When one worker said, "Now we pressure each other to do it right the first time," I had to remind myself where I was. But isn't this what team members ought to do, when we're all on the same side? Isn't the number of sides – one or two – the nub of the matter?" (Slaughter, 2013, Para. 37)

To understand the degree of workers' control in a company one should consider key issues such as how and if workers are involved in decision-making, and whether or not they own some, all, or none of the firm. Fig. 2.2 attempts to depict these distinctions graphically. We can judge the completeness (or not) of workers' influence and power in decision making and ownership of organizations along a continuum. This spectrum ranges from minimal "employee involvement" in Fig 2.2 through forms with degrees of profit sharing and participation in management; to labor managed firms and worker co-ops on the right end, where workers both *participate actively* in the running of the firm and *co-own* the firm and its means of production and share in the profits. In short, toward the left end of the continuum, we see more managerial oversight and less worker participation. On the right end, we find increasingly more workers' oversight and workers' control.

Sociocracy

Sociocracy has emerged as a practice that has systematized different tools of consent-based decision making that allow for "effective and efficient" management in organizations seeking to move away from centralized authority. Perhaps one reason why sociocracy is catching on is that it is amenable to organizations of all sizes due to its decentralized approach where decision making is conducted in "circles that are convened around specific aims" (Sociocracy for All, n.d., para 2). The model also includes specific suggestions for how proposals should be brought to circle meetings and guidelines for facilitation that help groups manage meetings effectively. Sociocracy blends aspects of network organizing with a form of modified consensus (consent) while being animated by a strong commitment to egalitarian, horizontal governance.

Unicorn Grocery, a worker co-op in the UK, has fully adopted sociocratic decision-making practices. From the beginning, the co-op operated in a non-hierarchical, flat model with small teams (similar to circles) charged with handling different parts of the operations and decision making was based on consensus. However, as the organization grew from 15 to 60 worker owners, the co-op realized that they needed to reevaluate their operations because decision making was starting to become onerous. Adoption of the model took nearly 4 years, and the co-op gradually incorporated sociocratic practices throughout the co-op. Teams with more than 15 members, were divided into smaller circles convened around more specific objectives, and meetings were conducted with an "action" focus, leading to greater productivity. The co-op also notes that "cooperative culture has improved with the implementation of sociocracy" (Brooks et al., 2021, para. 14).

TOWARD MORE INCLUSIVE AND EXPANSIVE ORGANIZATIONS

Multi-Stakeholder Co-ops

One way that inclusivity is being addressed in the cooperative movement is through discussion and development of "multi-stakeholder" cooperatives (MSCs). MSCs have become popular to cover a wide range of cooperatives where generally speaking, there is more than one category or class of membership. MSCs that include some kind of usually non-voting investor category are also termed "hybrid co-ops"; however, the MSC term is also used in some of those cases, too. A common multi-stakeholder form is found with a consumer co-op, such as a grocery store, which also has employee ownership. One of the first MSCs was Eroski, founded in 1958 and currently the Retail Division of the Mondragón network. With members consisting of workers and consumers, today Eroski is one of the largest retailers in Spain and the south of France.

Relationships between consumer-members and employee-members need to be addressed in by-laws, policies and practices. The "stake" is much more substantial, though, for an employee member-owner compared to a consumer member-owner, and this is a key debate highlighted in recent research by Imaz et al. (in press). They begin with the approximately 25% of the Mondragón cooperatives that are in one way or another multi-stakeholder and then extend their analysis to ask what "membership" truly means, especially in cooperative networks that may involve many different organizational arrangements.

MSCs are common in co-ops that provide social services, where local residents, marginalized groups that benefit from the services, management, suppliers, and employees can make up the membership base. MSC types now widely known as social cooperatives were founded by local citizens in Italy in the 1980s and were officially recognized in Italian legislation as welfare delivery organizations and a type of co-op in 1991 (Borzaga, Depedri, & Tortia, 2010; Borzaga & Defourny, 2001). Type-A social cooperatives provide other social services such as care for children, the elderly and disabled, and assist with immigrant integration. In the Type-B social cooperative, a unique form of state-supported work integration co-op, at least 30% of employee-members must be otherwise unemployed or unemployable people who also benefit from national insurance contribution exemptions. Most of Italy's social cooperatives also rely on member and nonmember volunteers (Becchetti & Borzaga, 2010). Both Type-A and Type-B social cooperatives have highly constrained distribution rights and therefore may be considered like nonprofit social enterprises, incorporated as a cooperative, with membership also open to users, volunteers, community leaders, and employees. This model, or variations of it, has been picked up in Sweden, the United Kingdom, Belgium, France, Portugal, and Poland. Québec refers to such organizations as solidarity cooperatives (*les coopératives de solidarité*) (Girard, 2008); in France, they are referred to as SCIC (*Société coopérative d'intérêt collectif*) (Vieta et al., 2016).

MSCs, especially those involved in providing social services, raise the question of uses of common resources, thus connecting their experiences with those of the commons. Multi-stakeholder efforts extend to cooperative farming, land conservation, and affordable housing with a variety of "agrarian and community commons" models being explored by a land trusts and cooperative development centers in the US (see, e.g., https://www.agrariantrust.org). The connection between multi-stakeholder arrangements and the commons is one of the key points of a recent study of MSCs by Margaret Lund and Sonja Novkovic (2022), where they not only explain all the major types of multi-stakeholder arrangements but also raise issues, including where the power and organizational boundaries lie in these systems. Lund, a cooperative consultant (personal communication, 2022) calls for more applied research, especially to look across many cases and types of MSCs to examine decision making both in terms of quality of outcomes and participants' views of process. Such work is crucial to understand multifaceted democratic arrangements.

The Commons

One of the oldest forms of economic cooperation, *the commons* have been described as "systems of production in community" characterized by a "robust class of self-organized social practices for meeting needs in fair, inclusive ways," and a "different way of being in the world and different ways of knowing and acting" (Bollier & Helfrich, 2019, p. 4; see also Helfrich, 2016). The primary scholar of the commons is the Nobel laureate and economist Elinor Ostrom (1990), whose work remains essential to any understanding of the commons, but the concept has been broadened to include the "commoning" of any type of what should be considered "non-rivalrous" and publicly accessible resource, from land to air to labor, and from data to knowledge. Thus, the Wikimedia Commons website (https://commons.wikimedia.org) offers millions of media files that are either free of copyright or licensed under Creative Commons or other "copyleft" licenses.

Drawing on feminist economics, commons theory, and value flows analysis, mixed with a sense of play, members of Guerilla Translation developed a model called "DisCO" (distributed co-operative organization). (Value flows analysis is used to track the movement of economic resources of all kinds in an economic system (P2P Foundation, n.d.).) In their co-op, members are compensated for three types of work: (1) paid work for clients, which they call "livelihood" work; (2) pro-bono work that contributes to the commons or to social movements, aka "love" work; and (3) "care" work, the often-overlooked work that maintains organizations and their members socially, psychologically, and physically. Members of Guerrilla Translation, for example, regularly contribute *pro bono* translations of articles to the "knowledge commons," in the interests of facilitating exchanges among activists and organizers. This approach is enabled by sustained and intensive discussion, both informally and in regular retreats, and by careful value accounting, for which they have considered creating specialized software based on blockchain (see Three Perspectives on Blockchain in Chapter 3).

DisCOs are "active creators of commons," says movement co-founder Stacco Troncoso (personal, communication, 2020). "Our thesis is that cooperatives formalize the practices of the commons that have been going on for millennia... So, ironically, the future of cooperatives is a rekindling of its past, getting in touch with this base of commoning." On the other hand, "talking about the commons also takes us into the future."

Unlike the typical behavior of market enterprises, DisCOs do not just draw down resources from the Commons. They reciprocate by adding to the commons as well as stewarding existing commons or creating new ones. These new resources are created through both paid livelihood work and value-tracked *pro bono* work. Commons may be digital (code, design, documentation, legal protocols, and best practices, etc.) or physical (productive infrastructure, deliberation spaces, machinery, etc.) (DisCO.coop, 2021).

femProcomuns (We Make Commons) in Catalunya (Catalonia) is a multi-stakeholder cooperative that sees co-ops as tools for commoning. "Cooperativised Activity Groups" (CAGs) carry out much of the group's work, following "commons criteria": for everyone (accessible, shared, replicable); produced by everyone (everyone contributes or can contribute to them); sustainable (we do not exhaust resources/reproduction/fair relationships); [and] managed by everyone (everyone participates or can participate in governance) (*femProcomuns*, 2022).

As *femProcomuns* member and self-described free knowledge activist Wouter Tebbens explains: "[W]e try to be in the social solidarity economy and at the same time in the commons and the digital commons, to really work on that convergence. In all projects that we develop, we try to be inclusive and generous to the ecosystem around us" (Tebbens, personal communication, 2021). So, for example, working together with members of various cooperatives, the CommonsCloud CAG, created a project to pool digital cloud resources – file storage, forms, email, project management, enterprise resource management, and office software – that is used by several organizations.

Although the mission of *femProcomuns* is focused on the vibrant solidarity economy of Catalunya, it is one of the founding members of Meet.Coop a transnational "commons-cooperative" organization providing open source video-conferencing. Other members are the tech cooperatives CollectiveTools (transnational), Platform 6 (UK), WebArchitects (GB), Koumbit (CA), and Hypha (CA). Though it started as an initiative of tech cooperatives, Meet.Coop also has user members, including platform cooperatives like the social networking site Social.Coop and NGOs like Friends of the Earth International, both with members in multiple countries. Meet.Coop is in transition to a multi-stakeholder model that will include both operational and user members in governance. The first step in that process has been the convening of a series of "Commons Hour" sessions, in which users share experiences and discuss strategies for building community governance, writing the group's handbook as they go.

WHERE DO WE GO FROM HERE?

Democracy is widely celebrated but hard to do in practice – on any level of society. In the context of work, where democratic pursuits have often involved great struggle, the achievements have come with a lot of effort as well as vision. Within even avowedly democratic workplaces, participatory processes are challenging and have to be renewed and revised (Azkarraga et al., 2012). We argue for a fundamental rethinking of the employer-employee relationship as one key to economic justice as well as enactment of democracy in daily life. As Wolff (2021) argues, worker ownership offers one of the best hopes for transcending old debates about private versus state ownership by "collapsing the difference between two groups of people within enterprises and unit[ing] them as one" (p. 203).

This can be part of "the organizational imagination" that is really not new. As Graeber and Wengrow (2021) have documented well, hierarchical *and* cooperative communities have existed, often side by side, dating back thousands of years. Some communities and civilizations have taken dramatic turns in the direction of horizontal relationship, rejecting their earlier pyramidal forms (sometimes literally in architecture as well as sociopolitically). It is time we began taking more seriously the cooperative possibilities at work and in our communities. Taking our commitment to innovation and experimentation further, as we will see in Chapter 3, we have nothing to lose by trying.

3

INNOVATION TO
TRANSFORMATION

INTRODUCTION

Innovation and entrepreneurship are two widely and enthu-
siastically used words in the business world. Virtually any
change can be considered and marketed as an innovation, and
anyone who starts a project or runs a business can claim
entrepreneur status. There are multiple terminological
spin-offs including: "open innovation," "green innovation,"
"intrapreneurship" for internal change, "extrapreneurship"
for projects that cross organizational boundaries, and
"teampreneurship" for collaborative projects (see, e.g.,
Ridley-Duff, 2021). Perhaps the most important variants, for
our purposes in this book, are "social," as in social innovation
and social entrepreneurship.

In this chapter, we discuss how worker cooperatives engage
in entrepreneurship and innovation in both conventional and
social senses (see, e.g., Logue, 2019). At the same time, we
explore how worker cooperatives, in conjunction with other
organizations and movements building economic and social

solidarity, serve as agents for deep social, economic, cultural and political change – the type of radical social transformation necessary to address the multifaceted crises we discussed in Chapter 1. We maintain that worker cooperatives, working together and as parts of a broader landscape of economic and social solidarity, can be important players in such transformations, and that their practices can transcend innovation and entrepreneurship, as commonly understood. To see how worker cooperatives do this we must first examine the conventional meanings and uses of these ambiguous but important terms.

Popular Images

Perhaps the first image that comes to mind when thinking of innovation is some kind of new, usually consumer-oriented, technology: automated factories, smart homes, self-driving cars, AI devices. "Entrepreneur" evokes some kind of wunderkind billionaire inventor like Steve Jobs, Elon Musk, or Jack Ma. The dominant figure remains overwhelmingly male and usually white, though the contributions of women and people of color are sometimes recognized, for example Oprah Winfrey or "Ice House" entrepreneur Clifton Taulbert (Schoeniger & Taulbert, 2010).

In business, innovation takes the form of new inventions, of course, but also copying, adaptation, revival, creative recombination, etc. Established businesses and government institutions typically insist on intellectual property rights, but as Ha-Joon Chang (2007) has shown, piracy and industrial espionage have also played key roles in the development of modern economies. The early textile industry in the US, for instance, was built on stolen British technology, and Apple's intuitive user interface liberally borrowed from a Xerox PARC design.

Innovation and entrepreneurship typically go hand in hand. Inventors become entrepreneurs, or entrepreneurs take an innovation of some kind and apply it, through creation or acquisition of new ventures and/or "exiting" by selling to an established corporation. The goal is success, fame, fortune, and power. One of the most compelling modern visions of innovation and entrepreneurship is the cyborg, an invention that takes on the role of a protagonist, whether in the form of Ishiguro's (2021) solicitous "Artificial Friend" Klara or Star Trek's all-assimilating Borg.

Entrepreneurs can also have bad reputations. Biotech entrepreneur Martin Shkreli, recently released from jail after serving a seven-year sentence for securities fraud, acquired the antimalarial drug Daraprim used also for AIDS treatment, then raised the price of a single dose from $13.50 to $750.00 overnight (Rockoff, 2015). The "billionaire space race" between Jeff Bezos, Richard Branson and Elon Musk, which one writer aptly described as a "tragically wasteful ego contest" (Silverman, 2021), is another glaring example. Rising questions and potential cracks in the neo-liberal model and the ever more urgent crises associated with climate change may have shaken the heroic image of the entrepreneur, but they also open up new, perhaps greener fields of innovation and entrepreneurship (Druon, 2015).

Another reason for the appeal of entrepreneurship is the freedom it implies: one is no longer a cog in the machine, but its creator. Some become "serial entrepreneurs" selling out to a larger company and going on to the next project. Others, like Sergy Brin and Marissa Mayer, become executives. How to "exit" is a key question for startup companies, especially in tech. The "Exit to Community" (https://e2c.how/) project helps startups transition to worker and community ownership.

When it comes to worker cooperatives, popular images are of something more modest, like a small cooperative bakery using artisanal methods. Cooperatives sometimes appear to be innovation-agnostic, even anti-innovation, or maybe just suited to niche markets for hipsters. Then again, perhaps such worker cooperatives are oriented to something different from what we typically think of in terms of innovation and entrepreneurship, less interested in economic growth for growth's sake than building a satisfying workplace or thriving communities: having less and being more, as the slogan goes.

People who live in countries where cooperatives are leading enterprises in their sectors may have very different images of worker cooperatives. Promotional videos put out each year by the Mondragón Corporation depict successful businesses that compete on the global stage side by side with conventional firms, employ cutting-edge technologies and are capable of impressive projects. The architecturally revolutionary Guggenheim Museum in Bilbao that opened in 1997, built by the Urssa cooperative, part of the Mondragón group, transformed what had been a somewhat depressed former industrial center into a revitalized city center. Interestingly, that project also involved an entrepreneurial approach to urban development policy that was widely copied in other cities, the so-called "Guggenheim effect" (Ceballos, 2004).

Isthmus Engineering and Manufacturing, in Madison, Wisconsin, is a successful worker-owned firm specializing in custom automation technologies for manufacturing. And Italy's SACMI (*Società Anonima Cooperativa Meccanici Imola*), founded in 1919, is a multinational manufacturer of heavy presses and other machinery for industrial customers. All are as representative of worker cooperatives as is the local bakery co-op.

There are even worker cooperatives of entrepreneurs and inventors. In the small town of Aztec, New Mexico, USA, a worker co-op called "4 Corners Invents!" runs a physical and virtual space for collaboration, mutual support, and pooling of resources. The new technologies they create, like solar devices and biodegradable materials of various types, are then marketed by the collective. In France, taking advantage of the 1995 law establishing Cooperatives of Activity and Employment (CAEs), entrepreneurs come together to address social and economic problems, notably unemployment and poverty. Members with diverse backgrounds and skill sets contribute certain assets to the cooperative, while accessing the resources of other members in return for a fee which is invested in the cooperative. The model, which includes a mix of collective and individual incentives, has been successful and adopted in other European countries (Ashta & Cheney, 2017).

Broad Terms

To make sense of cooperative practices of innovation and entrepreneurship and their place in the future of worker cooperatives, we need to examine the terms more closely. "Constant innovation" is the rule not only in business and technology but also in culture, science, medicine, politics, law, psychology, and nearly every other area of human activity. The ubiquity of innovation represents, in part, a kind of fetishization of change, shaped in no small part by the marketing assumption that new is always better. Broadly speaking, innovation is linked to a paradigm of endless growth and progress, and, as we shall see, is driven by competition for the purpose of capital accumulation.

Of course, innovation can be driven by altruistic motives. The Polio vaccine, Wikipedia, and alternatives to copyright like the Creative Commons licenses for content, are all examples of successful innovations shared without concern for monetary gain.

Innovation and entrepreneurship can also be utopian in reach. The great US utopian communities of the 1800s like Brook Farm, Massachusetts, New Harmony, Indiana, and The Oneida Community, New York, mixed new technological, social, economic, political, and cultural practices in the interests of achieving one or another version of the perfect society (Noyes, J.H., 1966). In other cases, utopia was "the only way out of no way." In the massive Palmares *quilombo* in Brazil, an autonomous proto-state which existed for nearly the entire seventeenth century and whose population numbered in the tens of thousands, Africans from various nations coexisted with Indigenous people, free Blacks, and some Whites, forging a new society on the basis of resistance to oppression, indentured servitude, and slavery (Gomes & Reis, 2016).

Science fiction is replete with examples of techno-utopias, liberatory and oppressive. Perhaps the most realistic balance between dystopian and utopian futures is struck by Kim Stanley Robinson (2012) in his novel *2312*, in which the cooperative "Mondragón Accords" define the prevailing socioeconomic framework in the solar system; yet a moribund capitalism still rules on the environmentally devastated earth.

CAPITALIST INNOVATION AND ENTREPRENEURSHIP

The history of innovation is often presented as a succession of long waves, each associated with a form of technology: agriculture, steam power and the factory system, railways, mass production, aviation, computerization, and the Internet (Neufeld, 2021; Taalbi, 2019). Each wave has involved transformations not only of technology but of the other factors of production – land, labor, management, and capital – and their combination. The invention of the factory involved not only the introduction of machinery but new ways of using land and waterways, new types of energy (steam, electricity), new types of labor (skilled mechanics and "unskilled" hands). The introduction of the factory system also brought with it many changes in labor and employee relations, including a deemphasis on craft knowledge, the definition of job by task, time delineation and pressures, and the extension of working hours.

New forms of business organization and new sources of financing were created to fund the creation of factories. And of course, all of these changes induced and integrated changes all along the line, as new techniques required new or improved inputs and enabled other changes in turn (Mantoux, 1929). And as we now know too well, the ecological repercussions of the Industrial Revolution and its descendants were as drastic as the social and political consequences, especially as merchant and then industrial capitalism spread to colonies and integrated millions of people and countless species into its accumulation process (Ahmed et al., 2013; Rodney, 2011).

Competition

The ability to invent and apply new ideas and techniques, or apply existing or outmoded techniques in new ways, has long been considered a defining human characteristic, as in the Latin expression *homo faber*. And yet innovation and entrepreneurship only began to find their modern meaning with the rise of merchant and then industrial capitalism (Godin & Lucier, 2014; Hales, personal communication, 2022; Williams, 1976).

What makes innovation and entrepreneurship central to capitalism today? The answer is found in the process of competition. Competition is commonly understood as the rivalrous seeking of benefit, something like a footrace. Competition is one of the principal forms of play, "*agon*," central to human culture and even that of other species (Caillois, 2001). But competition as we know it today frequently has an element of economic coercion as portrayed so graphically in the dystopian Korean drama *Squid Game*, where indebtedness and poverty drive people to play children's games in which losing means death and winning means walking away with a massive cash prize (Hwang, 2021).

In economics, competition "pits seller against seller, buyer against buyer, capital against capital, capital against labor, and labor against labor. *Bellum omnium contra omnes*" as Anwar Shaikh puts it (2016, p. 14). Cities, regions, nations, and empires compete. This "turbulent, antagonistic process" is capitalism's "central regulating mechanism" (2016, p. 14), determining profits, prices, and crises.

> *The profit motive is inherently expansionary: investors try to recoup more money than they put in, and if successful, can do it again and again on a larger scale, colliding with others doing the same. Some succeed, some survive, some fail altogether... In the battle of real competition, the mobility of capital is the movement from one terrain to another, the development and adoption of technology is the arms race, and the struggle for profit growth and market share is the battle itself. (pp. 14, 261)*

Shaikh (2016) contrasts "real competition" to the mainstream economic theory of "perfect competition" in which competition operates as an equilibrating force, leading to the optimal use of resources and systemic stability. Like Joseph Schumpeter (2008), the Austrian economist who made innovation and entrepreneurship central to the popular understanding of capitalism, Shaikh sees innovation, especially technological change, as a dynamic and destabilizing force that operates by means of "creative destruction." The emergence of new technologies creates dynamic forces that result in violent crises and massive loss of invested capital even as they create opportunities for new growth, in some cases, wiping out entire industries, at great human cost. In his memoir, film director Akira Kurosawa tells the story of his elder brother, a leader of the union of "*benshi*" narrators for silent films, who committed suicide when talkies took over (Kurosawa, 1983).

Competition compels firms to innovate. At the same time, because it requires new ideas or technologies to take the form of marketable products or services, it can present a significant barrier to the introduction and spread of innovations. Those that don't afford an obvious competitive advantage or opportunity for capital accumulation may be ignored or left undeveloped. Innovations in auto safety promoted by Ralph Nader in the 1960s – seat belts, padded steering wheels and dashboards – were introduced under public pressure.

Competition's creative destruction is not only a matter of soaring profits for some and bankruptcy for others. There are also broader impacts that conventional economists describe blandly as "negative externalities" or military strategists call "collateral damage." From the standpoint of workers thrown out of work, communities ravaged by plant closings, rural populations displaced by extractive industries, or ecosystems poisoned by industrial waste, such creative destruction can be a threat to survival (see Salgado, 1993, 2000). It should be noted that one of the leading sectors requiring a true "arms race" of constant innovation is the weapons industry that gives us "advances" in the capacity for destruction and death.

In his article *Of Flying Cars and the Declining Rate of Profit* (2012), the late anthropologist David Graeber lamented the fact that the flying cars and other technology he imagined in his childhood had not materialized. The "space race" of the 1960s created the impression that we were on the verge of a new frontier, especially in popular culture; however, what we got instead were largely advances in what Graeber calls, following Baudrillard (1983), "technologies of simulation," virtual reality headsets but with few changes to lived reality.

Capitalist competition can even be *anti-innovative*. Since the end of the Cold War in 1991, the argument of last resort in defense of growth has been TINA (there is no alternative). But TINA is really an argument *against* innovation – an attempt to push alternatives out of sight and to suppress imagination itself (Graeber, 2012).

This is a perverse effect of competition in contemporary capitalism. Rather than liberating creative forces at the broadest level, capitalist innovation can become an obstacle to change, especially the type of change we most urgently need: the fundamental transformation of the social-economic-ecological relations that are destabilizing us socially and environmentally.

Growth, Progress, and Time

Growth is often assumed to be good thing. Plants grow; children grow. But tumors grow too, as do landfills and inequality. Economic growth is the basic premise and overriding goal of business strategy and government economic policy alike, at least in countries like the United States. Growth is also the ultimate justification for competition: without competition, we are told, there would be stagnation and collapse. At the firm level, growth is measured by things like profitability, market share, and market capitalization. At the governmental or national level, it is represented by gross domestic product (GDP) or stock market indices. (See Chapter 5 for a discussion of alternative measures.) In both cases, the growth measure that counts above all others is growth in accumulated capital, whether that takes the form of more products, more property, or more money in the bank. As Piketty and Saez (2003) demonstrated so dramatically on the eve of the 2008 global financial crisis, as capital accumulates economic inequality grows.

The virtue of progress is normally unquestioned. The term's original meaning was simple: a step forward. For centuries, a "man of *progress*" was someone who "*walks*, who takes a look, experiments, changes his practice, tests his understanding, and continues in this way, forever" (Rancière, 1991, p. 109). Progress gained its current sense of a linear process of improvement, or a rise in station of an individual or a nation, with the advent of the enlightenment, colonialism, and industrial capitalism (Williams, 1985). Technology, education, science, biology, civilization, language, government, art, even freedom all came to be understood in terms of progress. While the toll of this progress on human and other life has been clear for centuries – the genocide of Indigenous peoples in the Americas is a still burning example – the threat it poses to overall survival has become increasingly clear in the last 50 years. At times, progress has also been claimed by those seeking emancipation and liberation. When Henry George (1879) wrote *Progress and Poverty* in 1854, his goal was to free progress from its association with economic inequality.

Concepts of progress and growth are also related to the modern understanding of time as a linear progression (Colombo, 2008). The marketing slogan "new and improved" and the constant rush from old to new lean on this linear notion, as do ideas of "traditional" and "vintage." Firms and individuals seek to get ahead, moving from past to future and from worse to better as measured by the accumulation of capital. Today is better then yesterday; tomorrow will be better than today.

There are alternatives. Instead of the arrow of rising growth, one can picture reality as a web of events, a complex network of interrelations. Recognizing the importance of images in economic thought, Oxford economist Kate Raworth (2017) devised a diagram she calls the "doughnut of social and planetary boundaries." The hole represents unmet social needs, or "shortfalls," like education, healthcare, and housing. The doughnut's outer edge represents the limits beyond which human activity overshoots sustainable use of planetary resources like water, climate, and biodiversity. The area between these two limits, the doughnut itself, is the zone within which humans can exist in a just, equitable and regenerative way.

The "doughnut" not only frees the question of economic goals from the narrative of linear progress, but also provides a powerful image of proportionality in practical, measurable terms based on the UN Social Development Goals (https://sdgs.un.org/goals). The focus is not on GDP growth but building thriving, equitable, democratic societies that operate within planetary limits (Raworth, 2017; compare Illich, 2005). What counts in this more holistic worldview is not linear forward motion but dynamic interrelations within systems. The doughnut allows for both growth and de-growth, increasing complexity or simplification (See Fig. 3.1 below). We return to this question in Chapter 5.

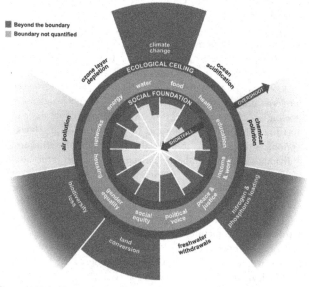

Source: Kate Raworth and Christian Guthier. CC-BY-SA 4.0 (Raworth, 2017).

Fig. 3.1. The Doughnut Model.

WORKER COOPERATIVES AND COMPETITION

It is important, when considering innovation and entrepreneurship in worker cooperatives, to take a step back and consider the playing field. The first thing that stands out is the massive infrastructure that supports conventional business development: the small business development centers, chambers of commerce, better business bureaus, etc. Then there is the financial infrastructure: banks, investment firms, and stock markets provide access to capital. Governments provide supportive regulations along with subsidies and tax breaks. There is also a massive educational and research infrastructure in place to perpetuate the practices that underlie standard capitalist enterprises, while cooperativism and related forms go largely unmentioned.

And yet, despite playing on an uneven field, worker cooperatives do manage to compete, and, as we mentioned in Chapter 1, have special competitive advantages (see also Webb & Cheney, 2014). First, because of their democratic character, goals, mode of organization and operations, worker cooperatives can make the most of solidarity between workers and with community and other stakeholders, the "C Factor," which has been shown to be an important element in the productivity of an enterprise (Razeto, 2019; compare Logue & Yates, 2005).

Second, the democratic structure of cooperatives requires greater transparency, effective communication, and teamwork based on personal autonomy and commitment. To play their roles in ownership, governance, and management, members need access to company information, opportunities for meaningful dialogue, and the power to shape how work is organized. These features dovetail with those identified as key factors of success in innovation and entrepreneurship by writers like Peter Senge, who popularized the reimagining of corporations as non-hierarchical "learning organizations" characterized by elements like openness, dialogue, creativity, and team learning (Senge, 2006).

Third, worker cooperatives are well suited for "scaling out" in decentralized or distributed form, much like a strawberry patch, replicating in ways that respond to the specific context, while building mutual support networks. This makes them adaptable and robust, encouraging the sharing of intellectual property and best practices. Namaste Solar Cooperative, Boulder, Colorado, USA, initially attempted to expand itself nationally before reconsidering and then founding the Amicus Solar Cooperative and the Amicus Purchasing Co-op, with dozens of member businesses (Sharpe, personal communication, 2022). In scaling out, as worker-owner and CEO Jason Sharpe emphasizes, it is important to foster systems of cooperative enterprise without being concerned that a co-op that is expanding necessarily owns others that are being spun off or developed (personal communication, 2021).

Fourth, worker cooperatives are well suited to building broader and deeper connections to organizations, communities, and people outside the enterprise itself, building and expanding economic and social networks (see Rossiter, 2006, on the creative, democratic potential of networks).

The competitive pressure on cooperatives is real. One way it is felt is through the pressure to innovate and grow or "scale up" in the conventional sense of those terms, which is often in opposition to cooperative values of solidarity, sharing, equity and mutual support. There is also a trend toward hybrid forms mixing cooperative and non-cooperative ownership, governance, and management which risks drawing cooperatives away from their ethical and economic center. For outside investors and entrepreneurs, investment in hybrid or new generation cooperatives can represent a "cooperative fix" for problems of capital accumulation and a way to acquire the benefits of the cooperative advantage without surrendering ultimate ownership and control, much like the "commons fix" described by De Angelis and Harvie (2014, p. 290).

When Worker Cooperatives Fail

Mondragón Corporation's industrial division offers a poignant example of the effects of competitive pressure: the famed worker cooperative Fagor Electrodomésticos (FED) which went bankrupt in the wake of the world financial crisis of 2007–2008.

Business failure is an essential part of competition and its creative destruction. The fact that worker cooperatives sometimes fail is not evidence that they are uncompetitive; on the contrary. It is because Fagor Electrodomésticos was competing at the forefront of a global industry that it was exposed to the risks and pressures that led to its failure. Moreover, worker cooperatives are less likely to fail than conventional businesses. Research in Canada, Uruguay, the US, Italy, and France shows that worker cooperatives are often more productive, have much lower failure rates, and longer survivability rates (Burdin, 2014; Olsen, 2013; Park et al., 2004; Pérotin, 2016; Vieta et al., 2017). Worker cooperatives are usually not as leveraged; thus, risk and investments are pooled among the membership, so the financial risk to members is limited. They are accountable to worker-members and to the communities of which they are a part. Why then do they fail less? Member interests and job security are less likely to be sacrificed in favor of outside investors. They are more creative in job-sharing, re-training, and other measures that preserve employment. Moreover, before jobs are lost, troubled worker co-ops tend to adjust salaries or withhold patronage refunds rather than undermine the stability of the co-op. In the case of FED, they may also get financial support from other worker cooperatives.

When Fagor Electrodomésticos declared bankruptcy some business publications declared it proof that cooperativism can't work, or at least isn't any better than capitalism (Bjork, 2013; Cheney, 2014). While the definitive account of this event has not yet been written, we see it differently. If it were a capitalist business, the failure of FED would have come as no surprise. It was a highly leveraged multinational manufacturer of "white goods" (household appliances), facing intense mature-market competition from larger, low-wage firms in the thick of a global economic crisis that wiped out all new construction in Spain, its primary market. Moreover, it can be argued that FED failed not because of its cooperative aspects but as a result of a series of major departures from cooperativism, especially the taking on of massive commercial debt to finance acquisitions of existing capitalist businesses.

The expansion of FED was part of a larger strategy of "multi-localization" (Luzárraga et al., 2007) which in most cases involved worker cooperatives becoming parent companies of non-cooperative subsidiaries. Fagor's acquisition of Brandt, in France, and Mastercook, in Poland, resulted in a hybrid form that Anjel Errasti (2015) has dubbed a "coopitalist multinational." While this strategy inevitably raises questions about the organizational consistency or integrity of the system as a whole, evaluation of the internationalization process must take into account global economic trends, diverse national economies, and local contexts and strategies (Azkarraga, 2007a, 2007b; Reuten, 2021).

If FED's coopitalist internationalization strategy weakened its cooperative commitments and exposed it to crisis, the bankruptcy also revealed the strengths of Mondragón's cooperative safeguards. Lagun-Aro, the cooperative employment security agency created by Mondragón but also open to cooperatives outside of the Mondragón group (Errasti et al., 2017; Ortega & Uriarte, 2015; Santos-Larrazabal & Basterretxea, 2021) provided co-op members with important job security protections. Following

Mondragón's policy of securing members' incomes as much as possible, FED members continued to receive pay. Within two years of the bankruptcy, all had found work in other Mondragón cooperatives or had taken early retirement with benefits. However, these protections applied only to members of cooperatives that participated in the Lagun-Aro system. Members of cooperatives that had left the Lagun-Aro system were not covered, nor were the thousands of wage workers employed by FED and its overseas subsidiaries (Santos-Larrazabal & Basterretxea, 2021).

Change and Innovation

"Change" is a key term associated with innovation. The literature on organizational change is also vast (see, e.g., Poole, & Van de Ven, 2021), and we cannot do it justice here any more than we can do with "innovation." Instead, we would highlight the distinction between first-order and second-order change, popularized by the provocative anthropologist Gregory Bateson (2002) and adopted in contexts from business to psychotherapy.

The most direct way to think about first-order change is changing so an individual or organization "doesn't have to change." In other words, an entity makes some innovative change in order to forestall a greater transformation. Like a chameleon, the company can "go green" – at least with certain initiatives – as a defensive adaptation to changing surroundings.

Second-order change is far less common but involves a more embracing and thoroughgoing transformation – the entity really does become something different from what it was. For an organization, like a co-op, this can mean that deep reassessment leads to adoption of new goals such as taking diversity or climate change seriously enough that ways of doing business are fundamentally altered (Zorn et al., 1999). Second-order change in democratic organizations can result from allowing a new wave or generation of worker-owners to remake the co-op in key ways, which can be a very challenging process, especially for any remaining founders.

Social Innovation and Entrepreneurship

Hybridism is also evident in terms like "social innovation" and "social entrepreneurship," which combine economic concepts with broader social concerns (see Nicholls & Murdock, 2012; Spear, 2009). In practical terms, social innovations can be described as "novel solution[s] to ... social problem[s] that [are] more effective, efficient, sustainable, or just than existing solutions and for which the value created accrues primarily to society as a whole rather than private individuals" (Phills et al., 2008). For example, Father Joachim Gitonga created the first SACCO (Savings and Credit Cooperative) in Murang'a, Kenya, the Mariira Cooperative Society, in order to overcome one racial barrier that kept people in poverty and excluded them from the cooperative economy (Okubasu, 2022). SACCOs are now common in Kenya and other African nations, meeting social needs and creating new financial relationships that enhance the capacity of social groups to act (Murray et al., 2010, p. 3). Social innovations can be socially inspired, have society as their object, be carried out through social organization, enhance the capacity or power of social groups, or some or all of these in combination.

In their 2010 collection of examples from hundreds of organizations around the world, Robin Murray and his coauthors identify over 500 "patterns" of social innovation practice that include socially oriented supply chains (#132), social silicon valleys (#285), and recognizing household time for social production (#503). Of course, there can be no authoritative list; new patterns are constantly being created, revived or adapted. Universal basic income policies like the one trialed in Dauphin, Manitoba, Canada in the 1970s, crowd-sourced citizen monitoring of radiation in the wake of the Fukushima nuclear disaster in Japan, or the "worker self-directed nonprofit" structure pioneered by the Sustainable Economies Law Center in California, are a few examples.

While social innovation and entrepreneurship are often associated with public agencies and non-governmental organizations, they occur across all sectors and in all types of organizations, from cooperatives and collectives to corporate R&D labs and the military (Roper & Cheney, 2005). Fossil fuel companies are just as likely to claim the status of social innovator as the environmental groups that oppose them. British Petroleum's (2001) rebranding as "Beyond Petroleum" and their creation of a carbon footprint calculator enabled consumers to measure their impact on global warming, but put the onus on individuals, not BP, to address climate change (Carpenter, 2020). This too is a reminder of how compartmentalization of "things social" or of public value can occur in any organization and emanate from many different motivations or political viewpoints.

Ultimately, social innovation and entrepreneurship embody a contradiction: they are "governed by a hybrid rationale combining market, personal development, and public interest" (Klein, 2013, p. 10). Social entrepreneurs often struggle to reconcile their social mission (personal and public) and the imperatives of competition. As long as the economic logic remains centered on capital accumulation, the social mission will be secondary. As the common refrain goes: "No [profit] margin, no mission." The obverse of that coin is: "No mission, no real value." But what if the social mission is joined to a different economic logic?

Platform Cooperatives

The Internet is a good place to find rival economic logics on display. Since the turn of the millennium, two highly visible

Internet business trends have dominated the economy: the growth of centralized proprietary Internet platforms like Google, Amazon, Facebook (Meta), Apple, and Microsoft (GAFAM), and the rise of the so-called sharing economy, represented by platforms like Uber, DoorDash, and TaskRabbit. These platforms have created a new area of business activity based on the astonishing collection of user data for private commercial use, on the one hand, and a new form of exploitation of precarious workers, on the other hand, that we can call "Platform Surveillance Capitalism" (Srnicek, 2016; Zuboff, 2019). They have also provoked a vibrant response: "Platform Cooperativism" (Schneider & Scholz, 2017).

Platform cooperatives are not another form of co-op alongside consumer, worker, or producer co-ops (see Chapter 1); in fact, they are better understood as online platforms in which a broadly cooperative approach is taken to ownership and governance, combined with a commitment to open-source tools, decentralization, transparency, and data privacy. In some cases, they are not cooperatives at all, taking a variety of forms of governance and ownership, often lacking a clear business model. They are typically multi-stakeholder in character and often transnational. Most use free-libre open-source software, meaning anyone can see and copy the code on which their platforms run. In many cases, they might better be described as cooperatively-managed commons (Hales, personal communication, 2020).

To take three examples: the bi-national (Nicaragua/USA) web design company Agaric is a Limited Liability Company under US law, with cooperative bylaws that govern its ownership and governance. FairBnB, an ethical alternative to the short-term apartment/house rental platform AirBnB, is a multinational worker cooperative registered in Italy, in the process of converting to a multi-stakeholder model. The Open

Food Network is a global network of national, regional, and local food sovereignty groups, some of which are cooperatives, sharing a platform that is developed and maintained by global collective funded by an Australian nonprofit organization. While Agaric and Open Food Network use and develop open-source software, FairBnB's main source code is proprietary. Increasingly, platform cooperatives like the Drivers Cooperative in the US are using distributed ledger, or blockchain, technologies as they create worker-owned alternatives to gig economy giants like Uber and Lyft.

Three Perspectives on Blockchain

In recent years, debate has raged about the role of a technology referred to by its basic protocol, a blockchain, or its principal application, cryptocurrency. Is it a Ponzi scheme? Is it the next Internet, web 3.0? A proper treatment of this rapidly changing technology and its applications is beyond the scope of this book. Here, though, are perspectives from three co-op practitioners familiar with the technology and its implications for worker cooperatives. First, two quick definitions: a *blockchain* is a computer program that records information and transactions in a distributed ledger, a kind of shared database that exists on many computers; *cryptocurrency* is money that exists only in digital form and is recorded in distributed ledgers on different servers (e.g., Bitcoin, Ether, and Holo).

Matt Cropp, of Burlington, Vermont, USA is the Executive Director of the Vermont Employee Ownership Center and is an organizer of several cooperatives, including the Vermont Real Estate Co-op, the Full Barrel Cooperative Brewery, and Social.Coop, an open-source microblogging platform. His interest in alternative currencies started in childhood, but it was Occupy Wall Street that stimulated his interest in alternative forms of economic and social organization, and got him experimenting with Bitcoin. Cropp is primarily interested in alternatives that are aligned with his cooperative and environmental values like Holo, and platforms like Moeda (MDA) and The Sun Exchange, which facilitate impact investing in social enterprises and clean energy development in Brazil and southern Africa.

Cropp believes cooperatives should adopt distributed ledger technology where appropriate, pointing to cooperatives like the ride-sharing platform Eva Coop in Canada that already uses it. He sees the potential for the technology to play an important role in fair trade, for example, enabling people to trace products and components to their origins and build in certifications and watchdog-type controls. The use of digital tokens for governance, as well as exchange, intrigues him but he thinks that for most worker cooperatives the technology is not needed. If the cooperative movement fails to engage in this space, building alternatives based on a clear set of principles and values and guided by a clear moral compass, he fears they may end up ceding the field to players who take an exploitative approach (Cropp, personal communication, 2021).

Alanna Irving of Wellington, New Zealand, is a cofounder of several platform cooperatives, like Loomio, Enspiral, and Open Collective, the online platform that enables communities to "collect and disburse money transparently to sustain and grow their projects" (Irving, personal communication, 2020). Open Collective is an example of what she calls "radicalizing technology," technology that lowers barriers to participation, especially for marginalized communities, designed for the transparency and distributed governance needed to build trust and cooperation. It's not about "leapfrogging" to a new way of doing technology or economy, she says, but finding steps that can be taken that are immediately practical and, importantly, accessible. Technology, like organizational form, should not be a cliff, but a stepping stone.

Irving is a self-described "crypto-skeptic." Like all new technologies, she says, distributed ledger technology (which includes blockchain) "exacerbates whatever is already going on" in society, "inequality if there's inequality, beautiful cooperation if that's what's happening." In the case of crypto, she says, a "libertarian-individualist frat boy mindset" prevails. "Tech space is already terrible for diversity and inclusion and the crypto space is 1,000 times worse."

"People doing organizational design with crypto," she says, are focused on the wrong questions. "They are excited by the parts of the problem which are quantifiable or cryptofiable and forget that the important or hard parts of the problem aren't quantifiable at all.…The hard parts of cooperating are all about building trust, not zero trust, about people, about connecting your vision with the outside world – and none of that is really solved by cryptocurrency itself. Luckily, there's more to the web3 space than cryptocurrency (e.g., distributed protocols like Secure Scuttlebutt that boost trust), and more to decentralized money than cryptocurrecy" (Irving, personal communication, 2021).

Stacco Troncoso, of Hervás, Spain, is a founder of the Guerrilla Translation and Guerrilla Media cooperatives and the Distributed Cooperative Organizations (DisCO) group. An artist, translator, and political activist, Troncoso has worked in the field of peer-to-peer organizing, commoning, and distributed organizations for some time.

Troncoso approaches distributed ledger technology from the standpoint of decentralization of power. "Decentralization is not just technological topography, but it means decentralizing what I would call the trifecta of power: colonialism, patriarchy, capitalism. Because DisCOs are small organizations by design, using blockchain [which typically requires a large network of environmentally unfriendly servers] would be ridiculous, even obscene I would say." On the other hand, in order to track and remunerate the various forms of value creation, which they categorize as Livelihood, Love, and Care work, Troncoso and his colleagues are working with coders to develop a federated value-tracking software they call the DisCO DECK that will enable them to largely automate their accounting.

Imagining a transnational network of DisCOs, Troncoso can see a role for distributed ledger technology, but he emphasizes sufficiency – use the technology only when it is really needed – and the role of human contact: "You can have the best team, with the best values baked into the technology, but that's meaningless without regular practices and freedoms which exist outside of the technology.…. The hard work comes from conversations, raging, crying, being supportive when you have a bad day" (Troncoso, personal communication, 2021).

Now numbering in the thousands (there is no reliable
directory), platform cooperatives offer a wide range of services
from asset sharing (cars, lodging), gig work, online markets,
and financial services, to farm and food system management,
and cloud storage and services, including social networking
and communications (Dey & Kumar, 2022). Loomio, for
example, provides a platform for participatory democracy
decision-making used by many cooperatives and other
organizations.

Unlike capitalist platforms which are typically centralized,
with software and data owned and controlled by one company,
platform cooperatives are independent and decentralized.
Decentralization can take various forms, as seen in Fig. 3.2. So,
on Twitter, which is *centralized*, user A is connected to user B via
a central hub (server). The alternative social network Mastodon
is *decentralized*, with users free to set up their own local instal-
lations of the software. It is also *federated*, meaning the various
instances on different servers are connected via a shared

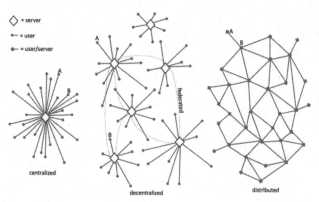

Source: Adapted from models in wide currency; courtesy, Emi Do.

Fig. 3.2. Types of Networks.

protocol, like email, so user A on one instance can communicate with user B on a different instance (as well as people on other platforms using the same shared protocol). In the case of the communications software Secure Scuttlebutt, the network is *distributed*, meaning that every user is like a server and information is "stored" on each user's phone or computer, so user A connects directly to user B. (For application of these concepts to governance and organization, see Community Rules (https:// communityrule.info/)).

Some see platform cooperativism as an antidote to youth unemployment and their hyper-exploitation by multinational tech corporations like Meta/Facebook (Perigo, 2022). Irma Lila Zentle Colotl of Ibero University in Puebla, México, sees platform cooperativism as a "very promising phenomenon... especially as an answer to problems like increasingly precarious work, youth unemployment ... [and] technological and educational exclusion" (Zentle Colotl, personal communication, 2021, see also Dave, 2022). Is creating jobs enough? Experience suggests that to offer a real alternative to surveillance platforms, platform cooperatives must become more cooperative, that is, they must cultivate processes of meaningful participation in governance and management as well as ownership.

COOPERATIVE INNOVATION: FROM COMPETITION TO TRANSFORMATION?

Historically, workers, peasants, and others have mitigated harmful market effects by taking their labor and other resources "out of competition." In labor unions, this is done by bargaining collectively with the employer. The wider this web of solidarity among workers, the greater the leverage of workers which can be used not just to negotiate terms and conditions of employment but to push for change on a wide range of issues, including government policy. Such widespread collective action is difficult to achieve but recurs in history. The wave of unofficial or "wildcat" strikes that swept China in the 2000s, the teachers' strikes in the United States in the 2010s, and the massive Indian farmers' protests of 2020–2021 are recent examples.

In principle, for worker cooperatives competition between workers and competition between employer and worker are structurally eliminated. Of course, this may not eliminate conflicts between management and labor in the workplace, depending on the structure and culture of the worker cooperative. Fagor Electrodomésticos was the site of an intense labor struggle in the 1970s. Thus, as long as the change remains limited to a single firm or a small group of firms, it will not pose a challenge to competition in the markets in which the cooperative operates. In a parallel manner, consumer, producer, and credit cooperatives all take consumption, distribution, and finance out of competition to some degree. As cooperatives and other solidarity enterprises (collectives, buyers' clubs, time-banks, etc.) network and inter-cooperate, they narrow the scope and influence of competition, democratizing the market (Razeto, 2017; see also Peredo et al., 2019).

With increasing freedom from and control over capital that may be gained by removing labor and other resources from competition, workers would be able to slow the process of capital accumulation and concentration, creating new possibilities for development of labor, consumption, technology, and relations with nature.

Democratizing the market requires organizing on two fronts: creating spaces or relations of solidarity, democracy, and freedom within spheres of capitalist control, on the one hand, while cultivating autonomous or independent spaces of economic activity on the other. The latter includes nonmonetary exchange, time banking, etc. (Baschet, 2016). For worker cooperatives aiming at social transformation as for other alternative economic organizations, competition is at once a game to be played and a table to be overturned. In both cases the stakes are autonomy, solidarity, and freedom.

Transformative Social Innovation

What is the best way to describe the kind of innovation and entrepreneurship involved in this type of social change? At their most ambitious, social innovation and entrepreneurship represent "second-order change," that is, an attempt to "radically transform some of the fundamental systems on which we depend – how food is provided, healthcare, housing, or learning – according to fundamentally different principles" (Murray et al., 2010, p. 107). For example, Mondragón Team Academy offers a radically different educational model drawing on the cooperative tradition that is "adapted to the new way society is organized [and] encourages 'teampreneurship' through experimentation" (Ashoka, 2022; Luzárraga et al., 2007). But do such second-order, *systemic*, changes amount to *system change*, also known as social transformation?

"Transformative Social Innovation" is meant to resolve the basic tension between social mission and economic logic, by focusing on second-order social innovations (see Avelino et al., 2017) like the Water Protectors campaign that seeks to change the system through multi-group organizing to block the construction of an oil pipeline across native lands, as in the case of the Keystone XL pipeline in the US.

But does adding another modifier to the term innovation really help us understand the relation of social transformation to innovation and entrepreneurship? Or does the search for supplementary terminology point instead to the need for new concepts or more concrete analysis? The labels may be too tethered to some meanings to serve as levers for major change (Raupp, 2014). We may need to cultivate a new language for the activities those terms commonly describe, one that better grasps and expresses the new sensibilities and new organizational forms described in this book. One such attempt at cultivating a new language is found in the notion of a New Cooperativism.

The New Cooperativism

Worker cooperatives innovate and are effective vehicles for entrepreneurship, in every sense of those terms. They do it by force of competition, and they do it for social motives. In cases like Earthworker Cooperative in Australia, Equal Exchange in the USA, Argentina's *empresas recuperadas*, and Cecosesola in Venezuela, they do it with a commitment to radical social transformation, showing that worker cooperatives can be creative and flexible in finding a way out of the dead-end of competition centered on the amassing of monetary wealth.

The "New Cooperativism" is a term that has been increasingly used to describe an emerging socioeconomic, political, and cultural "movement of movements," in which cooperative economic activities are located within and integrated with other social movements. Starting from an explicitly anti-capitalist framing of the role and potential of worker cooperativism, the New Cooperativism stresses that "collective actions, self-direction and struggles of the grassroots," including those of worker cooperatives, "can overcome contemporary capitalist limits to economic... life" (Vieta, 2010, p. 8; compare Larrabure et al., 2011).

The New Cooperativism captures how cooperatives, as part of a broader solidarity economy, are returning to their original radical roots. At the same time, it connects them to the responses and proposals advanced by other working people, communities, and social movements to the crises of neoliberal capitalism. As part of the broader social and solidarity economy, the New Cooperativism goes beyond the traditional aims of the co-op movement defined in terms of member benefit and concern for community to imagine and articulate practices that use cooperative principles and organizing strategies grounded in social justice, inclusion, the recognition of difference, the fluid nature of social relations, and practices of collective action to promote and create socio-ecological well-being.

Six Features of the New Cooperativism

Marcelo Vieta has identified six key features of the New Cooperativism (Vieta, 2018, pp. 59–60):

1. *It espouses values and practices of subsidiarity and community-led development.* It is entrenched deeply within surrounding communities and usually embraces clear objectives for local community development by and for the very people affected.

2. *It directly responds to crises.* It tends to emerge as bottom-up solutions by working people and grassroots groups to myriad shared challenges. It also provides proactive, community-led alternatives to the privatization of public goods and social services.

3. *It is ethical and sustainable.* Its ethico-political commitments emerge not from capital-centric frameworks but from everyday experiences and needs. Further, it is driven by more ethical and sustainable engagements with the other and the planet.

4. *It is inclusive.* Its protagonists emerge from or engage with broad coalitions of community members, multiple stakeholders, and social justice movements.

5. *It is horizontal, democratic, and co-managed.* Compared to both capitalist production and to more traditional co-operative experiences, it fosters more horizontalized work processes, more gender-sensitive divisions of labor, more directly democratic decision-making, and shared forms of co-management.

6. *It practices collective ownership and equitable distribution of social wealth.* Its means of social, cultural, or economic production are owned collectively rather than privately. Moreover, it aims at a more equitable distribution of social wealth and surpluses.

Other features might be added to the list. Ridley-Duff (2021), for example, has suggested three more: "(7) calls for multi-stakeholder governance... (8) strongly emergent forms of commoning; and (9) a renewed stress on (re-)enfranchising labor." Recently, Vieta has also begun to connect the New Cooperativism explicitly to notions of the commons (Vieta & Lionais, 2022).

We have discussed multi-stakeholder approaches and commoning in Chapter 2. What Ridley-Duff describes as "re-enfranchising labor" Vieta approaches through *autogestión* (self-management), which is both characteristic of the "new" cooperativism and deeply rooted in cooperative traditions (Vieta, 2016).

Timelines and Ruptures

While the term "New Cooperativism" suggests a continuation of the old/new opposition, Vieta (2010) stresses that "the new cooperativism's prefigurative potential is as much about rupture as about newness." Indeed the practices of the new cooperativism:

> ...articulat[e] the ways that people are collectively provisioning for their needs, producing and distributing goods and services otherwise in short supply, or meeting their desires for sustainable communities, as well as (re)imagining a different kind of world where such practices can proliferate. It is this... orientation of the new cooperativism that distinguishes it from reform-focused or more accommodative forms of cooperativism that remain caught in capitalocentric schemas. (p. 4)

And while the New Cooperativism emphasizes cooperatives, that is not to suggest that cooperatives are the sole or primary vehicles for the movements it includes. In fact, the New Cooperativism does not so much refer to a form or stage of cooperativism as to the integration of worker and other cooperatives into multi-institutional networks of movements for human liberation and natural recuperation. This is not a new idea. Arizmendiarrieta, who might be described as an original New Cooperativist, saw cooperatives as one tool among many. As Aguirre (personal communication, 2021) puts it, he "worked beyond co-ops... envision[ing] a system that was more cooperative than the cooperatives."

To take a current example, the Kola Nut Collaborative of Chicago facilitates the creation of multiple organizational forms: time banking, needs and offers exchanges, mutual aid projects, and worker cooperatives, all centered on cooperative economics and self-organization. Which form is used depends on the context, the people involved, and their needs and goals. At the center of the work is a popular education practice through which people develop movement skills, especially facilitation, a skill that is all too often left to professional consultants or nonprofit staff. Kola Nut cofounder Michael Tekhen Strode sees the socialization of movement skills among the people who are participating in the organizing process as the key to developing the collective capacity for social transformation.

The Earthworker Cooperative in Australia, to which we return later in this book, offers an inspiring example of rupture and re-centering, focusing their social, political, cultural and economic activity on the multifaceted crises associated with climate change. The radical trade union roots of the founding members enabled the group to set goals that transcend what might otherwise be a narrow cooperative mission, on the one hand, or a siloed social movement group, on the other.

Worker cooperatives have the marvelous capacity to operate both outside of and within the prevailing capitalist system, often thriving by developing new systems on their own terms, outside of the market economy – commons, time banks, alternative trade organizations, etc. – while competing within and working to transform power relations in the standard business world. In both settings, as the poet Antonio Machado (1982, p. 143) famously wrote, people "make the way as they go." That is, they progress in the original sense of walking, learning, and growing together.

WHERE DO WE GO FROM HERE?

While it is difficult to predict trajectories of movements, it is essential that we consider the long-term transformational potential of forms of organizing. In the landscape of cooperatives, it is often put forth that worker cooperatives offer the greatest structural and practical potential for economic and political transformation, even though many worker co-ops –

indeed like other types of co-ops – are not necessarily animated by a wider political concern.

We argue that by principle and design, worker co-ops are well suited to pursue organizational and business paths that are usefully revolutionary, and that such paths are increasingly essential for the survival not only of cooperatives, their members, and their communities, but also humanity and the biosphere, of which we are one element. To play this role, worker cooperatives must be constantly open to change: in principles, strategy, organizational forms/practices, governance, development practices, education, technology, and even the co-op form itself, which can be altered, transformed or combined with other forms. As Joxe Azurmendi (1992) puts it, interpreting Arizmendiarrieta's approach, "there can be no dogmatic formulas, no rest, nothing is untouchable, everything should be subject to revision, new and better formulas must always be sought... 'To live is to renew oneself'" (p. 576).

Although we have been attentive to language, we end this chapter without satisfactory alternatives for the key terms in currency: *innovation* and *entrepreneurship*. The Spanish word *formación*, which we could translate as self-organization, describes a process of education and collective action in which people develop individual and collective capacity and create organizations incorporating new social relations of production (Hales, personal communication, 2022).

Time will tell if the ideals and trends included under the umbrella of "New Cooperativism" will become a holistic approach in practice that inspires new waves of workers. Still, it puts us on the right path, if only by expanding our imagination, which starts with making what Fourier called an "*écart absolu*" (a radical break), even as we build bridges to the new terrain (Fourier, 1836, p. 242). As we shall see in the following chapters, the practices that make up a "new cooperativism" have implications for the relations of cooperatives to community, ecology, and education.

4

COMMUNITY TO SOLIDARITY

INTRODUCTION

When telling the story of the emergence of the Japan Workers Cooperative Union (JWCU), Sagara Takao, a director at JWCU, starts with a basic conflict that pitted workers engaged in public works projects against the communities where they worked. As part of an "unemployment countermeasures project," the government funded the construction of public infrastructure projects like local parks and school swimming pools. The creation of those projects was the result of the vigorous, at times combative, labor struggles of the postwar years, so the relationship between workers and the government was largely antagonistic. Moreover, the government clearly expressed its intention to bring the countermeasures to an end.

Workers resisted the termination of the countermeasures project; however, local community members saw the workers' tactics as evidence of laziness and remained sympathetic to the government's position. In response, All Japan Free Trade Union, which was the labor union for unemployment measures projects, changed its policy from "work as little as possible" to "be useful to the community and loved by the community." The labor union was converted to a workers' cooperative and spread into other areas of work, many involving public works or services. Nakanishi Goshu, the founder of both the union and the cooperative, JWCU, described this as a "democratic reform of unemployment countermeasures projects," and "good work" for workers and communities alike. This would become the guiding principle of JWCU (Sagara, personal communication, 2021).

Community in Its Many Forms

The word "community" is ubiquitous today, with a wide range of formal and informal uses. In the news, for example, commentators will loosely describe "the X or Y community" without really explaining whether there are meaningful connections among the people being grouped together. In the Japanese case just introduced, connections between the interests and identities of union workers and residents of the locality where they worked were missing from the start, leading to the problems that the cooperative-union JWCU began to address.

We also know not to take too seriously allusions to specific and precise communities, such as the "real estate community," "the medical community," or "the rockhound community." Using community in this way is familiar, yet it can project a false sense of coherence or unity. Most readers or listeners can readily understand how a potent term is appropriated for casual, taken-for-granted marketing purposes. In everyday discourse, however, we scarcely notice these uses that can cheapen the currency of the term like community by repeating it without focus or clear purpose.

This sense of community is very different from what one of the founders of sociology, Emile Durkheim (2014, 2018), described as values- and ethics-based bonds that hold groups together – whether they are defined by occupation, heritage, ethnicity, religion, or common purpose. Another early sociologist, Ferdinand Tönnies, captured the transformation of this social glue in the book *Community and Society* (1887/ 1957). At a time of increasing urbanization spurred by the Industrial Revolution, Tönnies observed that *Gemeinschaft* (community), a collective sense of belonging in social and familial bonds, was challenged by *Gesellschaft* (society), which privileges individual and self-interested social relations based largely on the division of labor, laws, and contractual bonds. Importantly, this distinction led to the severance of politics or political life from community, and then the latter became associated with the State.

While community is hard to define and conceptually fluid, we know when we are *in* community and when we are not: we can feel it. Community, moreover, both includes and excludes. Bauman (2001) reminds us that while community brings with it a warm feeling from invoking security and belonging, it can also be a social dimension of enclosure and limits. Community in our late-modern condition exists in a tension between our desire for autonomy and our need for togetherness and safety, between freedom of the individual and responsibility to the other.

These myriad conceptualizations of community serve to remind us of the concept's importance in academic language as well as the vernacular. In the oft-referenced *Community: A Critical Response*, Joseph Gusfield (1978) cautions against attempting to define community in any definitive or immutable way. Rather, he points to two major uses of the term: territorial and relational. The territorial usage, where community is used in the sense of location, physical territoriality, or geographical continuity, is more traditional and conceivable to us because these senses of community have been with humans a long time. Here, the importance of proximity and shared history in a space is stressed. In-groups and out-groups, frequently defined by territory, adherence to a piece of land and to surrounding landscapes, play a huge role in both collective and individual identity.

The second usage, the relational, points to the aspects of human relationships that define who is included in the community. By stressing relational connections, we are able to encompass groups and communities that do not necessarily share a space yet may engender and maintain powerful bonds. For Felipe Witchger, founder of Community Purchasing Alliance Cooperative and co-convener of US gatherings of the Economy of Francesco, a connection to faith communities and spiritual values allows individuals and groups to address issues that go beyond their own interests. Faith offers an "imagination that can put us in the mode to tackle these intractable challenges (such as climate change, inequity, or systemic injustices)" (personal communication, 2021).

The feeling of connection with future as well as past members of a group shows how powerful transcendent notions of community and identity can be. Deeper senses of community implicate interdependence, mutual assistance, trust building, and sustained attention to the well-being of individuals, households, and much larger collectivities. Relationally based communities often foster a feeling of belonging. However, this does not necessarily mean that the bonds of family, neighborhood, work, or activities are strong enough for the group to defend members under threat or for the group to control its own destiny through collective action.

Strong communities, containing a high degree of what has been called "social capital" (Putnam, 2000), feature dense network interconnections – as when many linkages connect those members of a neighborhood or organization. The idea of social capital, although covering a wide range of meanings and practices, has been valuable in calling attention to the social health of communities and societies, in ways often neglected by modern economics. On an empirical level, too, social capital can be operationalized, assessed, and interpreted using network analysis to reveal, for instance, how many people rely on certain social services in a city, or how a network of cooperatives and related organizations can have a wider circle of effects not immediately apparent from figures on sheer membership. Social capital theories can also help to underscore the strong bonds between cooperatives and territories, including the community-building and sustaining potential of cooperatives, while recognizing relations of power at play throughout (Bianchi & Vieta, 2020; Saz-Gil et al., 2021).

From the study of social networks, we should also keep in mind that a web of "weak ties" (Granovetter, 1973) such as sources for information, assistance, or new ideas, as well as "strong ties" represented in close personal and working relationships, are all part of the picture for social capital – and community – at any level. Importantly, such relationships can also lead to either reinforcement of the status quo, where the group is closed to new ideas and new forms of influence, or to challenges to accustomed practices, including innovative thinking and confrontation of fundamental inequalities.

Community, Society, and the State

It is important to keep in mind that in the eighteenth and nineteenth centuries when modern cooperativism arose, community was often used to describe a form of social organization which included functions of government and economy, as opposed to the modern form in which state and civil society are separate spheres. Associationism, socialism, and communism were all originally understood as communal in this sense, as underscored by social reformers and revolutionaries such as Robert Owen, Charles Fourier, Mikhail Bakunin, Peter Kropotkin, and Karl Marx, who once defined the alternative to the divided capitalist state and economy as "true community" (*wirkliche gemeinshchaft*) (Marx, 1844). Indeed, until the Russian Revolution of 1917, the defining event in the history of socialism was the Paris Commune of 1871, the uprising in which democratic systems of community and workers' control and self-government were briefly instituted before being crushed by the French military.

In the aftermath of the Russian Revolution, Communism became synonymous with state control and ownership of the means of production, including in the cooperatives that survived. Socialism, although having various forms, became chiefly associated with the social-democratic nations, like Finland, where cooperatives prospered with the support of extensive welfare states. Meanwhile, cooperatives in more strictly capitalist, as opposed to mixed, economies generally maintained a distance from the state and politics, adhering to ICA's fourth principle of cooperative autonomy: "Cooperatives are autonomous, self-help organisations controlled by their members. If they enter into agreements with other organisations, including governments, or raise capital from external sources, they do so on terms that ensure democratic control by their members and maintain their cooperative autonomy" (International Cooperative Alliance, 2015, p. 45).

In the colonies, the European powers sometimes employed cooperatives as a form of economic organization in imperial rule, as epitomized in the career of the fourth Earl Grey, president of the ICA from 1895 to 1907, Administrator of Rhodesia, and a fierce advocate of white supremacy (Rhodes, 2012). The nation states that emerged out of struggles for national liberation repurposed cooperatives as part of their decolonization and development strategies, again under state control (Rhodes, 2012). Colonial tea cooperatives in Africa and Asia are prime examples.

In the late twentieth and early twenty-first centuries, older notions of community re-emerged in movements around solidarity economy, commoning, and *buen vivir* and in political theories rejecting the old focus on state power. One of the most developed forms of this new associationism is the Zapatista movement in Chiapas, Mexico, where, in order to preserve and develop grassroots economic cooperation rooted in Indigenous practices, communities have had to defend themselves against state and corporate incursions, including militarily (Baschet, 2016; Santiago, 2021).

Community is seen not only as an alternative to the state. Many of the most interesting and promising developments in the relation of cooperatives to community are taking place in cities where municipal governments are strongly supportive of cooperative development: for instance, in Seoul, Korea; Barcelona, Spain; Preston, UK; Jackson, Mississippi, USA; and Montreal, Canada.

In Seoul, Korea, the administration of the late Mayor Park Won-Soon unleashed a massive program of support for cooperative development in 2012. According to cooperative researcher Minsun Ji (personal communication, 2021), 25,000 cooperatives have been created since 2012. "The government is ready to pour on financial support with the goal of increasing civil society organizational capacity." Around the world, from Finland to Rwanda, the Emilia-Romagna region in Italy to Puebla, México, local governments have created programs and promoted legal changes to encourage the development of worker cooperatives and other social enterprises. Still, these efforts are dwarfed by the support given to private sector corporations.

SOLIDARITY

A worker cooperative is just one tool that a community can use to build relationships of mutuality and solidarity. Because it involves shared ownership and direct democracy, it is a particularly powerful tool. While in the formal structure of worker cooperatives members have the roles of owner, worker, and patron, they are also community members, an important "fourth hat" that influences decisions that members make within their cooperatives (Mamouni et al., 2018). As a worker-member of the Venezuelan co-operative group CECOSESOLA observes: "We are not in a bubble; we are in this society, in these relationships ... [and] we change ourselves through work" (CECOSESOLA, personal communication, 2021).

As we noted earlier, the process of coming together for some can result in the exclusion of others. In *Collective Courage*, Jessica Gordon Nembhard (2014) observes that though cooperatives were critical to attaining racial justice through economic democracy for Black Americans after emancipation, it was usually a segregated freedom, as most cooperatives at that time were not integrated. In organizations like the Knights of Labor that welcomed Black workers. The attitude was: "We can't do it without Black Workers: if we don't all do this together, we won't win" (Gordon Nembhard, personal communication, 2021).

Although this suggests that a community can overcome perceived differences based on shared problems and a common enemy, there is also a deeper connection that needs to be explored. A connection based on pragmatic goals may not endure when that moment of need has passed. The bond must be based on a rejection of inequality and racial privilege by those who stand to benefit from inequality. Roediger (1988) points to DuBois' argument that white labor needed to "transcend the narrow parameters of 'Black and white; Unite and fight'" and be willing to "sacrifice... the... public and psychological wage of petty and not-so-petty racial privileges" (p. 289). The work of intersectionality – probing how various identities come together and what they mean in terms of privilege and power – in cooperative organizing and governance practices continues today and with greater urgency.

From this, we can see that concern for community is not enough; cooperatives also need to internalize and practice solidarity. "Solidarity" is often used when we refer to cooperative work that addresses this deeper sense of community, or that encompasses movement connections beyond the regular business. Commonly associated with labor and social movements in which groups work together with diverse allies who may not be directly known, solidarity conveys a stronger sense of "power with" than typically invoked by the term community. When people in mutual aid groups and networks say "Solidarity, not Charity," they are invoking this distinction: charity seeks to care for the injured; solidarity seeks to do that and build the power necessary to change the conditions that cause the injury. These purposes are not mutually contradictory. If co-ops want to build the collective capacity to transform social relations, they have to take care of people's immediate needs.

Solidarity is very much part of the histories and practices of worker cooperativism as it is of labor unions, which emerged together in many countries and still face many of the same strategic questions and challenges. Like labor unions, cooperatives face a continual choice: whether to focus on the narrow self-interest of members of an enterprise or to widen their scope to include the collective interests of all workers and other social movements. As Mondragón founder Arizmendiarrieta insisted:

> The simple creation and operation of cooperative businesses cannot be the goal ... whether the economic results are more or less satisfactory in our particular enterprises, we as cooperativists must continue being dissatisfied as long as the whole vast social-economic world is not aligned with the postulates of dignity of the worker and the needs of their work, to do otherwise would place us at risk of falling into an unforgivable myopia and lack of solidarity.
>
> (quoted in Azurmendi, 1992, p. 824)

The "C-Factor"

Solidarity has also come to be recognized as a key to the success of worker cooperatives and other explicitly solidarity-oriented enterprises. Razeto (2020) differentiates between two dimensions of worker organization in a cooperative or other solidarity enterprise: the working group and the solidarity group. As a "working group," people use their various capacities, specializations, experience, knowledge, and skills toward a common business outcome that serves a specific function. As a "solidarity group," they cultivate relationships and community with one another and build an organization based on democratic governance, shared commitment, investment, and objectives. As a working group, the cooperative seems similar to any other enterprise that is doing business: they want to achieve their desired outcome as efficiently and resourcefully as possible. But this is misleading, because at the same time, as members in a solidarity group, they are practicing democracy, solidarity, and equity, not just in "nonwork" activities like governance and community-building but also in the labor process itself.

Solidarity in the labor process is also *a source* of productivity, alongside the other factors of production: labor, land, capital, technology, knowledge, and management. Razeto's "C Factor" is simply solidarity as a factor of production (Razeto, 2020). "C" is used because in Spanish so many words which describe aspects of solidarity begin with the letter c, including *cooperación*, *compasión*, *confianza* (trust), *colaboración*, *coordinación*, *comunidad* (community), etc. In recent cooperative economic literature, the ability of worker cooperatives to draw on and regenerate the C-factor, and the productivity it adds, has also been referred to as the "cooperative advantage" (Birchall, 2003; Novkovic, 2008). It enables these firms to survive in the face of competition in the market.

In Argentina's worker-recuperated companies, another C-word rooted in solidarity takes central stage: *compañerismo* (Vieta, 2020). *Compañerismo* is a strong sense of solidarity through camaraderie that develops from having traversed difficulties together – such as having to take over a struggling business, convert it to a co-op, and learn how to become cooperators and self-managed workers. As Placido Penarrieta, one of the nine founders of the Buenos Aires print shop Chilavert Artes Gráficas, explains:

> *Before, under owner-management, there was always someone marking out the rhythm of your work. ... Things are now different. ... Before we were 'workmates' but today we aren't workmates anymore. We're now more like* socios *(partners, members, or associates), where the problem of one member affects us all. ... Before, if something happened to someone it was the owner's responsibility, but now, what binds us together is the fact that we're all responsible for this cooperative.*
> (cited in Vieta, 2020, pp. 498–499)

Traditional firms, hierarchical and fundamentally unequal, also draw on this source of collective productivity, which is why teams, participation, quality circles, empowerment, and similar buzzwords eternally reoccur in management theory and practice. It is difficult, however, to make solidarity the organizing factor in production as long as the firm is organized along capitalist lines. Unfortunately, the neglect of solidarity as a deeper, stronger sense of community can also occur in worker cooperatives, in part because the pressure of competitive markets, or the practical demands of the production or service work, generate a constant demand for attention to the other factors of production. It is also because some of the activities necessary to maintain solidarity – education, care, participatory strategic planning, decision-making – take the form of "non-work" (i.e., non-remunerated and unacknowledged labor). As cooperatives scale up, many fall back on a more hierarchical structure of management to achieve their "work group" aims, weakening the "solidarity group" in the process.

Trust

For deep cooperation and solidarity to grow and flourish at work, in communities, and in societies, trust is fundamental. This points to the maxim, "working at the speed of trust" (Brown, 2017). There is no effective substitute for the mutual knowledge and mutual understanding that can be built up with time and, for many people, this can only happen with some face-to-face interaction. Trust plays an important role in all organizations; in Dasgupta's *Economics: A Very Short Introduction* (2007) the second chapter is entitled "trust" and includes sub-topics such as mutual affection and "pro-social disposition." Part of such trust building relates to believing that others will "be there" as needed, will perform their duties competently and efficiently, and will treat personal information with discretion. Moreover, mutual trust is critical if a cooperative or network of cooperatives is going to weather difficult times, especially when the members agree to make sacrifices such as a temporary cut in wages or dividends in order to preserve jobs overall. In the wake of the 2008 financial crisis and the COVID-19 pandemic, this latter situation occurred in Argentina's worker-recuperated companies, such as at the print shop *Cooperativa Chilavert Artes Gráficas* (Ruggeri, personal communication, 2021) and at the Mondragón cooperatives (Exteberria, personal communication, 2021).

Violent and massive breaches of trust such as oppression, enslavement, war, and genocide may not be repaired for generations or even centuries because of either ongoing hostilities or historical trauma (Derezotes, 2014). This is why the "cooperatives of trust" in post-civil war Rwanda, described by Kyanzaire (2022), are so compelling. Jocelyne Alexandre and Josephine Murphy cofounded the nonprofit, Shelter Them, when they returned to Rwanda after having immigrated to Canada three years after the 1994 genocide against the Tutsi. The organization's mission is to empower underprivileged children and youth in Rwanda to be self-sufficient, and cooperatives have been an important tool to build up individual capacity while also fostering group solidarity. In describing how this works in practice, Murphy explains: "community strengthens people: I am independent and you are independent, and we are interdependent ... interconnected" (personal communication, 2022). Halfway around the world, Tanaka Shigeru, community organizer and executive director of Pacific Asia Resource Center (PARC), makes the same point, noting "if you want to be truly independent, you have to have many people to depend on" (personal communication, 2021). This lesson from the disability rights movement in Japan is applicable to anyone living in our complex and inter-woven societies today (Tanaka, personal communication, 2021).

CIRCLES OF COMMUNITY

The International Cooperative Alliance's 7th Principle, "concern for community," assumes a distinction between a cooperative's fundamental responsibility to meet the needs of its members and its responsibility to the wider community. The implication is that cooperatives start from a primary commitment to serving their members and then widen the circle of interests and concerns, leaving it "up to the members to decide how deep" the commitment should be and "in what specific ways" their cooperatives should contribute (ICA, 2015). A helpful way to illustrate this is with ripples around a stone tossed into a pond or lake. The widening circles may not be as definite as the inner ones, but they represent the potential for broader, greater effects, even some that may not be readily noticed.

And yet this center-out image can be misleading. In many cases, worker cooperatives *are* the ripples; that is, they are organizations created *by* communities seeking social and economic impact. People organizing around a particular need or goal choose worker cooperatives because of the specific features they offer: autonomy, democracy, equity, education, and concern for community and planet. However, because cooperatives are economic enterprises and must have a clear business idea and the operational practices needed to execute them, it is possible that the cooperative will become inwardly focused and adopt a narrow economic vision. In much the same way as with a profit-maximizing capitalist firm, this narrow economic vision can lead the inherent community character of the cooperative to be treated as an "externality." So, cooperatives too must face the challenge of maintaining and renewing a larger social mission and resisting the reduction of that mission to standard definitions of business success.

Virtual Communities

In the Internet era, especially since COVID-19, social theorists, project managers, and therapists, along with a host of others, have had to reconsider what community means for people who may seldom, if ever, share the same physical space. Micky Metts, a worker-member of a tech worker cooperative, Agaric, explains that though all members have a sense of ownership of the co-op, it is only once a year ("if that!") that they are able to convene on the same continent to re-align with one another in person, and usually only in conjunction with attending a conference (personal communication, 2021). Similarly, Meet.Coop formed online as a multi-stakeholder cooperative in response to a demand for an open-source web conferencing software during the COVID-19 pandemic. Many of the members of Meet.Coop have not met IRL (in real life) though they share a common goal and meet online regularly for the purpose of building community.

While we may be removed physically, we are still tied to the spatial notions of group gathering and belonging, such that we speak almost without a pause about *visiting* websites, admitting people to *rooms* in a videochat, etc. So, we lean heavily on spatial and geographic notions of community even when those are not really part of how a group is functioning. Multiple-player games and immersive workspaces are also vivid examples.

In addition to trust, the cultivation of a democratic culture is critical for ensuring that the democratic structures and institutions are sustained. As we discussed in Chapter 2, a democratic culture is one in which members are equal, in principle and in practice. It is understood that decisions that affect the collective are best made collectively and that inequality and privilege are incompatible with solidarity. Education also plays an important role in fostering democratic culture, and we return to this in Chapter 6.

Marina Sitrin, author of *Everyday Revolutions: Horizontalism and Autonomy in Argentina* (2012), noted in an interview for the website *Joyful Militancy* the ways in which the culture of a movement affects how individuals act within it.

> *I was honestly a bit surprised at how much people spoke of love and care as necessary to create the sort of world they desire. But now, in retrospect, the fact that the forms of organizing are all about social relationships—paying attention to power, making sure people are heard and can speak, prioritizing voices often excluded and ignored, organizing events with food, drinks, music and other tools that make them more social—were crucial and often just necessary for survival. Care is at the heart of the new forms of organizing.*
>
> (cited in Bergman & Montgomery, 2018)

As Sitrin's observation demonstrates, institutions and culture are produced and sustained through social relationships. This is why, according to one of his first students, José Mari Ormaetxea, Arizmendiarrieta often stressed "cooperatives are made by first making cooperativists" (Arizmendiarrieta, n.d., F2.1.21). When a worker cooperative cultivates solidarity among the worker-owners, solidarity becomes part of everything the worker co-op does.

Sometimes, crises at the level of the co-op and the community bring both together in a mutually beneficial relationship. Argentina's worker-recuperated companies and many other examples from around the world show how worker co-ops that emerged from crises, and that were supported by the community, give back for years after by opening up the space to community initiatives and redistributing wealth with the community. This new kind of "conscientization," to use philosopher and educator Paolo Freire's term, underscores how workers who come together in struggle to save jobs and form worker co-ops often become intimately aware of the plight of the community and its needs and "learn in struggle" to become not only new cooperators, but more responsive and equity-focused community members (Vieta, 2014, 2019).

Still, most cooperatives need to adopt specific intentional strategies to contribute to larger or deeper community movements, especially when the connection to members is not so immediate. These strategies might include building into their operating practices policies like dedicating a certain percentage of profits to agreed-upon community projects that reflect the type of movement work that they are engaged in. Other co-ops might center their work on social movements of some kind, while yet others might build movement work into the business model itself. In practical terms, some co-ops, like the fair trade worker cooperative Equal Exchange, allows members to work outside the scope of their position while they are still on the clock for the co-op (Shipper et al., 2013).

Of these various strategies, financial contribution to external projects is a familiar way in which many cooperative organizations show their commitment to wider circles of community. At Unicorn Grocery, the cooperatively owned store in Manchester, UK, the mission of the cooperative includes the advancement of food sovereignty. Although they use this framework when making operational decisions in their business, including procurement practices that prioritize purchasing from local producers and fair-trade products, they also recognize that the impact of such efforts is limited. For this reason, they support organizations doing the work their cooperative is not designed to do. Every year the co-op puts 1% of its wage bill toward a fund for projects involving environmental activism, support for refugees and asylum seekers, and expansion of community-based food production in the UK. An additional 4% is set aside for initiatives that promote sustainable livelihoods led by the communities experiencing the impacts of unfair world trade.

Coming back to the idea of community from the standpoint of solidarity, we can see how relations of compassion, care, cooperation, *compañerismo*, etc., on the one hand, and a vision of self-emancipation and social transformation, on the other, conjure up different images of community. Both relational and territorial, these visions of community go beyond classification of groups or networks in an existing socioeconomic order, to practices of community building that bring people together based on solidarity, democracy, and equity in order to transform social and economic relations on both a micro and macro level. In Latin America the term *economía solidaria* (solidarity economy, also known as social and solidarity economy or SSE) has been used since the 1980s to describe both the spread of solidarity across the global economy through the actions of organizers, and the sector of the economy in which solidarity is the organizing principle, instead of capital (Razeto, 2019). Perhaps the most ambitious effort to combine community in its most expansive sense with solidarity economy is the Andean-Indigenous concept and practice of *Buen Vivir*.

THE GOOD LIFE

Buen Vivir, known by various names in different languages – *Sumak Kawsay* (Quechua), *Suma Qamaña* (Aymara), *Ñande Reko* (Guaraní) – combines cultural, economic, legal, cosmological, ecological, and political perspectives and practices (Acosta, 2018). While it draws on wisdom that goes back

millennia (compare Aristotle, 2012, on *eudaimonia* or flour-
ishing), it is not some sort of timeless pure worldview linked to
a presumed unitary Indigenous identity. Nor is *Buen Vivir* a
single set of parameters or measures of well-being to be
applied universally. Instead, it is an evolving framework, with
many different expressions, for Indigenous peoples, other
communities, and socially oriented organizations.

In two countries, Ecuador in 2008, and Bolivia in 2009,
Buen Vivir has been enshrined in the constitution and made
the focus of state policies, including the well-known Rights of
Nature that have been used to protect rivers and forests. At
the same time, like the notion of "community" itself, the term
has been used as "an equivalent for anti-poverty policies or
interpreted as solely the demand of Indigenous people, or even
repeated as a slogan that ends up losing all meaning" (Houtart, 2011).

Rooted in the resistance and resilience of Indigenous peoples in the face of European colonization, US imperialism, and
contemporary neoliberalism, Buen Vivir is the articulation not
just of different social goals but of radically different
assumptions and even cosmologies, particularly in the relations of humans to the natural (i.e., other-than-human) world.
One part of that difference is the emphasis on plurality: on the
multiplicity of worldviews, notions of time, understandings of
nature and the place of humans in it. The alternative to the
universalism of the rationalist, instrumental, market-driven
values imposed by European colonial powers, is a "pluni-
versalism" (plurality + universalism) that recognizes multiple
experiences and histories and their interactions as well as the
tensions between local and global concerns (Baschet, 2016).
Buen Vivir explicitly incorporates ideas that are synergistic
with Indigenous practices that have remained resilient through
different environmental and social structures.

As David Bollier and Silke Helfrich have said of commoning, *Buen Vivir* involves an ontological shift – a different
understanding of existence, with different ways of being
(Bollier & Helfrich, 2019). Cooperatives are one of the key
forms used by Indigenous communities to make this shift in
economic and environmental relations. For example, coffee
and honey producers in Chiapas, of the cooperative group
Yomol A'tel, are selling through fair trade networks and
regaining control over how their land is used and their
economy is structured while remaining engaged with global
markets (Irezábal, personal communication, 2022).

Indeed, cooperatives are extensively deployed by Indigenous peoples throughout the Americas. Often, cooperative
forms of co-determining and co-organizing their socioeconomic and sociocultural endeavors merge ancestral ways
of doing with both contemporary solidarity-based and even
market-based economies (Kuokkanen, 2011; Peredo et al.,
2019). But Peruvian-Canadian organizational studies scholar,
Ana Maria Peredo, also warns that the cooperative form, if
not led by the Indigenous communities themselves, risks being
a neocolonial imposition on Indigenous peoples:

> *Indigenous peoples' economies are based on*
> *cooperation. However, oftentimes with good*
> *intentions, Western cooperative structures are*
> *imposed on them without consideration of cultural*
> *norms and practices. Cooperation and cooperative*
> *structures come in different forms. The cooperative*
> *movement needs to embrace them and allow for a*
> *diversity in organizational forms.*
>
> (Peredo, personal communication, 2022)

Aware of the concerns that Peredo mentions, many advo-
cates of *Buen Vivir* reject conventional conceptions of

economic development, and with this the assumed primacy of "growth" – capital, goods, and market accumulation. Until recently, such positions were seen as fringe or marginal views. As Eduardo Gudynas (2020), from the Latin American Center on Social Ecology, writes:

> *A strategy that does not depend on growth of the economy would seem to be unthinkable, even unimaginable. The only acceptable debate is over how to achieve and organize economic growth. Only discussions about levels 1 to 3 of development [theoretical models, sectoral programs, specific projects] are permitted, but not about the fundamental ideas that are found at level zero. It would seem that thinking about alternatives to growth is the terrain of marginal groups or the deluded. Just as the question of whether the obsession with growth might not be one of the causes of the social and environmental crisis is never seriously considered.*
>
> (Gudynas, 2020, p. 15)

Buen Vivir is not an attempt to wind back the clock of history, but in effect to reset it to zero. It rejects the limited choice between various strategies of development in favor of alternatives to development itself. While the objective is "not ... producing more, but producing to live better" (Acosta, 2018), *Buen Vivir* is not limited to determining the factors necessary for living well; it also expresses the need to resist, negotiate with, and where possible, overcome opposing forces.

One basic practice of *Buen Vivir* is building the collective capacity of communities and networks of communities to oppose corporate development in the face of crises. In their study of responses to COVID-19 in the Andean Mountains,

Córdoba, Peredo and Chaves found that strategies of reciprocity empowered individuals and communities to "present their visions of a diverse or mixed economy to the society at large to erode the dominance of capitalism" (Córdoba et al., 2021, p. 139).

So, when we speak of worker cooperatives as vehicles for community economic development, we should not let ourselves be limited to the prevailing definitions, assumptions and parameters. We should be prepared to go back to Gudynas' "level zero" – back to the point of production of solidarity and self-organization (Gudynas, 2020). Worker cooperatives are one essential vehicle for this generative type of world-building because they provide a practical means of provisioning that is, at the same time, a practice of education, self-management, and democratic governance. Because it is not limited to those who have traditional forms of wealth or operate within the status quo, cooperative development is available to those who are marginalized, providing spaces for the free exercise of their creativity in their pursuit of a good life. In the following sections, we explore how cooperatives contribute to two dimensions of the good life – food and health – in this expanded vision.

Food Sovereignty

When defining the good life, fair and equitable access to food is often a central element. The symbolism of food is also very important because it involves a direct connection to the earth and to the conviviality of shared meals, a quintessential expression of community. Almost no feeling is as powerful, no drive so strong, as that of hunger. Though we have the global capacity to produce enough food to feed the Earth's population, our food system continues to fail to distribute sustenance to all. With more than half of the world's population now living in urban environments, the process of food production and the people whose livelihood depends on it are no longer present in many communities. This alienation from farms and farmers continues to perpetuate the commodification of food, subjecting farmers to the whims of the market, while those dependent on charitable programs for food access are provided culturally inappropriate, poor nutritional food.

The concept of food sovereignty first came to international attention in the mid-1990s with the efforts of La Via Campesina, an international network of farmers and farmer organizations, which defends peasant farmers and addresses food insecurity among consumers. From the perspective of *Buen Vivir*, it is not enough to gain access to food to survive; it is also necessary to rethink our relationship to food and to the entire food chain. The movement gained momentum in 2007, when the International Forum for Food Sovereignty was held in Mali. There, the Declaration of Nyéléni (Food and Agriculture Organization, 2007), signed by representatives from over 80 countries, established a shared definition of food sovereignty: "Food Sovereignty puts those who produce, distribute and consume food at the heart of food systems and policies, rather than the demands of markets and corporations" (p. 1). At its core, food sovereignty champions the right of people to define their involvement within the food system – whether it is access to food (like cost and availability) or the ability to produce food (like having land and knowledge).

From the beginning, this concept was political in the sense of entailing a kind of deeply grounded empowerment. Then and now, it stands in contrast to widespread trade and agricultural policies, as well as the powerful interests that benefit from them. As Lynsey Miller, Director of Sales and a Vice President at the worker cooperative Equal Exchange stated in an interview with the National Cooperative Business Association, "A lot of what we do is share power…. [W]e want to share power more inclusively with more people (in the food chain) whether they are farmers, workers or consumers" (NCBA-CLUSA, 2020).

One of the oldest and most evoked forms of cooperation is the agricultural producer cooperative – where farmers come together to gain economies of scale for greater purchasing and selling power. For commodities like coffee, tea, sugar, chocolate, and bananas, small-scale farmers can participate in the food chain by forming cooperatives that serve as the aggregator, processor, distributor, marketer, or all of these functions. These kinds of cooperatives enable farmers to reduce their costs and challenge large corporations head-on, while retaining local ownership, culture, and values (Do, 2020).

Cooperatives like Milestone Cooperative Association in Holmes County, Mississippi, demonstrate that they can do much more. The cooperative, founded in 1942 and comprised predominantly of African American farmers, is in a region of the Mississippi Delta, US with a high rate of poverty. The co-op has partnered with local organizations to assist with low-income housing for families, bringing in fiber optic cable to provide high-speed internet connectivity for the community, and creating vocational training and work opportunities for those with developmental disabilities. Milestone serves not just the interest of their members' agricultural enterprises but provides much needed social services to their greater community (Mitchell et al., 2021).

Farm Worker Cooperatives

Unlike the Indigenous communities that collectively farmed much of the continent before their forced displacement, many contemporary North American farmers – including those who identify with the progressive-minded farm-to-table movement – have abandoned cooperation in pursuit of the "mythic virtue of rugged independence" (Newman, 2019).

However, with resource scarcity and barriers to land access increasingly presenting hurdles for young farmers, many are finding these trade-offs unrealistic. For some, like the Somali refugees who organized New Roots Cooperative Farm in 2006, the worker co-op model has offered a means to overcome the most improbable odds of getting and staying on the land. Others have been drawn to the model by a desire to rethink and reimagine their relationship to the land altogether. Judith Winfrey, who helped organize Love is Love Cooperative Farm Mansfield, Georgia in 2021, recounts that "it wasn't so much about the ownership and wanting to own a piece of land, but the permanency [and] having a long-term view for how a farm could be a piece of a community" (Mitchell et al., 2021). Like Love is Love, *Tourne-Sol* in les Cèdres, Quebec owns its land collectively. The five members who formed the cooperative farm in 2005 have come to gain appreciation for what they've built together, providing motivation to work through rather than walk away from conflicts. As Frédéric Theriault, one of the co-founders and worker-owners at *Tourne-Sol* says, "figuring out how to work together within the structure to allow for happiness and ease was maybe more desirable than slamming the door, starting over anew, and saying 'I'm starting my own farm and doing it my own way'" (Theriault, personal communication, 2022).

Further up the food chain, worker cooperatives are actively changing how food is procured and sold in a more traditional retail model. Unicorn Grocery, mentioned earlier, was founded on the principles of food sovereignty with the aim of building community wealth rather than private wealth, developing and growing a market for locally grown and organic, fairly traded foodstuffs. As Unicorn has grown, they have adopted procurement policies that reflect their commitment to environmental sustainability by reducing plastic and non-recyclable packaging and ensuring that their products are transported by freight overseas rather than by air (Kempson, personal communication, 2021).

Food access, especially in urban areas, continues to be an issue that societies grapple with as rural migration increases globally. An example of this is the increase in prevalence of food deserts, a phenomenon first identified in the 1990s, which refers to areas which lack sufficient access to food, especially healthy options. Food deserts occur primarily in low-income communities where there are few grocery stores and residents often rely on convenience stores. Community organizations attempt to fill in the gaps with food banks, urban farming initiatives and school lunch programs, but it is rarely enough.

ChiFresh, a food service worker cooperative of formerly incarcerated people, is one of the organizations that are addressing urban food insecurity in Chicago. When the COVID-19 pandemic started ravaging North America, members identified a growing need for emergency meals in their community. Rather than wait for government or nonprofit funding-based solutions, the group decided to fast-track the launch of their own catering business. Partnering with Urban Growers Collective, a non-profit urban farm, they contracted with the Chicago Food Policy Action Council to provide tens of thousands of ready-to-go meals. ChiFresh continues to change perceptions of who needs to be at the helm of organizations that are providing solutions. Camille Kerr, a co-op developer who helped found ChiFresh, explains: "worker ownership enables us to demonstrate what is possible, to change the narrative, to show what our economy could look like" (Kerr, personal communication, 2020).

As we see in our examples with food, when we imagine what is needed for our communities to live well it is not enough to think about what it means to have the bare minimum necessary to survive, but rather what is necessary for a community to thrive. In terms of health, we often turn to metrics that point to a lack of health: mortality rates, comorbidity, prevalence of chronic illnesses or malnutrition. However, when we think about what we hope for in terms of health, few wish for "lack of illness" but rather to "be healthy."

Health

The links between health, well-being, and employment were laid bare around the world during the COVID-19 pandemic. In the United States, many employees in sectors deemed "essential" like food and health were asked to set aside their own health concerns to do their job (Hammonds et al., 2020). The experience of workers at Amazon, deprived of bathroom breaks and suffering musculoskeletal injuries due to unrealistic productivity goals, highlighted how a company's actions can starkly contradict its public commitment to put "the well-being of our employees first." This was at a time when the company CEO's personal wealth grew from $80 billion to $190 billion (Kantor et al., 2021).

Long before the pandemic, research on employment as a determinant of health was already underway (Egan et al., 2007). In *The Health Gap*, Michael Marmot (2015) presents numerous case studies of the impacts of inequality on physical health outcomes. These include differences not just between high-income and low-income neighborhoods in various cities in the UK and US, but also differences in health outcomes between government workers based on their rank, with employees in greater positions of power having longer life expectancy than those with less power. Furthermore, studies have shown that employee health is positively associated with control over working environments and social support in the workplace (Baruch-Feldman et al., 2002; Spector, 2002). The mechanism presented by these studies is that the working environment can be a source of stress, which is a very significant determinant of cardiovascular, gastrointestinal and mental health.

We should consider health not just in responsive or corrective ways but also in proactive and holistic ways. Solidarity puts an even greater emphasis on promoting health as a collective and highly democratic set of responsibilities and practices. In Northern Italy, David Erdal set out to study the correlation between social and health effects and employee ownership (Erdal, 2014). He compared three small towns: one where no one was employed by a worker-owned business, one where 11% were, and another where 26% worked in worker-owned businesses. He found that in terms of crime, physical and mental health, the social environment and social participation, the town with the greatest percentage of workers employed by worker-owned firms scored most positively. What was even more striking was that life expectancy was two years longer in the town with the highest percentage of workers who worked in worker-owned businesses. Although this evidence is not conclusive, it is clear that the benefits of the cooperatives extend beyond just the worker-members to the towns in which they are situated.

The ability of communities to determine their own approach to healthcare is another way in which worker cooperatives contribute to community health. Community Pharmacy in Wisconsin, US, has a reputation for being a safe place to ask questions about health care options, accessing herbal librarians, and sharing experiences in living with different challenges related to health and well-being. Centering the health interests of marginalized groups within their community, Community Pharmacy made business decisions that were counter to state regulations to assure equitable access to supplies that individuals identified as necessary to be healthy. During the AIDS epidemic, the co-op offered free needle exchange and continues to this day to offer sterile syringes at cost to those who request them. Their commitment to a broader definition of health also meant that workers were able to purchase first aid supplies at cost to distribute to #blacklivesmatter protesters, acknowledging different factors at play in the life expectancy of their fellow citizens (GEO Collective, 2020).

A great deal of the work that is needed to reproduce human life and sustain society is not accounted for in the conventional understanding of labor. But without such work, the model would not be viable, as feminist economics has rightly pointed out (e.g., Nelson & Power, 2018; Pérez, 2021). Although care-giving and other pro-social work is essential for the sheer continuance of a healthy society, most such jobs are invisible, often performed by women in the home, without any economic representation, or in a very precarious and undervalued part of the labor market. The COVID-19 pandemic made this invisible work visible when the market was unable to support the most vulnerable in society. In many communities, citizen-led mutual aid groups sprang up to fill those gaps. In the UK, more than 500 groups registered to be part of a network coordinated by COVID-19 Mutual Aid UK which provided guidance in how to support those in self-isolation (Brooker, 2020). These groups, run entirely by volunteers, facilitated help with shopping, dog walking or phone calls between neighbors. Other mutual aid groups in the US organized to re-distribute stimulus checks, an idea that was adopted and spread through the hashtag #share-mycheck. These groups were able to provide much needed financial aid to undocumented families or those who did not qualify for government assistance. Indeed, in Canada, cooperatives have been documented to be among the first businesses to respond to community needs during the first weeks of the pandemic (Vieta & Duguid, 2020).

WHERE DO WE GO FROM HERE?

Community is a catch-all term used to describe everything from shared geography, shared interests, shared demographic characteristics, or other more superficial points of similarity. It can also refer to a deeper sense of solidarity based on values, strategic goals, or collective vision. Community can also be thought of as a process, not just a static entity or condition. The processes contributing to community include collaboration, communication, conflict management, co-creation, and indeed cooperation. People not only belong to communities; they create them. We have seen how worker cooperatives can be spaces for building community, networks in which multiple communities intersect, and vehicles for organization of community at all levels, from the workplace to the world.

Seen as a business, a worker cooperative like Community Pharmacy might be described as a community of worker-owners focused on the concerns and needs of their customers, selecting and stocking items for their pharmacy that they know their customers need. A grocery store like Unicorn focuses on their regional customer base while at the same time investing in and cultivating relationships with local and internationally based farmers and producers, thereby changing relationships within the food chain. In organizations like *femProcomuns*, discussed earlier, a worker cooperative or a collective may be one of many groups within a larger socioeconomic project.

As we look to the future and consider how worker cooperatives can impact our relationship to community, we can start to see cooperatives as spaces for building a different social economy and for re-shaping our fundamental relations to ourselves, each other, and our world. We can see that how we think about who is included in our communities can change the scope of who we consider when examining the impact of our enterprises. Our challenge, then, is to move not only from the individual to the community but also to the greater "we" that includes the nonhuman whole of the Earth.

5

COOPERATIVE ECOLOGY

INTRODUCTION

In this chapter, we reflect on some of the ways that cooperatives – notably, worker-owned-and-governed cooperatives – can help to address the environmental crisis, internalize as well as spread ecological practices, and play a significant role in efforts toward resilience and even restoration. We do not presume that worker co-ops, especially acting in relative isolation, can bring about the kind of widespread and dramatic change needed. Worker co-ops, however, can be part of the desperately needed work for a just and less traumatic transition. Zamagni (2014), for example, explains how cooperatives create new spaces for widespread cooperation across sectors of the economy where otherwise transnational corporations tend to crowd out grassroots and innovative business forms. By design and in practice, worker and multi-stakeholder co-ops can pursue transformational organizational and business paths – increasingly essential for the survival not only of the economy but also of civilization as we know it.

It is not a matter of weighing economic progress against confronting climate change (Stuchtey et al., 2016). There are millions of jobs to be created in an economy that adapts to the new reality. We argue that there are enormous roles to be played by cooperatives of all types in a transformed economy that recognizes and responds effectively to the limits of growth and pursues the path to sufficiency and resilience (SSG, 2014; Novkovic & Webb, 2014). Taking up the role of co-ops for the transition, legal scholar Melissa Scanlan (2021) has drawn strong connections between democratic organization and decarbonization, illustrating how co-op and related laws in nations can encourage environmental measures and recommending principles to be incorporated in worker and other co-op by-laws. For example, she recommends including "a clear commitment to environmental sustainability, circular economy, biodiversity, organic and regenerative agriculture, and renewable energy" (p. 287). As we explain below, these measures and more are critically needed, and they are far too rare in key organizational documents, policies, and practices.

CRISIS, URGENCY, AND THE GRAND DELUSION

Humanity is facing the greatest set of challenges in history, not only because today's crises are multiple but also because they are existential (Heinberg, 2021; Korten, 2007). Dramatic climate change alone calls for the most extraordinary types and scales of cooperation ever seen. Yet, a great deal of economic practice and reporting continues to act "as if" somehow traditional calculations in strategy, for-profit maximization, and market expansion can yield anything more than extremely short-term results in the face of a rapidly accelerating climate crisis. The widespread belief, even if usually implicit, is that economic, technological, and organizational principles – said to be guided by the "invisible hand" of the market – achieve a kind of magic that is outside the reality of Earth systems. This magical thinking is evident at all levels of contemporary society, from everyday conversations to international agreements.

As discussed in Chapter 3, "Western" industrial-technological-consumer culture and most major institutions are plainly ill-equipped for long-term survival, especially given the addiction to growth and modern notions of progress, in both material and discursive practices (compare Hamilton, 2003; Klein, 2014). The metabolism of our civilization is unsustainable (Max-Neef, 2010). A telling – and for many observers – astonishing statistic is that an individual's or household's level of affluence is far more predictive of carbon footprint than are any of their beliefs and attitudes about climate change, contradicting the often-felt superior position on climate mitigation and climate justice from those who align themselves with progressive views (e.g., Moser & Kleinhückelkotten, 2018).

Even after dozens of international conferences and summits on climate change, political and economic debates about facing the crisis frequently devolve into questions of "What can we realistically do?" Or "We can't afford to make changes too fast" Or "We can't hurt the economy in addressing climate change." At international summits, such as COP26 in Glasgow in the fall of 2021, an added barrier to action arose as a combination of finger-pointing at some nations and concerns for equity. Although both responses are justified, they contribute to paralysis or very incremental action (McKibben, 2021). In a tragic way, the image of the scale shown in former US Vice-President Al Gore's documentary *An Inconvenient Truth*, where the Earth is in one hand and a bag of money is in the other, still hasn't effectively tilted in the Earth's favor (Guggenheim, 2006).

It is convenient for many believers in anthropogenic climate change to think of denial as a binary matter. It can be self-satisfying and legitimizing to take the position of agreement in principle without making any significant changes in practices or policies. However, we argue that there is not one but are in fact many forms of denial–and not all of them involve disbelief in science surrounding the climate crisis (Thunberg, 2021). In other words, denial is not simply an either-or matter. Rather, psychologists, sociologists and communication scholars have found that distinctions between types of denial are important with respect to climate change because, as Norgaard's (2011) in-depth study of Norway reveals, the vast majority of self-identified believers in the severity of anthropogenic climate change do not take actions that in any significant ways change their life patterns. Denial is thus profoundly relevant, for example, to all sorts of groups, associations, and organizations, including educational institutions and value-driven businesses such as worker and other cooperatives (Cheney & Planalp, 2019; compare Monbiot, 2022b).

Within such a context, is it realistic to continue with business as usual, make minor tweaks in policy, or delay a transition away from fossil fuels and industries that contribute greatly to greenhouse emissions? Where then is *the true realism* here, when we are confronting mass extinctions (Kolbert, 2014), wide scale desertification and floods, and rapid advancement toward 1.5 degrees Celsius in the overall warming of the planet (Klein, 2014)? We would say, along with millions of others, that transformations at every level of production and consumption are absolutely necessary; but, along with such moves, *changes in the very ways we think about and do work* are critical as well (OECD, 2020). This means that a transformation in organizational structures and a wide array of practices is essential (Extinction Rebellion, 2019). As we will argue, addressing climate change and a grassroots economic and political revival are tightly interwoven, and inspired democratic businesses can make a difference.

Drilling down to the level of specific business and organizational practices, however, we find that few organizations of any type have fully internalized the environmental crisis that surrounds us. Certainly, there are nonprofits, governmental agencies, and businesses that have dedicated themselves to addressing climate disruption, species extinctions, and environmental restoration. Still, the responses to these crises are inadequate – limited in their scope and realizations. This was a big part of the impetus for the youth-driven Sunrise Movement, notable for its effectiveness in connecting the climate crisis to a variety of issues and lobbying lawmakers for dramatically new policies (https://www.sunrisemovement.org/). In our own interviews for this book, we were surprised to find that the internalization of ecological principles by cooperatives and other related organizations was not as pervasive by now as we had expected. Still, we have found many concrete reasons to be hopeful and will profile some of those cases and organizations.

The external pursuits and the internal operations of business are of a piece. Most of us will readily criticize the "family friendly" assertions of a business that at the same time does not allow for flexible schedules for employees who have family and other care-giving responsibilities. In this instance, employees or consumers might insist that the company bring its practices in line with its promotional activity. When it comes to the environment, however, things get more complicated because of the many environment-related issues that can affect internal and external organizational orientation, operations and performance. Indeed, advances regarding environmental policies and commitments with programs like "green product lines," eco-efficiency, sustainable development, and carbon trading simply do not offset the rapid rate of environmental decline (Cole et al., 2015).

The Social and the Environmental Absorbed into "The Economic"

In Karl Polanyi's brilliant work, *The Great Transformation* (1944), he argues that the transformation to a "market society" is the first time in human history that society has become a servant of the economic system. Land, nature, money, and human beings and their work are now all mere goods for buying and selling, subject to the law of supply and demand. The social is subordinate to and subsumed by capital within a generally *laissez-faire* market model. The economic sphere is in this way severed from society, and the social dimensions of life are then recast in chiefly economic terms, thereby "leaning" on the economy for their value, as opposed to being seen as having intrinsic worth.

This economic dominance over other realms became more so – and explicitly – as the marketing function came to be an embracing principle for the organization, its workers, and of course, extending to consumers. In the 1990s, George found through his interviews and field observations at Mondragón that such emphases were becoming more pronounced in co-op policies and practices, as well as talk on the street and in homes. The entire co-op organization became dedicated to marketing – such that everyone, across departments, was expected to think of the consumer all the time – and people were more likely to be comfortable referring to themselves as consumers rather than citizens or other terms (Cheney, 2006).

Consequently, what has become commonly understood as economic (neo)liberalism undermines the very foundations of society and sociability. Today, self-regulating market mechanisms, including the consumerist ethic, can tear apart the community fabric and the old forms of sociability – for example, with elimination of town squares and plazas – along with strong bonds to the land (see Tönnies' distinction between community and society in Chapter 4).

Capitalism's crisis is not a matter of compulsive greed or the systematic political plan of certain social classes but might well be termed historical "sleepwalking" through the many forms of accumulation of capital and goods seemingly without limits. Both Marx's (1976) and Polanyi's (1944) analyses show us that the decision to reinvest profits chiefly to generate more profits – which may be a decision made by any type of business, including a cooperative – is at the basis of socio-ecological exploitation.

Cooperatives, too, often participate in this self-destructive sleepwalking. Marx (1981) theorized this in his ambivalent view of worker co-ops: workers collectively managing enterprises in order to produce commodities for markets "naturally reproduce in all cases, in their present organization, all the defects of the existing system," becoming "their own capitalist" (p. 571). That is why conventional cooperativism engaged in competitive markets potentially also destroys the bases that make societal continuance possible – by the fouling of our own nest (Vieta, 2020). As Moore (2015, p. 291) declares, we are at "the end of cheap nature" – not that it was ever cheap in reality.

Modern economic theory and practice, for the most part, has understood and treated the economy as if it were a closed system: goods are exchanged by adjusting prices that are in turn regulated by the mechanism of supply and demand. The reality, however, is that the economy is an open system (Daly & Farley, 2010). The system is open at the "top"; it has no alternative but to work with inputs of energy and materials. At the same time, it is open at the "bottom"; it is a system that produces waste (carbon dioxide, for example). Yet, all these supposed "externalities" such as strip-mined land or polluted water are inextricably part of the big picture of corporate and governmental impacts (e.g., Hawken, 2017).

Even cooperative economics has traditionally excluded such externalities, and this has been generally true with worker co-ops as well. The exclusion was understandable during earlier times for worker co-ops in the nineteenth and early twentieth centuries, when the focus was on the economic and social security of member-owners. But today, the organization's perspective must be broader. This includes solidarity not only with the community but also with the Earth, which all measures of sustainability must ultimately take into account.

Sustainability Solutions Group (SSG), Vancouver, Canada

SSG is, to our knowledge, unique. It is a worker cooperative consisting of over 30 members and associates who focus entirely on sustainability analysis, planning, and tools. SSG's members are a diverse group in terms of education and expertise as well as gender and ethnicity. What unites them all is a mission to create decarbonized, healthy, equitable communities for everyone. The co-op was founded in 2004 and has participated in hundreds of projects since that time, principally in Canada, but also in the United States. Projects range from neighborhood planning to energy audits to much broader systemic examinations of entire communities and regions.

In 2014, SSG issued a report on co-ops and climate change that was sponsored by the International Cooperative Alliance

(SSG, 2014). Although climate change has become even more evident and better understood in the intervening years, the report was notable because of how it linked what is often called "the cooperative difference" to climate disruption mitigation strategies. This report not only details particular ways co-ops, including worker co-ops, have instituted environmentally friendly and ecologically oriented practices, but also outlines ways in which co-ops can collaborate to share resources, scale up their efforts, and expand their impact. In addition, the report takes the seven established cooperative principles and recasts them somewhat in terms of ecology and the environment.

In our interviews, two worker-owners of SSG discussed how environmental concerns are "baked into" the organization, not only in terms of the substance of projects but also in terms of self-assessment of internal practices. This is one way that SSG distinguishes itself from many other co-ops – worker-owned, consumer-owned, or producer-owned. Sustainability for SSG is not just one of many themes or goals; it is what the co-op is about. If there was an area they highlighted for further attention, given the limits of time and the demands of their expanding client base, it was messaging about the climate emergency at the broader level.

Still, the representatives of SSG expressed the wish for more members and more time to deal with popular education and messaging. They are heartened by the fact that recent polls show greater public acceptance of the realities of anthropogenic climate change, yet the interviewees lament that most people still do not see climate disruption as an emergency that implicates every level – from local to global (Cripps, 2022).

OUR SEVERANCE FROM THE EARTH

The only viable path toward mitigating harms, let alone moving to a regenerative relationship with nature, is through

ecologizing the economy. Cooperatives and other organizations must overcome the framework of economic activity and
organizational practice that is underpinned by the illusion that
we are disconnected from physical reality and somehow
exempt from the laws of nature. The entire landscape of social
and economic organizing needs to change in accordance with
ecological as well as democratic principles.

In a manner parallel to the abstraction of the economy
from the social and the planetary in much of economic and
market theories and discourse (Cheney et al., 2010), organizational theory and organizational studies generally have
persisted in the view that the main component of "the environment" of an organization is in fact other organizations.
Organizational frameworks should shift to an "organizational
ecosystem" that includes land, water, air, and, of course,
bodies at work.

The same principles and effects apply to technology. From
casual uses of the term "post-industrial" to the advertising of
technologies as if they were floating above the Earth, the
empirical realities of toxic substances, emissions, and over-
flowing landfills are pushed out of humanity's collective vision
(Cheney et al., 2011). In linguistic and persuasive terms, this is
an extraordinary effort at defining a vision through labels
(Burke, 1969); in economic and social terms, it represents a
powerful extension of the very types of alienation Marx first
described in the mid-nineteenth century (compare Ollmann,
1977; Sayer, 1990). Here it is alienation from our very nature
– our very being as part of nature.

The extraction of natural resources and the emission of
waste per capita continue to expand. It is simply not true that a
thorough "dematerialization" of the economy is actually taking
place; there is no overall reduction in material and carbon use,
just their constant relocation and expansion (Peters et al.,

2011). While many economic sectors of the global North have seen growth in a knowledge-based economy, even that is reliant on extractive industries, carbon-based fuel provision, manufacturing, and long-haul transportation and distribution, made possible in part by the reliance on ever-cheaper labor from the global South. Ours is not a society with few smoke-stacks or exhaust fumes despite promotional images to the contrary from advertising by the major fossil fuel corporations. A grand illusion has been created: that somehow the post-industrial society, the knowledge economy, and the information society are freed up from material concerns and consequences (Castells, 2010; Ellul, 1964).

An implicit reliance on growth underlies schemes that appear to have it all, such as carbon off-setting. Shell's Drive Carbon Neutral program, for instance, asserts that "you don't even have to change the way you work" because emissions can be completely offset through their "portfolio of nature-based solutions projects" (Shell Oil, 2019). When we dig deeper into how some of these programs operate in practice, we often find them falling far short of their claims even as they offer comfort to the informed and concerned consumer who is conscious of the problem yet is relieved to learn that widespread and massive changes aren't really needed after all (Monbiot, 2022).

An example of how a business can be productive and still not require limitless production is RESOURCE, the worker co-op based in Tasmania, Australia introduced in Chapter 2. RESOURCE states their purpose is bigger than profit, subsi-dizing unprofitable activities if they are aligned with their mission: create jobs, minimize waste, and promote waste minimization. This means collecting and recycling e-waste and domestic recycling which is vulnerable to commodity price fluctuation. In 2017, the co-op increased the number of worker-members, which gave them the capacity to expand into offering deconstruction – as opposed to demolition – services. Their first deconstruction project resulted in materials reclaimed and incorporated as features in the new building, while other materials were sold and reused locally or recycled and used in road base. In this way, they show that "growth" in the organization does not have to result in increasing impact on the planet.

Another way we've been severed from the earth is in the concept of "the consumer." The meanings and roles of the consumer are not straightforward, and they have a history in the modern world for at least 500 years (Trentmann, 2016). Still, over the course of the twentieth century, the consumer's role and the term itself became taken for granted in many domains and readily applied by individuals as well as organizations, with "consumer" replacing terms like "citizen" and "people" in political as well as economic discourses (Miles, 2005). In response to this sweeping trend, some writers and organizations aimed to make the role more "aware and active" by speaking of ethical, critical or political consumption (see Devinney et al., 2010). Such efforts are ongoing, and their successes are debated, especially because many value-driven organizations, even in the environmental realm, fall into offering non-essential goods as incentives or perks for contributions to a cause. Nevertheless, there have been significant efforts to mobilize consumer boycotts and "buycotts" (see, e.g., Kendall et al., 2007).

Some cooperatives have entered this space, not only to try to make consumption activities more mindful but also to broaden awareness of the political and environmental implications of goods, services, and transportation. In 2022, Mandela Grocery Cooperative and Rainbow Grocery Cooperative of California stopped selling products from Amy's Kitchen, a popular maker of organic prepared foods, in solidarity with workers in a dispute over labor violations and dangerous working conditions (Lawrence, 2022).

Italian Cooperatives and Political Consumption

RiMaflow is an Italian worker-recuperated company similar to Argentina's *empresas recuperadas*. Located in the northern industrial belt of the Province of Milan, RiMaflow emerged in 2013 as a consequence of the former owner of the Maflow factory pulling out of the Italian car-parts manufacturing market. A group of former employees, supported by their union, occupied the plant and converted it to a co-op (for specifics on the RiMaflow case, see Azzellini & Ressler, 2014; Orlando, 2020). RiMaflow has become a hub of community activism and support; its workers have positioned the worker co-op at the heart of social justice issues in the workplace and in the environmental sphere more widely throughout Italy and internationally.

One of the most important of these wider initiatives is *Fuorimercato*, meaning both "out of the market" and "out with the market." *Fuorimercato* is an alternative food justice, eco-sustainability, and dignified employment network of consumer and worker co-ops and collectives which the RiMaflow workers spearheaded. It brings together critical consumer groups, sustainable agricultural cooperatives, migrant workers, artisans, and precarious workers from across Italy by fostering solidarity exchanges and alternative production initiatives. The network has strong connections with *Via Campesina* (a global movement of small farmers and agricultural workers) and Brazil's *Movimento dos Trabalhadores Rurais Sem Terra* (MST, Brazil's landless workers' and peasants' movement). *Fuorimercato* positions itself outside the established market and promotes accessibility to good food at a fair price.

One of the most crucial things facilitated by Fuorimercato is the creation of a grassroots-driven logistical network for commercializing members' products which fosters a type of "political consumerism," striving to ameliorate consumers' awareness of what is purchased and how it is produced while taking into consideration certain key concepts such as fair trade and sustainability. Moreover, the network proposes an innovative approach to finding alternatives to the capitalist system of production and distribution by uniting the work of *recuperation* (of workplaces, of the economy) with workers' rights, mutualism, and the satisfaction of basic life needs. Over time, *Fuorimercato* (together with RiMaflow) has expanded its network internationally (Orlando, 2020).

Genuine Progress

The standard measure of economic health is the GDP, which as typically formulated and applied, adds increments for things that generate monetary value, which include not only what are conventionally considered to be additions or advances, like a new product introduction, construction of a new neighborhood, expansion of services by a city, but also negative phenomena such as new cancer cases, more oil spills, and even many corporate lawsuits and penalties. The assumption is that increased economic activity in any form is a plus. This is why the counter-marketing group Adbusters.org (2007) often asserts, cleverly, that "Economists need to learn how to subtract."

The problem with GDP is not just the way it measures economic growth but the equating of economic growth to societal well-being, including life satisfaction or happiness. As an "economic snapshot" of a country (www.investopedia.-com), it leaves out a great deal of the overall picture.

The commitment to continuous economic growth under-mines the foundations of productive work, reproductive work, *and* the natural foundations on which these are based. That is the triple structural conflict of capitalism: the conventional extraction, production, and waste model not only harbors conflict between capital and labor, but also conflict between economic growth and the human work of reproduction of daily life (mostly by women), and a fundamental conflict with nature (Mies, 2014). The idea that "economic health" is reliant on growth ignores both the social undershoot and ecological overshoot that Raworth (2017) describes in the Doughnut Model.

The concept of *green growth* seeks to address the ecological overshoot while maintaining economic growth, through innovation and investment in emerging or expanding sectors like renewable energy technologies or new food sources. However, it doesn't address the dynamics of growing inequalities within and between nations.

Degrowth, on the other hand, seeks to increase global well-being while improving ecological conditions, locally and globally, through the equitable reduction of production (GDP) and consumption on a global scale, especially in countries of the North (D'Alisa et al., 2015). However, it is not obvious that a reduction in GDP would lead to a decline in poverty, inequality, and the destruction of natural resources. GDP has declined many times in the past with no such result.

Post-growth also seeks an economy and a society in which economic growth is no longer the goal, but unlike degrowth does not emphasize reduction of production. The focus instead is on social and environmental policies that contribute to genuine well-being without regard to the impact those policies have on GDP. Post-growth stresses "dematerialization" of production (reducing materials used and waste generated), "decommodification" (reducing the scope of the market and its influence on social life), and "decentralization" (moving to community self-management and sovereignty over food systems, energy, communications, etc.)

We need better measures because we want to pay attention to the things that matter and to know if we are moving in the right directions. Genuine Progress Indicators (GPIs) measure social and ecological well-being by looking at factors including the following:

- affordability of housing

- access to excellent health care

- access to child and elder care

- incidence of mental illness

- support structures for children

- soundness of local food systems

- educational achievement of women

- degrees of racial and class segregation/integration

- criminal recidivism rates

- levels of participation in community groups and organizations

- the number of parks per capita

- environmental degradation and restoration

- network embeddedness

Alongside such GPI measures, the Gini Coefficient of economic in/equality, using a formula based on income distributions, is often included (https://en.wikipedia.org/wiki/Gini_coefficient). In other words, GPIs include within their conceptual and practical reach, a wide net of factors and domains for assessing what individual and collective life in a community or country is like. These factors include reported life satisfaction or happiness, which has been shown to be a major concern because of its complicated relationship to affluence and surprisingly low numbers for some of the most "developed" nations (on policy implications, see Diener, 2000; on cooperatives and happiness, see Kaswan, 2014).

LIMITS OF THE GROWTH FRAMEWORK, EVEN FOR COOPERATIVES

The main challenge ahead is to move toward an ecologically sound and socially just economy and society, while coping with the already unavoidable consequences resulting from decades of failure to take action.

The Mondragón Corporation is like many other organizations in that it values productivity and growth fueled by materials, energy, and human labor. What surprises many visitors to Mondragón is that it has not been on the cutting edge of environmental initiatives, despite its stress on innovation and its presence in the green business sector. Their heritage does contain the seeds of a more ecological approach (Sampaio et al., 2012), although those are tiny and for the most part have not flourished. Frugality and community-oriented sacrifice characterized the society which helped to support the cooperatives during their early years between the mid-1950s and mid-1970s.

At Mondragón, the rush toward widespread economic development in all quarters grew alongside an emphasis on the dignity of the person and democracy at work. Solidarity within and across generations, including mechanisms for sharing capital, meant that the cooperatives continued to stress internal dynamics and their relationships to the market but without necessarily embracing a broader environmental commitment. Indeed, even from an *internal* community perspective, the idea of material limits and value-driven sacrifice were later minimized as many people defined themselves as consumers with more individualistic career aspirations (Azkarraga, 2003).

In other words, conventional cooperativism such as Mondragón's emphasizes distributive justice for members and communities yet does not question the continuous accumulation of capital and its destructive implications.

For many cooperatives around the world, a reframing of growth and a shift to an ecological perspective would seem natural and vital. Cooperatives and especially worker cooperatives are primed for contributing to a transformation of how we think about and assess the well-being of a neighborhood, city, rural region, state, province, or nation. Worker co-ops do, in meaningful ways, decommodify work and labor; they are committed to their local communities; moreover, cooperatives can lead societies in an ultimately more satisfying and sustainable direction.

EXPANDING SCOPE OF VISION: THE ULTIMATE STAKEHOLDERS

A widening vision of ecological concerns encompasses several popular perspectives and trends that include the economic space of cooperatives but apply far beyond. They are markers along the path toward the full-scale internalization of ecological principles by business in general and by cooperative businesses in particular.

Corporate social responsibility (CSR) has been a widely used term with its associated policies and practices since the late 1970s (Sethi, 1977). What unifies the perspective is the idea that traditional investor-owned capitalist businesses should not confine their chief obligations to owners or shareholders. Nonetheless, CSR is frequently framed as something that a business, especially a large corporation, should engage in "safely" if it contributes to the bottom line of maximizing profit to owners and maximizing the success of managers (e.g., May et al., 2007). There are exceptions to this. Some private companies such as Patagonia strive for a type of constant improvement in terms of taking the environment into account. In 2022, Patagonia's owners converted the corporation into a business purpose trust linked to a private foundation (Erskine & Matthew, 2022, September 9).

The Triple Bottom Line (Elkington, 1995) drew a lot of attention because it implicitly challenged the notion that there is only one bottom line. The first bottom line of profit is supplemented by a second, social bottom line (the well-being of employees and the internal workings of the business and the community), and a third, environmental bottom line (its health and sustainability). Many national-level and multinational corporations, as well as smaller businesses, have been influenced by this perspective, and to some degree it is institutionalized in the UN Global (Corporate) Compact of 1999 (Verbos et al., 2017).

Another trend is the designation of benefit corporations or B corporations. For companies who demonstrate social and environmental commitments, B Corp status is conferred by a global non-profit. As of February 2022, there were over 5,000 certified B Corps in 80 countries and over 150 industries (B Lab, 2022). Importantly, sometimes employees pressure their B Corp employers to bring their business's practices further in line with their publicized, self-declared goals (Kopaneva & Cheney, 2019).

Stakeholder theory has also held an important place in business ethics for 50 years. The basic idea is that organizational decision making should take into account those groups and institutions that have a "stake" or are affected in substantial ways by its operation. Stakeholders include both internal groups or audiences, such as employees, and also customers, suppliers, partners, even competitors, in effect including the larger community (on stakeholder theory, see e.g., Freeman et al., 2010). A Stakeholder approach underlies the drive to bring as many relevant parties to the table as possible to discuss potential policies and actions. Such *multi-stakeholder* listening or planning sessions can be focused on issues such as land or water and indeed often are. Stakeholder theory, however, has been criticized for implying a somewhat naïve view of power, in that not all stakeholders come to the table with equal resources or opportunities to be heard and to exercise influence.

As we have discussed, cooperatives have been increasingly using "multi-stakeholder" models over the past decades (Birchall & Sachetti, 2017; Michaud & Audebrand, 2019). Stakeholders may include various member types or constituents within a co-op, or those involved in collaborative community projects. Italy's social cooperatives consider beneficiary groups, their families and other local stakeholders as members (Gonzales, 2010). The stakeholders of the Midwest USA's Fifth Season Cooperative (http://www.fifth-seasoncoop.com) include producers, processors, and distributors for a regional food hub, in addition to the hospitals, schools and businesses that they serve.

As discussed in Chapter 4, even rivers, mountains, forests, and deserts may become stakeholders when the effects of an organization's policies on them are taken into account. This may be another worker cooperative advantage: the organizational form tends to be rooted in the territories where they are situated, opening them up to ecological sensitivity.

Italy's Community Cooperatives

After several years of economic, social, and environmental crises, as well as the continued withdrawal of the Italian state the provision of social welfare and public benefit services, more and more Italians are turning to self-organizing socially and ecologically responsible economic activities focused on solving local problems. Communities across Italy are turning to the community cooperative model, which draws from traditional practices of the commons and the country's long-standing cooperative movement while recasting the organization of their social services provision and the protection of their local cultural practices and ecological inheritance (Borzaga & Zandonai, 2015).

Constituted legally as social cooperatives, community cooperatives are bottom-up, multi-stakeholder initiatives established by a network of territorial stakeholders using the cooperative organizational form in order "to manage local commons, regenerate community assets, administer quasi-public services, or produce goods in order to support local communities in their own development projects" (Bianchi & Vieta, 2019, p. 2).

In the Italian context, community cooperatives emerged from the rich cooperative traditions in the country but with a shift in focus from "mutuality" (the mutual interests of specific groups) to the broader interests of society, including consumers, producers, workers, and other community stakeholders, such as residents and migrants (Mori, 2017). Community co-ops, as such, tap into cooperatives' capacity to satisfy, at the same time, the socioeconomic, sociocultural, and ecological needs of communities and regions (Bianchi & Vieta, 2020).

Italy's Community cooperatives are concretizing many of the sustainable development goals (SDGs) too. They are reviving traditional cultural and economic practices while preserving local ecological spaces and creating new jobs via eco-tourism. Two eco-tourism community co-op initiatives of note which are also revitalizing remote villages with declining populations include Cooperativa Valle dei Cavalieri in the village of Succiso Nuova in the region of Emilia Romagna and Cooperativa Brigì in the village of Mendatica in the Alpine area of the Liguria region. Community co-ops have also been used for local clean energy production and use, such as the village-wide solar energy and clean water projects in Melpignano, Puglia. Community cooperatives often encompass cultural and ecological preservation, opportunities for decent jobs, more equitable forms of economic development, innovative ways to regenerate infrastructures and local assets, and the provision of services for communities in marginal areas or critical situations (Bianchi & Vieta, 2019).

Wider Solidarities, Wider Networks

Traditionally, a worker co-op can be a somewhat closed system because its first responsibility is to the worker-owners. Worker co-ops organize production differently, democratizing power, and distributing surplus fairly. They also "socialize knowledge," to use Arizmendiarrieta's phrase, and cultivate solidarity within the firm. But they do not necessarily dispute the imperative of economic growth as they are induced to compete in a largely capitalist market.

A major conference, Imagine 2012, issued a declaration that included the following language on *environmental stewardship*: the need to "redefine economic success on a finite planet" and that "cooperatives recognize that the human species is an integral part of an interconnected and interdependent world and that respecting nature and life in all its expressions is not separable from respect for the dignity and value of each person" (Imagine 2012, 2012). It remains to be seen how far-reaching this commitment will be, but the step taken in the declaration is an important challenge to all cooperatives.

Assemblies, a variety of research, and lay writings have endorsed *environmental stewardship*, even though it remains a minority perspective. One argument in support of environmental stewardship is based on evidence of societies that have survived and even flourished without significant growth (Kallis et al., 2018). These include traditional Indigenous societies with more balanced, collaborative, and sustainable economic practices (Kuokkanen, 2011).

In order to overcome institutional resistance, we envision a very different notion of markets along the lines of economist Michael Schuman's (2020) concept of "comparative resilience." This would include vital "community-based markets of resiliency" in each region, extending the notion of transition towns (Hopkins, 2009) to networks of production, distribution, consumption and funding. These networks would include organizations in the social economy as well as consumers and workers. These would operate in line with democratic, solidarity-based and ecological criteria. Markets would then be one among many mechanisms of production, distribution, and resource allocation. They would not operate autonomously but rather in collaboration with governments, civil society, households, neighborhoods, and organizations in the social economy (compare Gray & Purdy, 2018). Worker cooperatives are poised to play important roles in this new economy because of the commitments, investments, and participatory activities of worker-owners (Smith & Rothbaum, 2014).

FROM NETWORK EMBEDDEDNESS
TO ECOLOGICAL EMBEDDEDNESS

A transition rooted in cooperation means rethinking and redirecting many practices that are based on expansion to ones based on interdependence, sufficiency, and stability (Jackson, 2017). Here the practices of permaculture, forest gardens, and holistic farm management demonstrate that it is possible to create systems that produce, evolve, and thrive while maintaining and enhancing naturally regenerative processes and relationships. Indeed, organizational theory itself, which also applies to cooperatives, can benefit through revision according to lessons from natural systems rather than relying implicitly on mechanistic metaphors of organizational structure and process (see metaphors of organization in Morgan, 1996).

Cuba's *organopónicos*, for example, take a holistic approach (Ewing, 2008; McNamara, 2018). These urban-based cooperative farms use bio-friendly seeds and fertilizers and feed much of the country's towns and cities. Locally based and run by members of the neighborhoods where they are situated, *organopónicos* took off in Cuba after the collapse of the USSR and the end of its dependence on subsidized fossil fuels. Emerging out of the severe socioeconomic crises that submerged Cuba into its subsequent "Special Period" throughout the 1990s and into the 2000s, local communities, the country's mostly agricultural co-op sector, and the Cuban state co-organized the creation of hundreds of cooperatively run *organopónicos* that are still thriving as of this writing.

Another example of cooperative sustainability is Organagardens Cooperative, a landscaping and gardening cooperative in Colorado Springs, USA formed through the conversion of a private landscaping company started by a permaculture specialist. What set Organagardens apart from other businesses in its area was its combination of cooperative organization and permaculture, "the conscious design and maintenance of agriculturally productive ecosystems which have the diversity, stability, and resilience of natural ecosystems... the harmonious integration of landscape and people – providing their food, energy, shelter, and other material and non-material needs in a sustainable way" (Permaculture Research Institute, 2022). The cooperative dissolved in late 2022 but left a legacy of innovative practices. In addition to reinvesting in the cooperative, surplus was used to compensate members for three types of work: labor that is billed to clients, work that sustains the cooperative, and work that they do that contributes to social movements. The integration of landscape and people was central to the work they do, and to their vision of the cooperative. Members studied permaculture and shared what they learned, helping clients and fellow gardeners gain a new understanding of their place in the landscape (Noyes, 2020).

Satoyama: Landscapes as Social-Ecological Systems

In rural Japan, there is a word that embodies forestry, agriculture, and water management: *satoyama*. These spaces, which combined human interference with natural processes, were largely lost with industrialization and globalization. Since the start of this century thousands of satoyama revitalization projects have been launched bringing young people back to the rural areas where they engage with other species and elements in a collective process of "making livability" (Tsing, 2015, p. 263). At Next Green Cooperative, a forestry worker cooperative in Toyooka, Japan, workers focus on creating a forest kindergarten and enjoying the therapeutic effects of being out in nature, over "productive" forest management. As one of the worker-owners of Next Green explains, "maintaining and cultivating a healthy forest so that it exists in the future will only be valuable if the next generation has an appreciation for it" (Next Green, personal communication, 2021). In this way, when worker co-ops seek not only to re-make forests and revive rural communities but to address growing anomie among young people, they are "re-making persons as well as landscapes" (Tsing, 2015, p. 263; Sagara, personal communication, 2020). Experiential, participatory, and mutual learning is central to the process and groups are reported to have "developed a 'do, think, observe, and do again' principle, elevating collective trial and error to an art" (Tsing, 2015, p. 264).

The cultivation of networks among different types of organizations, including worker, consumer, and producer cooperatives, as well as other types of economic organizations, offers the chance to build a new economic arrangement. This "deep networking" may include cooperative producers marketing their goods through fair trade channels, depositing their capital in socially responsible financial institutions, and consumer cooperatives supplying their members and customers with cooperative products. "People should consume what the social market produces, produce what the social market consumes, and fund themselves and invest within the social market. So, it is about comprehensively practicing the principle of intercooperation" (Garcia, 2010, p. 63).

Perhaps the most striking example of the kind of cooperativism we are describing here is the Earthworker Cooperative and the additional cooperatives it has helped form: Earthworker Energy Manufacturing Cooperative, Redgum Cleaning Cooperative, and the energy provider Cooperative Power

Australia. Earthworker was formed by radical labor union activists in the Latrobe Valley, Australia's traditional industrial and coal mining area and site of many labor struggles. Dave Kerin, a former union construction worker with a history of labor, environmental, and anti-war activism, has long understood the importance of building networks of solidarity and mutual support among workers and communities. The Building Labor Federation, of which he was a member, was a key player in the so-called "Green Ban" actions in the 1970s to defend cherished environmental sites. Kerin understands the climate emergency and the fact that people cannot wait for governments or corporations to take action. The new economy has to be built immediately by the people who will work and consume in it, starting with the production of energy.

Kerin stresses that the idea is not enough to tell people about the urgency and possibility of changing the economy now, but to do that work with them. He calls us "to move beyond protest into production" because "we just don't have the time left to convince everyone." The goal is to create worker cooperatives as part of a larger movement to carry out the immediate changeover to renewable energy. Earthworker helped convert a solar water heating manufacturer into the Earthworker Energy Manufacturing Cooperative in 2014.

The movement is not limited to unions, yet they play a key role because it will take the power of organized workers to make the necessary changes in the energy sector in the face of corporate and government opposition. Having played the role of a second-order cooperative, facilitating and coordinating the formation of worker cooperatives, the next step for Earthworker is to establish a cross-sectoral general assembly. This will "put what has been a worker cooperative until now into its proper perspective, which is – it's the organization that encourages and allows for engagement by communities, whether they're geographic communities or faith-based communities or unions or whatever ..." (Kerin, personal communication, 2022).

Kerin hopes that people in other countries will want to create their own Earthworker cooperatives, and the Australian group is already collaborating with workers from worker-recuperated firms in Argentina. "We want to take that global and we are looking at the establishment of worker cooperatives as companies that are autonomous but cooperating with other cooperatives and [we are] providing the structure for them to be able to do that." There is a campaign to treat labor union pension funds as capital belonging to workers to be invested in renewable energy and other projects. They are also working to establish what they call "Social Sector Fair Trade Agreements" – an alternative to Free Trade Agreements – starting with the creation of a "distribution network in Australia for Timorese Co-operative Coffee" that includes "unions, faith communities, geographic communities, small towns, etc."

WHERE DO WE GO FROM HERE?

In the face of the global shocks that are already here, what are the factors that would bring resilience, both to society as a whole and to cooperative organizations and communities? How can we re-imagine and re-organize in order to transition towards the social-ecological economy we urgently need (Munshi et al., 2022)?

We know that a certain amount of human-caused disaster is already inevitable. For example, climate change is difficult to slow, much less halt or reverse. Disasters will affect different communities differently; cooperatives, too. The degree of vulnerability/resilience of each worker cooperative and community is very different, depending on multiple factors. Among these factors is their main business activity; a solar energy cooperative will be affected differently than an automobile parts manufacturing cooperative. Another factor is their degree of embeddedness in the global market; a fair-trade cooperative may face great increases in transportation costs. To face the coming disasters and crises, cooperatives can play a leading role in establishing systems of intercooperation and mutual aid. When Indigenous communities in Colombia "lost their main income by being unable to sell their agricultural products in the urban centres" as a result of the COVID-19 pandemic (Córdoba et al., 2021, p. 6), they took collective action. For instance, the "Minga of Food" (a traditional cooperative exchange system) organized by the *Consejo Regional Indígena del Cauca* expanded to include "bartering amongst communities of different agroecological zones and fair markets to secure access to food within the Indigenous communities and to strengthen networks with other social movements" (p. 6). Cooperatives need to build more of these networks of intercooperation right now and make immediate and drastic changes to prevent future disasters.

The deep economic democracy promised by cooperative work and the strong embrace of ecological principles are closely intertwined. In fact, participatory democracy is in some ways suggested by strong ecological bonds, just as participatory democracy can generate greater inclusiveness with respect to other species and the Earth as a system. To create truly open democracy, it is necessary to be aware of the Earth and the space and sustenance it gives humans for their lives and projects (Williams, 2004).

Criteria for a Cooperative, Resilient, and Restorative Society

Joseba prepared the following list, based on his research, community work, and activism within the cooperative and environmental movements. This should be considered a work in progress that any individual, group or organization can adapt for their needs.

Culture

1. Organizational and societal cultures of empowerment, mutual encouragement, well-being, gratitude and joy are featured.

2. Creative, constructive, nonviolent conflict management is pursued. Silence, pauses, deliberate breaks are all valued not only for rest but also for their capacity to produce insight and breakthroughs.

3. Mindful local consumption and living habits are part of formal and popular education.

4. Cooperatives and networks are embedded in the larger social-solidarity economy movements; democratic education is actively and widely pursued.

Economic Activity

5. Centered at local and regional levels to the extent possible. This is known as the "principle of subsidiarity."

6. Based on a circular systems model, with a high degree of reduction and reuse of waste. Economic activity is not materials- or energy-intensive; it maximizes renewables.

7. Guided primarily by the satisfaction of needs rather than the call for market expansion.

8. Real estate development is designed for energy efficiency and low energy consumption.

9. Local currencies are established and widely utilized. Sufficient reserve funds are maintained, based on critical financial resources, goods and services.

Intra/Intercooperation

10. Creative and practiced techniques for intra-organizational cooperation (for work sharing, flexible working hours, stress reduction, high level of economic equality based on adequate pay intervals, etc.).

11. Active mechanisms of intercooperative cooperation, offering mutual support, work sharing, relocations, common funds, joint resource management.

12. Participation in trans-cooperative networks such as social markets (meeting and trade spaces constituted by different actors of the social and solidarity economy) is encouraged.

Technology and Transport

13. Low-tech technologies are revived and used to their maximal applications.

14. High level of innovation and adaptation, with the capacity to direct economic and productive activity toward products or services important for the resilience of society.

15. Reduced mobility of goods and persons in the production process; thus, prioritizing proximity and public/collective transport between place of

residence and work; telework is accordingly
organized for sociality and well-being along with
efficiency.

Work and Governance

16. Cooperative governance is vibrant, legitimized, and
democratized. Management is conducted in ways
that maximize horizontal empowerment, shared
information, democratic participation, transparency,
and inclusion of differences. There is a high level of
internal cooperation and a low level of internal
competitiveness.

17. Shared leadership, polycentric, and multilevel
governance systems are employed across
institutions.

18. Bureaucratic procedures and regulatory mechanisms
are streamlined and adaptable.

19. Consensual plans are established to face vulnera-
bility to possible disasters. Management of all types
of networks is conducted so as to reduce the spread
of negative impacts, for example, through the
modularity of systems.

20. Inclusion of these criteria in key organizational
documents like by-laws (see Scanlan, 2021).

6

COOPERATIVE EDUCATION

INTRODUCTION

When Ana Aguirre was in Middle School her dream was to be a sea captain, an old dream in the Basque country where she was born. Discouraged by a teacher who told her that her physics skills were not sufficient to continue on that path, she turned her attention to a new program being launched by Mondragón University: LEINN – Leadership Entrepreneurship and Innovation (Mondragón University is part of the largely cooperative Mondragón Corporation).

The Mondragón cooperative experience started with a youth study group organized by the village priest, Arizmendiarrieta, and education has always been central to the project. Mondragón has multiple educational institutions and programs, including the Polytechnical School, the Otalora training center, the *Arizmendi Ikastola* (primary and secondary school), and the educational devices manufacturer Alecop (which also provides students hands-on training in cooperation, manufacture, and services). Today, nearly all of them are faculties within Mondragón University, also a cooperative. To facilitate the creation of cooperatives by young people for educational purposes, Mondragón lobbied the Basque government to create a new legal category of "Junior Cooperatives" (CSCE EKGK, 2021).

In 2009, her first year at Mondragón University, Aguirre and the other "teampreneurs" in her group formed a worker cooperative called Tazebaez (TZBZ), Euskera for "And Why Not?" The co-op, which still exists today, nearly 15 years later, offers a myriad of services from product design and facilitation to consultation for businesses and organizational teams, cooperative and non-cooperative. Being a worker-owner gave Ana the opportunity to channel her leadership drive in the direction of collaborative work with her peers, creating, building, and managing their cooperative enterprise together. Not hesitant to acknowledge their failures, TZBZ advertises the number of failed projects alongside their successes. In 2021, they became part of the emerging global network of DisCO Cooperatives we describe in Chapter 2.

Since graduating, Aguirre became active in the Youth Network of the ICA (she was elected President of the Global Youth Network in 2022). She became a coach for Mondragón Team Academy and in 2020 started collaborating with the PCC (Platform Cooperative Consortium) in NYC as coordinator of the *Platform Cooperatives Now!* course jointly sponsored by Mondragón University and The New School. As a member of TZBZ, Aguirre has worked for Mondragón Corporation, helping communicate the cooperative experience to visitors to Mondragón, which hosts thousands of visitors each year.

Education is not just about building the skills needed to run a cooperative business; it is also about maintaining the collective capacity to renew and reinvent the cooperative model itself. Aguirre tells of a conversation she had with Antonio Cancelo, the founder of the Eroski cooperative grocery chain, who was happy to learn that she was a fan of the writings of

José María Arizmendiarrieta. "It's great that you keep prais-
ing Arizmendiarrieta for being the leader and the thoughtful
mind of the movement," he said, "but who's thinking *now*?"
(A. Aguirre, personal communication, 2021).

In this chapter, we consider the role of education across the
areas of cooperative practice we have surveyed in this book
and reflect on implications for the future.

TEACHING COOPERATION

Cooperative education begins with communication, and
especially with dialogue or conversation. The first questions to
consider are who is in the conversation and where does it
begin: that is, in what context, with what methods? In many
cases, cooperative education and organizing begins with an
educator and a group of current or potential cooperative
members, the participants. The educator may be a fellow
member, a manager, a professional co-op developer from an
outside group, or an academic from a local university. The
curriculum and methodology can be more or less formal, from
a university course, to a workshop series, to non-formal and
apprenticeship-based learning (Noyes, 2009).

Learning in worker cooperatives can also be non-formal,
that is, explicitly educational but not structured in formal
certificate- or degree-based programs with the familiar
educator-student relationship, or informal, where the learning
is often tacit and happens by doing things (Vieta, 2014). Non-
formal learning can happen in peer-to-peer approaches, where
people take turns being the "educator." In self-study the
educator and learner are one.

Informal or tacit learning, where the person may not even
think of what they are doing as learning, is another important

area of cooperative educational practice, generally thought of as learning-by-doing. Like any workplaces, worker cooperatives are inherently sites of informal learning, but with a twist: members not only learn how to do the daily activities of their work but also learn how to participate and how to cultivate and practice democracy at work and beyond, as we will discuss a bit later.

Mondragón's LEINN program, for example, integrates formal, non-formal and informal learning. Based on the *Tiimi Akatemia* founded by Johannes Partanen at Jyväskylä University in Finland, LEINN is a four-year undergraduate program with three main elements:

- Students form team learning cooperatives which start functioning businesses;

- There are no teachers and students; instead there are coaches and "teampreneurs"; and

- Students use the money they make through their cooperative businesses to help pay for international "learning journeys" to Europe, North America, and Asia.

Readings are drawn from the "Book of Books," a compilation of hundreds of titles on Innovation, Entrepreneurship, Social Economy, Sustainability, Leadership, and more (Mondragon Team Academy, 2014). The program design provides opportunities for learning innovation, entrepreneurship, and cooperativism by doing, including practicing democratic decision-making skills. Informal learning is built into the model, with an emphasis on making tacit knowledge explicit through frequent reflection and self and group assessment (Kumakura & Noyes, 2015; Nonaka & Takeuchi, 1995).

In general, communication may be one-way, as in lecture or broadcast, or it may be part of a give and take, as dialogue and conversation suggest. Dialogue is widely understood to be interactive communication that builds trust and mutual understanding. In many cases it also plants the seeds for joint projects. Dialogue involves "common participation, in which we are not playing a game against each other but *with* each other. In a dialogue, everybody wins" (Bohm, 1996, p. 7). Dialogue may take place one on one or in a small group; in a conference, it often occurs informally in the hallways. It may begin in many ways: with a question, a presentation, a case example, a joke, a book, a video, a gesture, or an argument. Dialogic techniques are a key tool for building grassroots democracy, especially within groups that seek to be inclusive and allow for diversity to be heard and to flourish (Mindell, 1995).

Educators and Participants

The role of the educator, then, can be assumed by different people and take different forms: professor, coach, mentor, peer educator. In non-formal cooperative education, the educator's activity is often described as "facilitation" rather than teaching, the idea being that where teaching typically implies a top-down, or at least one-way, process of knowledge transfer from educator to "educand," facilitation is the organization of a collaborative learning process that is many-to-many and dialogic. Facilitation thus allows for the emergence of unplanned parts of the process. It is the responsibility of the facilitator to help a group identify, understand, and reach their objectives. It is a multi-faceted role that may involve designing agendas or activities, moderating discussions, keeping track of time, providing resources and information, working with discomfort, addressing conflict, ensuring a safe space for all participants, and more (Arnold et al., 1991, p. 148).

Participatory Learning

Cooperative education is often described as "participatory," usually in reference to the teaching techniques used. A lecture is less participatory; a role play is more. But the educators are not the only agents in the learning process. Cooperative education stands or falls on the participation of the learners. Yet participation, in learning as in work, refers to a complex, often paradoxical, set of dynamics and relationships as discussed in Chapter 2 (see Stohl & Cheney, 2001).

Analyzing the "fallacies and phases" of participation in the workplace, Alfonso Vázquez (2001) first notes that our primary form of participation as workers is simply the work we do. Books like *Rivethead* (Hamper, 1986), *L'Établi* (Linhart, 1981), and the classic *Working* (Terkel, 1974) feature the many ways in which people participate as workers, the informal learning that takes place, and people's different interpretations of the work they do. The scope of workers' knowledge, control, and decision making is typically limited. Participation is often restricted to just the second of the three phases that Vásquez explains:

1. Participation in the *origin*, at the point when the stage is being set, decisions begin to be made and meanings are generated,

2. Participation in *operations*, that is the processes as they unfold, the conditions and limits of that participation having been elaborated ahead of time, and

3. Participation in the *results*, including in the benefits or losses in the case of wealth generation, as well as the evaluation of performance and the identification of needed changes. (2001, p. 108)

In education, too, participation is often limited to the operational phase – participation in carrying out or performing an activity that has already been imagined, designed, and initiated by a teacher, within a structure already determined. Think of the call center worker going through their script, or the student memorizing historical events. These are the most extreme examples. Less common are situations where participants have some form of input in setting the theme of the course or organizing the work, participants have little or no part in shaping the outcomes. There may be some reward, for the purpose of incentivizing operational participation, and feedback may be sought. But control remains out of their hands.

As an alternative to more "paternalistic" forms of participation, Vásquez proposes "self-organized forms" in which people participate fully in all three phases. In smaller worker cooperatives, members typically participate in all phases; however, in larger co-ops, members may delegate strategic planning and decision making to board members who in turn appoint managers (see Chapter 2).

Effective facilitation of participatory learning is complex and takes some learning in itself. There is a tendency toward professionalization: formalization, standardization, and certification. Thus, cooperative development and education programs are often designed and facilitated by consultants hired by the cooperative or provided by non-profit organizations (GEO Collective, 2019). At the same time, Mike Strode, of Kola Nut Collaborative and Open Collective, emphasizes the importance of sharing facilitation skills:

> *People identify a problem in their community and then they want to collaborate to solve that problem. Now what either ensures that collaboration will continue over the long term or break down very quickly... is facilitation. And I'm not really talking about... some identified leader... It's the responsibility of the group to have these facilitation skills and facilitation dynamics so that if anyone is lacking in their needs for a space, someone can identify that, or the person who has the needs can feel comfortable giving voice to those needs.*
>
> (M. Strode, personal communication, 2022)

Participation in all phases of the learning process, with participants exercising democratic control, is a powerful learning approach that is well suited to worker cooperative culture and structure (Shor, 1987).

Play in Cooperative Education

In cooperative education programs, the role of play tends to be relegated to breaking the ice, team building, or taking a break from more "serious" learning. Play seems frivolous; but, as Huizinga (2016, p. 19) pointed out, "while it is pointless, it is not without meaning." Board games and card games have long been used for educational purposes – the quintessential capitalist game *Monopoly* was in fact copied from *The Landlord Game* designed by Elizabeth Magie for the purposes of teaching the anti-capitalist theories of nineteenth century reformer Henry George. Recent games like *Co-opoly* (TESA, 2017) and *Commonspoly* (ZEMOS98, 2018–2021) introduce cooperativism and commoning through cooperative game play in which teamwork is the key. Game design has also been widely applied to processes like participatory budgeting (Lerner, 2014).

Role playing games and Live Action Role-Playing (LARP) offer other means through which participants can experience the dynamics of cooperation, including decision-making, strategizing, conflict resolution, creative problem-solving and other skills, in a low-risk setting. Similarly, speculative fiction enables writers and readers to imagine an alternative reality. Speculative fiction is increasingly being used by educators for exploring philosophical, education, ethical and political challenges presented by our current economy and new technologies (Shaviro, 2014; Weaver, 2010). Researchers studying this approach noted that "speculative fiction offers a unique and necessary tool for inquiring into the very nature of life in times of accelerating social, environmental, and technological change, by tentatively enabling us to think beyond the constraints of human cognition and knowledge" (Rousell et al., 2017, p. 7).

During the first years of the COVID-19 pandemic, members of the cooperatively owned social media platform social.coop experimented with collaborative speculative fiction, meeting online to co-create a radio drama about a fictitious cooperative, loosely modeled on the DisCO cooperatives, set in the near future. Participants created characters and improvised scenes in which they confronted challenging situations often based on ones that participants had dealt with in their own lives. The collaborative, unstructured process was immersive, and, importantly, fun – providing participants the "warm cookies" that Vincent Russell (2020) has identified as important to creating and maintaining affective bonds in a group. At the same time play led to in-depth discussions of cooperative principles and organizing methods in the face of challenges like distributed ledger technology and co-optation of cooperative approaches (Do, 2021).

Another form of play, the performance of skits and dramas, is used by Chipukizi Voice of Drama (VOD), a worker cooperative formed by current and former students at the Cooperative University of Kenya (CUK). Co-op members write and perform short plays illustrating solidarity and inclusion and showing how cooperation can provide answers to common social and economic issues. Drama has been an important tool of social commentary and organizing in former colonies, especially in the transition after national liberation (Mollel, n.d.; Ngugi, 1991). Chipukizi VOD's plays help their audience understand how cooperative values are relevant both at work and in society at large. Chipukizi is an example of what CUK President Esther Gicheru calls "pre-cooperative groups" (E. Gicheru, personal communication, 2021): self-organized projects created by students to meet their immediate needs while putting their cooperative values into practice. Youth face multiple problems, including unemployment and drug abuse, and they are not interested in the "old-style," mostly producer-owned cooperatives, she says. But with the introduction of worker cooperatives "there is a lot of hope that we can save this generation." Gicheru stresses autonomy and what may be called "protagonism" in organizations; in worker cooperatives like Chipukizi VOD, young people practice "self-reliance [and] democratic decision-making ... they are not relying on somebody else to make decisions and tell them to do this or that."

COMMUNICATING COOPERATIVISM

Cooperative educators often have a strong commitment to cooperativism and an ideological orientation to some kind of social change. But, because cooperative education can take place in many different contexts, the interests, experiences and aspirations of the participants should not be taken for granted. When engaging members of cooperatives and communities, executive director of the US Federation of Worker Cooperatives (USFWC), Esteban Kelly, stresses the importance of meeting individuals "where they are" while moving toward a broader movement consciousness (Kelly, personal communication, 2020).

After many years in the cooperative movement in the state of Chiapas, Alberto Irezábal worked with cooperativists from urban centers around México City. He found "different expressions of social and solidarity economy" that required different narratives. "When you're working with Indigenous and rural communities," he observes, "*harmony* takes center place in the conversation and a central place in the approach that you have to have in terms of these dialogues and these reflections." In urban areas where people "come from a more individual paradigm and worldview," the term that moves people is *dignity*, "collective dignity... has an impact on your family's well-being and your role as a worker" (Irezábal, personal communication, 2021).

Meeting people where they are can enable activists and organizers to broaden the circle of conversation and make their work, values, and goals known to people who are not already interested and to those who may be skeptical or opposed. Rebecca Bauen, director of the Democracy at Work Institute (DAWI), notes DAWI has formed diverse partnerships with city governments, financial institutions, and policymakers (personal communication, 2021). Bauen notes that DAWI is "moving outside of a small, niche market of people who have had an interest in workplace democracy for the sake of democracy," to those who are interested in goals like retaining businesses in communities, promoting minority ownership, and reducing the wealth gap.

The United Nations' sustainable development goals (SDGs) are an example of language that is carefully designed to meet people where they are without presuming that they share your understanding or background (https://www.un.org/en/sustainable-development-goals). In fact the goals are deliberately framed in ways that make them accessible for educational purposes. Ana Aguirre has found the SDGs to be useful in her work because they are "talking a language that a lot of people understand [...] they are simple. People get it" she says, "You don't need to know about sustainability... You just understand that there are 17 problems, and we need to solve them and that's it!" (A. Aguirre, personal communication, 2021). This is why Kate Raworth – the savvy communicator who gave us the "doughnut economy" – uses the SDGs to describe the social shortfall that needs to be overcome, for example #6 Clean Water and Sanitation, the meaning and importance of which is easily grasped (Raworth, 2017).

There is always the risk that while adapting one's language may make it easier to find common ground and establish dialogue with people who are skeptical about worker cooperativism, it can simultaneously water down precisely the things that make worker cooperatives different and important. Sometimes, effective communication is provocative; choosing the best moments for that kind of language requires sensitivity to context as well as value commitments. Graffiti, images, slogans, and direct action can be effective ways of challenging the status quo and inspiring change. Think of the impact of the 2011 occupations, from Tahrir Square to Madrid, the slogans "We are the 99%" and "Black Lives Matter," or the "School Strike for Climate." Effective communication often combines invitational and participatory interaction with movements of challenge and provocation.

Personal and relatable narratives are another way that cooperatives are educating a wider audience about cooperatives. Though cooperatives are not well represented in the media, when media studies professor Nathan Schneider wrote *Everything for Everyone: The Radical Tradition that Is Shaping the Next Economy* (2018), there was no shortage of podcasts and internet radio programs for him to share stories of the many successful co-operative examples he wrote about. Through podcasts such as *Upstream*, *The Laura Flanders Show*, *Team Human*, as well as in features with publications like *The New York Times*, *Fortune Magazine* and *Quartz*, Schneider is able to popularize cooperative values and educate a wider public audience on the history and current applications of cooperatives (https://nathanschneider.info/press/).

Storytelling is often most effective when it is least polished. The Sustainable Economies Law Center has mastered the art of crude animation and unpolished role plays in their education about cooperative organization, recognizing that a stick figure acting out a scene is disarming and empowering. The viewer thinks, "I could draw that!" – exactly the point SELC educators are trying to make (Sustainable Economies Law Center, 2015).

Storytelling can also be a useful classroom tool. Mondragón University's Fred Freundlich uses the story of "Elena, Isabel and the Bike" to engage participants in reflection on the meanings of property, ownership, and the creation of value. It begins like this:

> *Elena needed a bicycle. She bought one for 50€, but it was in bad shape. She had nowhere to store it, so she left it chained up in front of her house. Isabel lives nearby and knows how to repair things …*
> (Freundlich & Arnáez, 2014, p. 2)

The story is paused at regular intervals for participant debate: Isabel repairs the bike, and another person comes along and wants to buy it. Who decides whether to sell or not? Who gets the money? Paolo Freire, who we will introduce later in this chapter, described the facilitation of critical inquiry through the use of open-ended questions, for which there are no pre-determined answers, as "the pedagogy of the question" (Bruss & Macedo, 1985). The process of debating and considering different viewpoints is also a form of practice of working with differences of opinion (see also Flanagan, 1954).

Just as important as storytelling and questioning is listening. When members of Solidarity NYC wanted to map New York City's solidarity economy, they embarked on a "deep listening" project, conducting a series of 30 interviews with people they describe as "first responders to the crises that confront our communities... a group whose wisdom is rarely collectively tapped" (Solidarity NYC, 2013, p. 2). By first responders, they did not mean emergency services personnel, but community members who deal with economic, social, and ecological crises such as Hurricane Sandy. Their subsequent report shared the "pragmatic vision for New York City grounded in values of cooperation, mutualism, ecological sustainability, social justice, and democracy" that the subjects articulated (Solidarity NYC, 2013, p. 2).

Bridging Gaps

While language can serve as common ground, it can also exclude. Miguel Yasuyuki Hirota, co-founder of the *Instituto de Moneda Social* in Spain, focuses his activism on overcoming linguistic barriers in the solidarity economy and co-op worlds. As he notes, the cooperative movement is as much divided by language as it is united. International conferences are often held in English and global organizations may be primarily English or Spanish speaking, leaving cooperative movements of tens or even hundreds of thousands of people excluded or represented by a handful of people.

Many cooperatives are addressing the language access gap. MayFirst.coop, a web-hosting and internet activist organization that has members in Mexico and the United States, ensures that all meetings, publications and communications are bilingual. Rural cooperatives in México are often multilingual, operating in local Indigenous languages while using Spanish or English in marketing to consumers. Although the 2021 ICA World Cooperative Congress in Seoul, South Korea, provided simultaneous translation in English, French, Spanish and Korean for many of its sessions, that still left out nearly every other country in Asia. Hirota describes this type of exclusion as a "weakness in intercultural work" (M. Hirota, personal communication, 2020). He is hopeful that use of Internet tools, particularly videos with subtitles in multiple languages, may help. "Videos are very important because they can show how solidarity economy practices are done in every part of the world" (M. Hirota, personal communication, 2020). His Spanish-language video on solidarity economy in Barcelona offers subtitles in dozens of languages (Hirota, 2020)

Generational and other cultural gaps can also present a challenge. Earthworker's Dave Kerin is an admirer of Mondragón's Arizmendiarrieta (Kerin, 2021), as well as the contemporary Franciscan thinker/practitioner Richard Rohr. Kerin sees education as the key to the regeneration of the values and understandings on which their movement-cooperative project depends. Reflecting on his efforts to move young activists "from protest to production," Kerin observed, "it's hard not to sound like a lecture" (personal communication, 2021). The key, he has found, is to demonstrate that he and the organization take the leadership of young people seriously: "that's the thing that could kill the whole thing, getting that wrong..." Respect, shown not just in words but in deeds, is one way to bridge the gap.

In 2003, the ICA launched the Global Youth Network aimed at bringing together young cooperators worldwide. The network has published several reports since then, and in 2021 released *Cooperative Spring: A Co-op Youth Toolkit*, the product of a research project on the role of youth in the ICA and the broader cooperative world (International Cooperative Alliance Global Youth Network, 2021). In part, it was frustration with discussions that seemed closed to them and not relevant to their concerns that led the Youth Network to produce a toolkit that points to youth as the source of new skills, enhanced creativity, innovation and problem solving, entrepreneurial thinking, new working patterns and a different attitude toward risk: "if we accept the ideas of reconceptualizing work as organizational innovation, young people may have an extremely important role to play in driving progressive change at different levels of an enterprise structure" (ICA Global Youth Network, 2021, p. 25).

In the interest of bridging generational and cultural gaps, the document includes a glossary of cooperative terms with a section titled "Dirty Words." "Throughout the cooperative movement today," they write, "you will not find much explicit conversation of capitalism, colonialism, globalization, and related topics outside of youth, poor, and worker-oriented spaces" (p. 60). They attribute this gap to six factors that include: the cold war experience which shaped much of the current leadership, the system of presumed virtue (the sense that having once declared a cooperative identity, no further reflection is needed), and expectations to conform to norms of conversation. Their key point is that these and other challenging topics should be discussed openly in the cooperative movement, in community meetings, and workplaces, just as they are among their group.

Worcester Youth Cooperatives

In Worcester, Massachusetts, in the midst of the COVID-19 pandemic, six high school students launched the Worcester Youth Cooperatives (WYC). Concerned about "homelessness, the opiate pandemic, hunger, and other systemic problems" in their working class and immigrant community, which were exacerbated by the virus, the students linked up with a mutual aid group and other community allies to organize three cooperative "serve the people" solutions: a hydroponic farm co-op, a delivery co-op (for home delivery of farm products and other items from food pantries) and a project called S.O.S. Worcester, "focused on developing deep relationships with the most vulnerable members of their community in the course of providing access to life-saving resources and even free basic medical services to the streets" (Worcester Youth Co-ops, 2022, para 1).

Our core message is "youth are not the future, WE ARE THE PRESENT." We do not need to wait until adulthood to organize resources and make decisions that create, impact and uplift communities. We value education and we understand that learning and teaching... don't start and end in the classroom. We also recognize that people do not need specialized degrees to identify problems and design courses of action and a rhythm of socio-economic life that becomes healthy communities.

(WYC, 2022, para 4)

The centerpiece of their work is the "Dare to Co-op Academy" (DTCA), a free 24 week "learning experience" open to youth and young adults based on Luis Razeto Migliaro's manual "How to Create a Solidarity Enterprise" (Razeto, 2020), which they are rewriting as they go, adapting it to their specific context and concerns.

LEARNING TO DEMOCRATIZE POWER

In 1930, Ella Baker toured the USA, organizing study groups devoted to the study of the history, principles, and methods of the consumer cooperative movement. Best known for her later work as an organizer and strategist for the NAACP and the Student Nonviolent Coordinating Committee (SNCC), Baker was a co-founder of the Young Negroes' Cooperative League (YNCL). On her tour, which was designed to "act as an antidote to some of the hopelessness that the Black community felt," Baker would spend a couple of days with each community, listening to people, studying their economic problems, and sharing examples and techniques to help them develop co-ops and organize new YNCL councils (Gordon Nembhard, 2014, p. 89).

Mondragón's Arizmendiarrieta also saw education and cooperative education as an antidote to the hopelessness that followed the Civil War in Spain and World War II. He saw education not just as an instrument for co-op development or promotion, but as the essence of worker cooperativism itself, as reflected in his words: "It has been said that cooperativism is an economic movement using educational means. It could just as well be said that it is an educational movement using economic means" (Arizmendiarrieta, 2022, #218). Education was not simply about building successful cooperatives or training workers or managers, but about upending the structures of inequality and exploitation that had caused such harm, through the development of individuals in community. This meant moral education as well as "hard" skills; before starting the first cooperative, he set up a technical school and led study groups on Catholic Action (Molina, 2005, p. 239). Arizmendiarrieta communicated about the values of cooperativism through sermons, conversations on the street, and the newsletter *Trabajo y Unión*. While he dismissed thought without action, he never lost the commitment to education as a process of cultural and spiritual growth and transcendence, culminating, ultimately in "cooperation with God" (Azurmendi, 1992, p. 272). It was this deep and expansive vision of education that guided his work with the five young men who would become engineers and founders of Mondragón's first manufacturing cooperative, Fagor.

At the time Fagor was being established at Mondragón in the late 1950s, Ella Baker was in Atlanta helping to organize the Student Non-Violent Coordinating Committee (SNCC), where she would perfect the educational approach for which she is famous, epitomized in her saying "strong people don't need strong leaders" (Gordon Nembhard, 2014; Wynne, 2016). Baker's approach, inspired in part by the work of Miles Horton and the Highlander Folk School, is a variant of what is often called popular education, a method in which the learners identify their shared concerns, analyze the roots of their problems, develop strategies for action, and act to transform their world, then begin the process again. It is like a spiral, growing outward, always moving through questioning and dialogue.

While it is not known whether Baker ever met him, her work paralleled that of Paulo Freire, the Brazilian educator and theorist famous for creating an approach to teaching literacy skills that has since spread to nearly all continents (Watson, 2014). Friere's approach, most famously articulated in the book *Pedagogy of the Oppressed* (2018), which was on Arizmendiarrieta's bookshelf, was further developed and practiced in South and Central America, the Philippines, South Korea, and Southern Africa, especially in its relation to social and political movements. In Mexico, the Zapatista practice of *accompañamiento* (accompaniment) exemplifies an ongoing learning relationship based on equality and dialogue. Likewise, the *caracoles* (snails/spirals) integrate popular education in a direct-action approach to governance, production, and service provision, aka world-making (Obando-Arias, 2013).

Transforming Relationships

Worker cooperatives continuously "negotiate their boundaries vis-a-vis the status quo" (Parker et al., 2014, p. 361): that is, with the economic, cultural, political and environmental contexts in which they find themselves. "The relationship between any so-called alternative and what we commonly refer to as 'the mainstream' is likely to be dynamic" (Parker et al., 2014, p. 361). The same holds for worker cooperatives as alternative forms of education. As we explained above, learning takes place within a cooperative and outside of it, and can be experiential and informal, formal or non-formal, and instructional, horizontal/peer to peer, and autonomous. All contribute to the "formation" of cooperativists.

In worker cooperatives with a comparatively hierarchical management structure, educational and training practices reflect the organizational culture. Frequently, there are different types of training for board members, managers, rank-and-file members, and non-member employees. In addition, managers or executives may be recruited for their academic background, previous management experience, and leadership qualities, while workers or employees are typically hired based on their ability to perform the assigned tasks, be responsible and consistent, and work well with others. A key factor is whether the new leader or manager enters with a strong commitment to cooperative principles. This has implications for hiring practices as well as ongoing cooperative education.

The assumptions, attitudes, and expectations that people bring to the workplace are greatly shaped by their experiences in other organizations and institutions, such as schools, military service, summer camp, churches, clubs, sports teams, community groups, etc. In each of these settings, people learn to play various roles. When they enter the workplace, they can easily fall into familiar roles in response to the power relations that they find or anticipate finding there. This is true of managers as much as workers, with managers typically having greater authority to shape workplace relationships. As Mondragón University business professor Fred Freundlich observes, even in worker cooperatives "managers who are hired to make decisions, as they see it," may create little space for worker participation, "leading to a negative circle of lowered expectations and participation" (personal communication, 2022). It is important to add that the research on participation reveals that people who are engaged in explicitly participative programs and become disappointed in the results are among the most dissatisfied members or workers going forward (Stohl, 1995).

The same kind of socialization takes place in many of our roles as clients, customers, patients, neighbors, even voters (Asimakopoulos, 2014). Some people acquire the skills and attitudes suited to supervision, management, supervision, and direction, while others become acculturated to comparatively passive roles: waiting, following directions, and performing tasks (Giroux, 2022). As a manager or employee, each person may end up contributing to an undemocratic and unequal distribution of knowledge and power. Of course, this is not to say that as students or employees people are without agency or power. Indeed, as the teenage Étienne de la Boétie (2015) saw with such clarity, the decisive factor in the reproduction of inequality and subordination is not external coercion, but "voluntary servitude," the acceptance and assumption of a subordinate role.

As we saw in Chapter 2, organizations are complex and subcultures of democratic practice – in a department, unit, or branch – often exist even within a business that is more hierarchical. Conversely, an avowedly democratic organization, like a co-op, may have pockets of more traditional hierarchical structure, especially depending on the individuals involved. Pursuing authentic participation and protagonism in work processes, management, and governance while modifying and even deconstructing traditional ownership and management hierarchies can help to build a countervailing force from within the workplace itself.

Worker cooperatives are cultivating a new language for the activities that common business terms fail to capture – a language that suits the new sensibilities and organizational forms described in this book. As discussed earlier, the DisCO cooperatives talk about, and remunerate members for, Livelihood, Care, and Love work, tracking all the contributions, monetary and not, made by members.

According to Rob Evert, Co-President of Equal Exchange, the cooperative has put effort into creating a new language that addresses the contributions of their multiple stakeholders. The cooperative, which emerged from the Central America solidarity movements of the 1980s, rests on three "legs": farmers, workers, and consumers. Though it was clear from the get-go what they needed to do to strengthen their farmer and worker legs (that is, invest in farmer cooperatives and make day to day working conditions better), it was less apparent how to engage the people who buy their products. The co-op recognized that the purpose of the initiative was not to secure a sales niche, but to "see people in their entire holistic being," not just as consumers. The term they subsequently introduced was "citizen-consumer," and the commitment was to seek "honest, credible, real input, not just [the] bogus kind of surveys" (Evert, personal communication, 2022).

> *We think of our consumer hat being in play when we are choosing products without factoring in the issues of democracy, food justice, and the earth. We each do this all the time. But when we put on our citizen-consumer hat we are actively opening up a litany of issues to grapple with, including democracy, food justice, and the earth. And to do this reasonably effectively we cannot be individual actors making personal choices. We will ultimately need to be organized—just as our farmer partners are organized—so that we can drive change together.*
> (Equal Exchange, 2022, para 21)

So as not to "lurch from one campaign to another," Equal Exchange started by building a community, beginning not with workshops on by-laws and governance, but with "a lot of listening." The outcome of the process was that the three outsider members of the cooperative's eleven-person board who were originally brought in to "prevent navel gazing," were replaced by three citizen-consumer members. Their responsibilities are "not only to represent their constituency that elected them but, like ... all workers who are on the board ... to look after the well-being of the wider organization" (Evert, personal communication, 2022).

Consumer-Citizens

Consumer education and organizing is crucial for the democratization of food systems and for guaranteeing food safety,
regenerative practices, and fair treatment for workers. But is
"citizen-consumer" the best term to capture the role we should
all play in our food systems and other markets? While citizen
originally meant simply "city dweller" or "denizen" and
served to unite residents in democratic movements, it has
evolved into a complex concept with multiple meanings. In the
twentieth century, particularly in the US, it has come to mean,
above all, a person with a legal status vis-à-vis the State. Thus,
residents of a country without this status may be considered
"aliens" with restricted rights to political, economic, and civic
participation. This can also occur within a country, as in
China's *hukou* (household registration) system, which created
the vast underclass of "undocumented" workers, mostly rural
people who moved to the cities and on whose backs China's
manufacturing boom was built (Chan, 2001). Worker cooperatives are an important option for documented and undocumented immigrant workers in the United States who face
discrimination or outright exclusion from the labor market
(see, e.g., Ji & Robinson, 2012).

DEEP PARTICIPATION

As John Curl reminds us in his history of cooperative movements in the United States, there is an "utter disconnect
between the promotion of American democracy as exemplary,
and the reality of its absence in almost every facet of American
economic and daily life" (Curl, 2012, p. 243). For Esteban
Kelly, the "proliferation of sites of democratic practice,"
particularly, but not only, in the form of worker cooperatives,
is one road to increased participation in and understanding of
democratic   principles   and   practices   (Kelly,   personal

communication, 2020). This was a notion well understood by Carole Pateman: "participation develops and fosters the very qualities necessary for it; the more individuals participate the better able they become to do so" (Pateman, 1970, pp. 42–43). Because worker cooperatives democratize decision making as well as ownership, they necessarily contribute to democratization of the economy. From a position that breaks through boundaries between work and political life, the act of being a worker-owner engaged in a collective process is in and of itself an education in democracy (see Lindenfeld & Rothschild-Whitt, 1982).

This learning-by-doing approach is a form of democratization in that it eschews traditional top-down instruction and embraces learning through "unhampered participation in a meaningful setting" (Illich, 1970, p. 39). Think of a study circle: the participants join as equals, each brings experience, resources, concerns and aspirations. The agenda is determined jointly, readings are proposed and selected by the group, and members take turns facilitating. Evaluation of the learning process and assessment of learning is done by the participants themselves.

Religious institutions have organized Base Communities using this approach around the world, sowing seeds of grassroots self-organization that led to labor and other movement organization, particularly in South Korea, where student activists took factory jobs and organized small groups that became the seeds of the union revival (Koo, 2001). Many of today's cooperative and trade union leaders came up through the South Korean grassroots democracy movement of the 1980s (Ji, personal communication, 2021). They develop a consciousness compatible with democratization in a broader sense – one characterized by self-reliance, community solidarity, mental flexibility, and an openness to experimentation, through a process Freire (2018, p. 35) called "conscientization."

The mere use of participatory learning techniques like brainstorming or role playing does not necessarily amount to democratic practice (Alexander, 1990; Vargas & Bustillos, 1988). The television show *The Office* satirizes the manipulative use of participatory techniques by a manager who is simply trying to get employees to say what he wants to hear (Daniels, 2005–2013). The outcomes of a democratic participatory education process cannot be determined ahead of time: they depend on the issues raised, goals set, and decisions made by the participants along the way. This approach is a tacit education in democratic functioning. Ira Shor (1987, p. 96) puts it succinctly: "the practice of democracy in study is the study of democracy in practice."

The practice of democracy in learning is also a practice of power, as Arizmendiarrieta stressed in his call to "socialize knowledge in order to democratize power" (Azurmendi, 1992, p. 240). Knowledge that in conventional organizations is held by managers or directors can be redistributed among worker-members in a cooperative. Information that is closely guarded can be made more transparent. In this regard, financial and organizational literacy in worker co-ops is especially important, as prioritized by Namasté Solar in Boulder, Colorado, USA (Sharpe, personal communication, 2021). Because of its unique features and culture, the worker cooperative provides fertile ground and a resilient framework for ongoing education in democracy, and for the formation of what Bernstein (1982) has called "a participatory-democratic consciousness" (p. 69).

Formal practices don't have to be rigid, as exemplified by the annual multi-day Enspiral retreats, which Nati Lombardo confesses can feel "chaotic," with parts of the program left open to be co-created by members on day one. The result is a retreat that is focused as much on building relationships as it is on defining roles and responsibilities. Such approaches not only build understanding of the organization but also cultivate what Lombardo describes as a "social fabric ... built on trust" (Bartlett & Lombardo, personal communication, 2021).

Formal and non-formal cooperative education can be internal and/or external. The central body of the Japan Workers Cooperative Union, for example, offers workshops and consultation for members and managers of its worker cooperatives (T. Sagara, personal correspondence, 2021). Cooperatives often seek formal training from university-based programs, such as the University of Wisconsin Center for Cooperatives in the US, or Saint Mary's University's Master of Management, Co-operatives and Credit Unions in Canada, or the Cooperative University of Kenya. Non-profit cooperative development programs like the Democracy at Work Initiative (DAWI) in the US or the Comparte Network in Latin America and the Caribbean also provide formal and non-formal education and organizing support. In Kenya an NGO called Global Communities, backed by USAID, does train-the-trainers education with rural cooperatives and provides evaluation metrics.

Some cooperatives, like the Japan Workers Collective Network, provide support and coordination for peer-to-peer learning they call *tomoiku*, combining the characters for cooperation and education. US cooperative developer Jim Johnson sees peer-to-peer approaches as an important alternative to the professionalization of co-op education, one that enhances self-organization and self-education (personal communication, 2020).

Peer-to-Peer, Learning in Struggle

Cooperative members also learn through independent inter-actions with fellow members, on and off the job, and through involvement with organizations and institutions outside the cooperative. For example, the worker cooperativists in Chiapas referred to above draw on a long tradition of cooperative culture as well as recent practices like the *caracoles* (Obando-Arias, 2013). They do not leave their values, understandings, and skills at the cooperative's door but bring them to bear in both daily work practices and larger decision-making processes.

Informal learning-by-doing in the context of worker self-organization often has a political dimension. For workers who occupy and recuperate their factories, like the door and window makers at Republic/New Era in the USA or the makers of ceramics at Zanón/FaSinPat in Argentina, the workplace and the community become "schools for struggle." Learning in struggle on and off the job, workers become more socially aware and politically active participants in their local, national, and even international networks (Vieta, 2014; see also Luxembourg, 1986). When cooperatives are created in a context of crisis, they are especially likely to develop a polit-ical orientation (Vieta, 2020).

The relevant question, then – for clarifying what distin-guishes cooperative workplaces in terms of process – is which practices and features do the most to develop and maintain the socialization of knowledge and the democratization of power.

Being of and for the Planet

In a well-known popular education activity called the Problem Tree, learners fill in a large outline of a tree, starting with the leaves, which represent the immediate problems they face, followed by the branches, which are the immediate causes of those problems. On the trunk, deeper causes are listed. The tree is complete when the root causes are filled in. Having analyzed their problems this way, participants can identify questions for further research and begin to strategize about action (Noyes, 2007). Variations include making a parallel "solutions tree" or multiple problem trees to reflect rival analyses and interests. This framework can be used to analyze climate change, as in the "Problem Cocoa Tree" used by Fair Trade Schools (2022). Interestingly, the trees are often drawn, roots and all, as if they were not planted in the earth and with no reference to their natural surroundings – as if analyses and strategies could be devised without reference to the role that nature might play in our problems, our thinking, and our solutions.

As we noted in Chapter 5, we were surprised to discover when researching this book how few worker cooperatives had rethought their basic strategy and practice considering the climate and associated crises. This absence can be seen in cooperative education, as well. A search of the Ed.Coop website (May, 2022), which is an excellent resource for cooperative educational resources, turned up nothing specifically dealing with climate change or ecology. Even in materials related to agricultural cooperatives, climate shows up as a metaphor: business climate. There are exceptions in the cooperative world, as we will see below, but the question stands: what would it look like to incorporate ecology, environment, and the climate emergency in cooperative education, to fill in the actual ecosystems that surround and sustain the cooperative organism (see Davis, 2019)? If the climate emergency "changes everything," how does it change cooperative education?

In Chapter 5, we profiled several cooperatives whose business model is essentially that of an education project. Sustainability Solutions Group, through their consultation with local governments, raises consciousness while facilitating the creation of context-specific solutions to problems related to the climate emergency. Namasté Solar contributes directly to public understanding and implementation of renewable energy, and Equal Exchange works as a nexus of consumers and farmers grappling with the effects of climate change on agricultural production around the world. RESOURCE educates the public about waste minimization directly through workshops but also in the ways that they find new ways to re-examine and reframe materials in the waste stream, such as through art.

These and other examples are of cooperatives whose work is directly impacted by and/or aims to mitigate climate change by choosing business practices that counteract extractive, exploitative and polluting production forms. Yet, to create the systemic change necessary to center ecology in how we approach living, cooperatives must think beyond the boundaries of their own enterprise. Creating a viable and sustainable cooperative culture of solidarity, equity, and democracy requires a shift in values and language within the cooperative (Parker et al., 2014).

Stepping outside of mainstream culture – with respect to growth, accumulation, consumerism, admiration for autocratic leaders, etc. – enables us to discover openings for change. In terms of both "messaging" and participatory engagement, this means doing one's best to choose moments to counter such trends and, when possible, creating spaces for people to come together to visualize different ways of doing things. Visualization exercises and what's sometimes called "future perfect thinking" (i.e., "we will have created this new project") can be helpful in breaking through barriers that are real or perceived when pursuing cooperative business and other socially inspired initiatives.

For Alberto Irezábal (personal communication, 2021), to reinvent work, it is essential to make space for reflection and to instill a sense of transcendence. Traditional businesses, he argues, "spend a lot of money and they spend a lot of work in terms of creating loyalty within their workforce and creating a sense of past and future. And, usually, with some years, they lose the interest of many of the workers [who] actually see no sense of the working." He contrasts this type of education with what he experienced when becoming a board member of the *Yomol A'tel* coffee cooperative in Chiapas. The process involved traveling from village to village, meeting with members, and fasting and staying awake for 24 hours of community prayers and reflection. By "walking the work" in the company of other members "you make a profound commitment to accountability and collective responsibility before everybody, and it becomes their responsibility to walk with you in terms of that commitment" (Irezábal, personal communication, 2022). He notes that in rural settings it is easier to recover an identity that is not only social, or even human, but embraces other species and elements, as in the cosmological vision called, in Tseltal, *Lequil Cuxlejalil*; or in Spanish, *Buen Vivir* (Pieck et al., 2019).

Leo Sammallahti, a marketing manager at co-op Exchange, a global platform for cooperative investment, cautions: "The cooperative movement needs to be careful that it doesn't over-promise and then under-deliver in that cooperatives can't... internalize all these negative externalities, such as climate pollution or stuff like that... But I do think that generally businesses that have a long-term view on things like cooperatives do, they will outperform others when it comes to [the] climate crisis" (Sammallahti, personal communication, 2021).

As we saw in Chapter 3, the New Cooperativism positions cooperatives as just one vehicle among many for building networks to achieve transformative social change. It is informed by a commitment to the empowerment of individuals, organizations, and communities through a wide range of practices. Those practices include various approaches to education both within and beyond the boundaries of cooperative enterprise – from consciousness-raising activities, participation in social action, and sharing of information and skills, to formal training and leadership development (Pyles, 2013). Like any structure, tool, or system, cooperatives find their richest use in conjunction with other tools, each contributing to the process of enhancing life on this planet.

PROLOGUE TO THE POSSIBLE

This book began with our own personal journeys and how we learned of the potential of cooperative businesses that are owned, governed, and managed by workers. Cooperativism is an important and often overlooked model that gives us a glimpse of what economic activity and work life could be, not only for individuals but also for communities and entire societies. The journey of this book project took us – virtually – to both familiar and new places around the world. Although we cannot claim to be comprehensive, we have tried to collect a wide range of interesting and inspiring examples, while also surveying recent academic, practitioner-oriented, and popular literatures. Additionally, the many interviews we conducted have brought worker co-operative projects to life for us, and we hope for you as well.

When it comes to both business and organizational structures, there is a failure of imagination along with the market pressures we have described. Despite the celebration of creativity and innovation within the framework of contemporary capitalism, despite the hype around technological advancement and the growing range of consumer goods and services, despite the common talk about people being able to invent and reinvent themselves, many of the results in terms of unhappiness, waste, and inequality are empirically hard to deny.

People are often surprised to learn that worker cooperatives not only exist but also thrive. We have discussed this one model in depth because of its unique characteristics and their transformative power.

Like any business or organizational form, worker co-ops are best seen in their *relationships*, including internal work relations but also relationships with other types of businesses and organizations. We have referred to various types of co-ops, union-co-op arrangements, B Corps, ESOPs, mutual aid organizations, commoning, time banks, bartering, fair and alternative trade organizations, conscientious consumption, multi-stakeholder collaborations, and informal solidarity networks like those that can be found in times of need or crisis at the neighborhood and community level. In their different ways, these forms try to break out of the strict mold that too often has been taken as the only way to organize work and economic activity. Worker co-ops are a key part of this mold-busting movement.

Business as usual is clearly not working well. This becomes clearer if we shift our gaze from narrow and immediate measures of success, like quarterly earnings or strategic planning for the coming year, to the well-being of our towns, cities, and our common home, the planet. After the global economic crisis that began in 2007–2008, many observers, including former officials in global financial institutions, expressed hope that the industrialized world would "wake up" and begin to do things differently. Unfortunately, the talk as well as the concrete practices largely returned to what was considered normal in many countries.

The crises in front of us now are multiple and grave. Where both the health of democracy and the health of our planet are concerned, we are running out of time and long past the moment where we should try to do our work and channel our productive energies differently. Slogans like "People over profit," "Planet or plastic?" "We are the 99%" and "Another world is possible" are catchy but also telling. They can grab and redirect our attention and energies; but then focused and transformative action must follow.

We have no illusions that the economic landscape will suddenly be sprouting with millions of worker co-ops. Nor do we assume that most readers will become members of worker co-ops. But instead of focusing on the typical, we would like to shift discussions toward the special cases that have the tried and tested capacity to be much more. We hope you find the cases and initiatives in this book as inspiring as we do. We welcome your feedback and dialogue.

REFERENCES

Ackoff, S., Bahrenburg, A., & Shute, L. (2017). *Building a future with farmers II: Results and recommendations from the National Young Farmer Survey*. National Young Farmers Coalition. https://www.youngfarmers.org/wp-content/uploads/2018/02/NYFC-Report-2017.pdf

Acosta, A. (2018). Buen vivir: A proposal with global potential. In H. Rosa & C. Henning (Eds.), *The good life beyond growth: New perspectives* (pp. 29–38). Routledge. https://doi.org/10.4324/9781315542126

Adbusters: ABTV. (2007). *Gross Domestic Product – Economists must learn to subtract* (Adbusters) [Video]. YouTube. https://www.youtu.be/0q-lEATP-9Y

Ahmed, M., Anchukaitis, K. J., Asrat, A., Borgaonkar, H. P., Braida, M., Buckley, B. M., . . . Zorita, E. (2013). Continental-scale temperature variability during the past two millennia. *Nature Geoscience, 6*(5), 339–346. https://doi.org/10.1038/ngeo1797

Alexander, N. (1990). *Education and the struggle for national liberation in South Africa*. Skotaville Publishers.

Alves, S. (2014). *Food for change* [Film]. Home Planet Pictures.

Anderson, B. (2006). *Imagined communities: Reflections on the origin and spread of nationalism*. Verso Books.

Appiah, K. A. (2008). *Experiments in ethics*. Harvard University Press.

Aristotle. (2012). *The Nicomachean ethics* [R. Bartlett & S. Collins, Trans.]. University of Chicago Press. (Original work published ca. 350 BCE).

Arizmendiarrieta, J. M. (1963). Puntos de vista sobre las cooperativas de Mondragón. *Cooperación*, *36*(1). https://www.tulankide.com/en/print-edition/august-1963

Arizmendiarrieta, J. M. (2022). *Reflections*, #218 (The Interpreters Cooperative of Madison, Trans.). Solidarity Hall.

Arizmendiarrieta, J. M. (n.d.). *Notas. Las cooperativas se hacen haciendo primero cooperativistas*. Eusko Ikaskuntza. https://www.eusko-ikaskuntza.eus/en/documentary-collection/documentary-collections/do-20461/

Arnold, R., Burke, B., Jame, C., Martin, D., & Thomas, B. (1991). *Educating for a change*. Doris Marshall Institute.

Ashoka. (2022). *Jose María Luzárraga Monasterio: Ashoka Fellow*. https://www.ashoka.org/en-us/fellow/jose-maria-luzarraga-monasterio

Ashta, A., & Cheney, G. (2017). Opportunities and challenges in the diffusion of social innovation: French cooperatives of salaried entrepreneurs. *Review of Social Studies*, *7*(4), 19–52.

Asimakopoulos, J. (2014). *Social structures of direct democracy*. Haymarket Books.

Avelino, F., Loorbach, D., Wittmayer, J., Lin, C.-J., & Bulut, N. (2017). *A Manifesto for transformative social innovation*. Transformative Social Innovation Theory. http://www.transitsocialinnovation.eu/blog/a-manifesto-for-transformative-social-innovation

Azkarraga, J. (2003, July). Cooperativism and globalization: The Basque Mondragón cooperatives in the face of changing times. In *Fifth international symposium on catholic social thought and management education*. Universidad de Deusto.

Azkarraga, J. (2007a). *Nor bere patroi. Arrasateko kooperatibistak aro globalaren aurrean*. Central Publications Service of the Basque Government.

Azkarraga, J. (2007b). *Mondragon ante la globalización: la cultura cooperativa vasca ante el cambio de época*. LANKI-University of Mondragon.

Azkarraga, J. (2018). Slaying the dragon together: Modern Basque cooperativism as a transmutation of traditional society. In A. Hess & X. Arregi (Eds.), *The Basque moment: Egalitarianism and traditional Basque Society* (pp. 217–253). Center for Basque Studies, University of Nevada.

Azkarraga, J., Altuna, L., Kausel, T., & Iñurrategi, I. (2011). *La evolución sostenible (I) una crisis multidimensional*. Mondragon Unibertsitatea.

Azkarraga, J., & Cheney, G. (2019). Mondragon: Cooperatives in global capitalism. In S. Berger, L. Pries, & M. Wannoffel (Eds.), *The Palgrave handbook of workers' participation at the plant level* (pp. 205–222). Palgrave Macmillan.

Azkarraga, J., Cheney, G., & Udaondo, A. (2012). Workers' participation in a globalized market: Reflections on and from Mondragon. In M. Atzeni (Ed.), *Alternative work organizations* (pp. 76–102). Palgrave Macmillan.

Azkarraga, J., & Desmarais, A. (2017). Youth producing food for an alternative society: Insights from the Basque Country. In A. A. Desmarais, P. Claeys, & A. Trauger (Eds.), *Public policies for food sovereignty* (pp. 199–216). Routledge.

Azkarraga, J., Sloan, T., Belloy, P., & Loyola, A. (2012). Eco-localismos y resiliencia comuntiaria frente a la crisis civilizatoria. *POLIS, Revista Latinoamericana, 33*, 1–23.

Azurmendi, J. M. (1992). *El hombre cooperativo: Pensamiento de Arizmendiarrieta*. Otalora.

Azzellini, D. (2021). Workers' control and self-management. In H. Veltmeyer & P. Bowles (Eds.), *The essential guide to critical development studies* (pp. 366–374). Imprint Routledge. https://doi.org/10.4324/9781003037187-52

Azzellini, D., & Ressler, O. (2014). *Occupy, resist, produce*. RiMaflow. https://www.azzellini.net/en/filme/occupy-resist-produce-rimaflow

B Lab. (n.d). *Make business a force for good*. https://www.bcorporation.net. Accessed on June 3, 2022.

Barrat, T., Goods, C., & Veen, A. (2020). 'I'm my own boss...': Active intermediation and 'entrepreneurial' worker agency in the Australian gig-economy. *Environmental Protection Agency: Economy and Space, 52*(8), 1643–1661. https://doi.org/10.1177/0308518X20914346

Baruch-Feldman, C., Brondolo, E., Ben-Dayan, D., & Schwartz, J. (2002). Sources of social support and burnout, job satisfaction, and productivity. *Journal of Occupational Health Psychology, 7*(1), 84–93. https://doi.org/10.1037/1076-8998.7.1.84

Baschet, J. (2016). *Adieux au capitalisme: Autonomie, société du bien vivre et multiplicité du monde*. La découverte.

Basterretxea, I., Cornforth, C., & Heras-Saizarbitoria, I. (2022). Corporate governance as a key aspect in the failure of worker cooperatives. *Economic and Industrial Democracy, 43*(1), 362–387. https://doi.org/10.1177/0143831X19899474

Bateson, G. (2002). *Mind and nature: A necessary unity.* Hampton Press.

Battillani, P., & Schröter, H. G. (2012). Demutualization and its problems. In P. Battilani & H. Schröter (Eds.), *The cooperative business movement, 1950 to the present* (pp. 150–174). Cambridge University Press. http://dx.doi.org/10. 2139/ssrn.1866263

Baudrillard, J. (1983). *Simulation.* Semiotext(e) of MIT Press.

Bauman, Z. (2001). *Community: Seeking safety in an insecure world.* Polity Press.

Becchetti, L., & Borzaga, C. (2010). *The economics of social responsibility: The world of social enterprises.* Routledge.

Benhabib, S. (2004). *The rights of others: Aliens, residents and citizens.* Cambridge University Press.

Benson, H. (2004). *Rebels, reformers, and racketeers: How insurgents transformed the Labor Movement.* Association for Union Democracy.

Bergman, C., & Montgomery, N. (2018, February 7). Care is at the heart: An interview with Marina Sitrin. *Joyful Militancy.* https://joyfulmilitancy.com/2018/02/07/care-is-at-the-heart-an-interview-with-marina-sitrin-2/

Bernstein, P. (1982). Necessary elements for effective worker participation in decision-making. In F. Lindenfeld & J. Rotschild-Whitt (Eds.), *Workplace democracy and social change* (pp. 51–85). Porter Sargent.

Bernstein, P. (2012). *Workplace democratization: Its internal dynamics* (2nd ed.). Kent State University Press.

Bianchi, M., & Vieta, M. (2019, June). Italian community co-operatives responding to economic crisis and state withdrawal a new model for socio-economic development. In *UNTFSSE international conference in Geneva* (pp. 25–26). http://dx.doi.org/10.2139/ssrn.3410314

Bianchi, M., & Vieta, M. (2020). Co-operatives, territories and social capital: Reconsidering a theoretical framework. *International Journal of Social Economics*, 47(12), 1599–1617. https://doi.org/10.1108/IJSE-03-2020-0135

Billiet, A., Dufays, F., Friedel, S., & Staessens, M. (2021). The resilience of the cooperative model: How do cooperatives deal with the COVID-19 crisis? *Strategic Change*, 30(2), 99–108. https://doi.org/10.1002/jsc.2393

Birchall, J. (2003). *Rediscovering the cooperative advantage: Poverty reduction through self-help*. Cooperative Branch, International Labour Organization.

Birchall, J., & Ketilson, L. H. (2009). *Resilience of the cooperative business model in times of crisis*. Sustainable Enterprise Programme, International Labor Organization. https://www.ilo.org/wcmsp5/groups/public/--ed_emp/--emp_ent/documents/publication/wcms_108416.pdf

Birchall, J., & Sachetti, S. (2017). The comparative advantages of single and multi-stakeholder cooperatives. Euricse Working Paper No. 95–17. European Research Institute on Cooperative and Social Enterprises. https://euricse.eu/wp-content/uploads/2017/09/WP-95_17-Birchall-Sacchetti.pdf

Bjork, C. (2013, December 26). Recession frays ties at Spain's co-ops. *Wall Street Journal*. https://www.wsj.com/articles/SB10001424052702303290904579276551484127412

Blasi, J., Freeman, R., & Kruse, D. (2017). Evidence: What the US research shows about worker ownership. In J. Michie, J. Blassi, & C. Borzaga (Eds.), *The Oxford handbook of mutual, co-operative, and co-owned businesses* (pp. 211–226). Oxford University Press.

Bloom, P. (2016). *Authoritarian capitalism in an age of globalization*. Edward Elgar.

de la Boétie, E. (2015). *The politics of obedience: The discourse of voluntary servitude*. Ludwig von Mises Institute. (Original work published 1577).

Bohm, D. (1996). *On dialogue*. Routledge.

Bollier, D., & Helfrich, S. (2019). *Free, fair, and alive: The insurgent power of the commons*. New Society Publishers.

Borzaga, C., Depedri, S., & Tortia, E. (2010). Testing the distributive effects of social enterprises: The case of Italy. In G. Degli Antoni & L. Sacconi (Eds.), *Social capital, corporate social responsibility, economic behaviour and performance* (pp. 282–303). Palgrave Macmillan. https://doi.org/10.1057/9780230306189_11

Borzaga, C., & Zandonai, F. (2015). Oltre la narrazione, fuori dagli schemi: i processi generativi delle imprese di comunità, in La morfogenesi dell'impresa di comunità. *Impresa Sociale, 5,* 1–7.

Bregman, R. (2017). *Utopia for realists: How we can build the ideal world*. Hachette UK.

Brooker, M. (2020, March 16). The birth of COVID-19 mutual aid. *The Ecologist*. https://theecologist.org/2020/mar/16/birth-covid-19-mutual-aid

Brooks, D., Kempson, A., Scott, K., & Simmonds, M. (2021). *Sociocratic governance in Unicorn Grocery Co-op*. Sociocracia Practica. https://www.sociocracyforall.org/the-use-of-sociocracy-co-op-governance-in-unicorn-grocery/

Brown, A. M. (2017). *Emergent strategy: Shaping change, changing worlds*. AK Press.

Bruss, N., & Macedo, D. (1985). Toward a pedagogy of the question: Conversations with Paulo Freire. *Journal of Education, 167*(2), 7–21.

Burdin, G. (2014). Are worker-managed firms more likely to fail than conventional enterprises? Evidence from Uruguay. *Cornell ILR Review, 67*(1), 202–238. https://doi.org/10.1177/001979391406700108

Burke, K. (1969). *A rhetoric of motives*. University of California Press.

Caillois, R. (2001). *Man, play, and games*. University of Illinois.

Carini, C., Gotz, I., & Turri, S. (2020). *World cooperative monitor*. EURICSE. https://euricse.eu/publications/world-cooperative-monitor-2020/

Carpenter, S. (2020, August 4). After abandoned 'Beyond Petroleum' re-brand, BP's new renewables push has teeth. *Forbes*. https://www.forbes.com/sites/scottcarpenter/2020/08/04/bps-new-renewables-push-redolent-of-abandoned-beyond-petroleum-rebrand/?sh=5f205a871ceb

Castells, M. (2010). *The rise of the network society* (Vol. 1, 2nd ed.). Wiley Blackwell.

Ceballos, S. (2004). The role of the Guggenheim Bilbao Museum in the development of urban entrepreneurial practices in Bilbao. *International Journal of Iberian Studies, 16*(3), 177–186.

Chan, A. (2001). *China's workers under assault: Exploitation and abuse in a globalizing economy*. Routledge.

Chang, H.-J. (2007). *Bad samaritans: The myth of free trade and the secret history of capitalism*. Bloomsbury.

Cheney, G. (1997). The many meanings of "solidarity": The negotiation of values in the Mondragón worker-cooperative complex under pressure. In B. Sypher (Ed.), *Case studies in organizational communication: II* (pp. 68–83). Guilford.

Cheney, G. (1998, May–June). Does workplace democracy have a future? *Work, 7*(3), 15–17.

Cheney, G. (2002). *Values at work: Employee participation meets market pressure at Mondragón*. Cornell University Press.

Cheney, G. (2006). Democracy at work within the market: Reconsidering the potential. In V. Smith (Ed.), *Worker participation: Current research and future trends* (pp. 179–204). Elsevier.

Cheney, G. (2014, January 6). Alternative look at Spanish co-ops. *Wall Street Journal*. https://www.wsj.com/articles/alternative-look-at-spanish-coops-1389042582

Cheney, G., Christensen, L., Zorn, T., Jr., & Ganesh, S. (2011). *Organizational communication in an age of globalization* (2nd ed.). Waveland Press.

Cheney, G., Lair, D. J., Ritz, D., & Kendall, B. E. (2010). *Just a job? Communication, ethics and professional life*. Oxford University Press.

Cheney, G., & Noyes, M. (2018). Review of the book *A global history of cooperative business*, by G. Patmore & N. Balnave. *Labor History, 115*(1), 186–188. https://doi.org/10.5263/labourhistory.115.0186

Cheney, G., & Planalp, S. (November 14–17, 2019). Climate-change denial and discourse in professional communities. [Paper presentation]. National Communication Association Annual Conference, Baltimore, Maryland, United States.

Cheney, G., Zorn, T. E., Jr., Planalp, S., & Lair, D. J. (2008). Meaningful work and personal/social well-being: Organizational communication engages the meanings of work. *Annals of the International Communication Association, 32*(1), 137–185.

Chugh, A. (2021, November). What is 'the Great Resignation'? An expert explains. *World Economic Forum.* https://www.weforum.org/agenda/2021/11/what-is-the-great-resignation-and-what-can-we-learn-from-it/

CICOPA. (n.d.). *COVID 19: How cooperatives in industry and services are responding to the crisis.* https://www.cicopa.coop/news/covid19-how-cooperatives-in-industry-and-services-are-responding-to-the-crisis/

Ciulla, J. (2000). *The working life: The promise and betrayal of modern work.* Three Rivers Press.

Clay, J. (2013, July 4). Can union co-ops help save democracy? *Truthout.* https://truthout.org/articles/can-union-co-ops-help-save-democracy/

Cole, G. (1944). *Century of co-operation 1844–1944.* George Allen and Unwin for the Cooperative Union Limited.

Cole, L., Herbert, Y., McDowall, W., & McDougall, C. (2015). *Co-operatives as an antidote to economic growth.* Sustainability Solutions Group. https://www.ssg.coop/wp-content/uploads/2015/04/Co-operatives-as-an-antidote-to-economic-growth.pdf

Colombo, C. (2008). Temps révolutionnaire et temps utopiques. *Empan, 1*(69), 17–26.

Cooperation Jackson. (2022). *Our principles*. https://
cooperationjackson.org/principles

Córdoba, D., Peredo, A. M., & Chaves, P. (2021). Shaping
alternatives to development: Solidarity and reciprocity in the
Andes during COVID-19. *World Development, 139*. https://
doi.org/10.1016/j.worlddev.2020.105323

Cornforth, C. (2004). The governance of cooperatives and
mutual associations: A paradox perspective. *Annals of public
and Cooperative Economics, 75*(1), 11–32.

Cornforth, C., Thomas, A., Lewis, J., & Spear, R. (1988).
Developing successful worker cooperatives. Sage.

Cripps, E. (2022, February 12). Here's how to demolish the
most common excuses for climate crisis apathy. *The Guardian
US Edition*. https://www.theguardian.com/commentisfree/
2022/feb/12/excuses-tackle-climate-crisis-apathy

CSCE EKGK. (2021). Ley de cooperativas de Euskadi. https://
www.csce-ekgk.coop/es/publicaciones/ley-de-cooperativas-de-
euskadi/

Curl, J. (2012). *For all the people: Uncovering the hidden
history of cooperation, cooperative movements, and
communalism in America*. PM Press.

D'Alisa, G., Demaria, F., & Kallis, G. (2015). *Degrowth: A
vocabulary for a new era*. Routledge.

Dachler, H. P., & Wilpert, B. (1978). Conceptual dimensions
and boundaries of participation in organizations: A critical
evaluation. *Administrative Science Quarterly, 23*(1), 1–39.

Dahl, R. (1985). *A preface to economic democracy*. University
of California Press.

Daly, H., & Farley, J. (2010). *Ecological economics: Principles and applications* (2nd ed.). Island Press.

Daniels, G. (2005–2013). *The office* [TV Series]. NBC Universal Television.

Dasgupta, P. (2007). *Economics: A very short introduction.* Oxford.

Dave, M. (2021). Resilient to crises: How cooperatives are responding sustainably to COVID 19-induced crises. *International Journal of Rural Management, 17*(1), 13S–39S. https://doi.org/10.1177/0973005221991624

Dave, M. (2022). *Kerala plans to launch 4,000 platform co-ops to upskill unemployed youth.* Platform Cooperative Consortium. https://platform.coop/blog/kerala-plans-to-launch-4000-platform-co-ops-to-upskill-unemployed-youth/

Dave Grace and Associates. (2014). Measuring the size and scope of the cooperative economy: Results of the 2014 Global Census on Co-operatives. *United Nations Division of Social Policy and Development.* https://www.un.org/esa/socdev/documents/2014/coopsegm/grace.pdf

Davis, J. (2019). *Against the ecosystem.* Grassroots Economic Organizing Blog. https://geo.coop/blog/against-ecosystem

De Angelis, M., & Harvie, D. (2013). The commons. In M. Parker, G. Cheney, V. Fournier, & C. Land (Eds.), *The Routledge companion to alternative organization* (pp. 280–294). Routledge.

Deller, S., Hoyt, A., Hueth, B., & Sundaram-Stukel, R. (2009). *Research on the economic impact of cooperatives.* University of Wisconsin Center for Cooperatives.

Derezotes, D. (2014). *Transforming historical trauma through dialogue.* Sage.

Derrida, J. (2011). *The beast and the sovereign, vol. I (The seminars of Jacques Derrida)*. University of Chicago Press.

Devinney, T. M., Auger, P., & Eckhardt, G. M. (2010). *The myth of the ethical consumer*. Cambridge.

Dey, K., & Kumar, A. (2022, March 28). *Unlocking the potential of platform cooperatives*. The Hindu Business Line. https://www.thehindubusinessline.com/opinion/unlocking-the-potential-of-platform-cooperatives/article65267406.ece

Diener, E. (2000). Subjective well-being: The science of happiness and a proposal for a national index. *American Psychologist, 55*(1), 34–43. https://doi.org/10.1037/0003-066X.55.1.34

Do, E. (2020). Japan: Cooperatively facilitating membership engagement—employee-led initiatives at JA Hadano. In M. Altman, A. Jensen, A. Kurimoto, R. Tulus, Y. Dongre, & S. Jang (Eds.), *Waking the Asian Pacific co-operative potential* (pp. 171–181). Academic Press.

Do, E. (2021, November 28–30). *Envisioning a co-operative future collaboratively: Speculative fiction as a form of cooperative identity formation*. [Paper Presentation]. World Cooperative Congress ICA Cooperative Research Conference, Seoul, Republic of South Korea.

Doughnut Economics Action Lab. (2020). *The Amsterdam City doughnut: A tool for transformative action*. Circle Economy. https://www.circle-economy.com/resources/the-amsterdam-city-doughnut-a-tool-for-transformative-action

Druon, E. (2015). *Ecolonomy: Doing business and manufacturing differently*. Triarchy Press.

Dufays, F., O'Shea, N., Huybrechts, B., & Nelson, T. (2020). Resisting colonization: Worker cooperatives' conceptualization and behaviour in a Habermasian perspective. *Work, Employment & Society*, *34*(6), 965–984.

Duffy, M. (2021, May 10). Women-dominated child and home care work is critical infrastructure that has long been devalued. *The Conversation*. https://theconversation.com/women-dominated-child-and-home-care-work-is-critical-infrastructure-that-has-long-been-devalued-159029

Durkheim, E. (2014). *The division of labor in society*. Free Press.

Durkheim, E. (2018). *Professional ethics and civic morals*. Routledge Classics.

Egan, M., Bambra, C., Thomas, S., Petticrew, M., Whitehead, M., & Thomson, H. (2007). The psychosocial and health effects of workplace reorganisation. 1. A systematic review of organisational-level interventions that aim to increase employee control. *Journal of Epidemiology & Community Health*, *61*(11), 945–954. https://doi.org/10.1136/jech.2006.054965

El-Youssef, H., & Elkington, J. (1995). Towards the sustainable corporation: Win-win-win business strategies for sustainable development. *California Management Review*, *36*(2), 90–100. https://doi.org/10.2307/41165746

Elkington, J. (1995). Towards the sustainable corporation: Win-win-win business strategies for sustainable development. *California Management Review*, *36*(2), 90–100.

Ellerman, D. (2021). *Neo-abolitionism: Abolishing human rentals in favor of workplace democracy*. Springer.

Ellul, J. (1964). *The technological society*. Vintage Books.

Equal Exchange. (2022, January 11). The citizen-consumer dilemma: Part One. Equal Exchange Resource Center. https://

www.info.equalexchange.coop/articles/the-citizen-consumer-dilemma-part-one

Erdal, D. (2014). Employee ownership and health: An initial study. In S. Novkovic & T. Webb (Eds.), *Co-operatives in a post-growth era: Creating co-operative economics* (pp. 210–220). Zed Books.

Errasti, A. (2015). Mondragon's Chinese subsidiaries: Coopitalist multinationals in practice. *Economic and Industrial Democracy*, *36*(3), 479–499. https://doi.org/10.1177/0143831X13511503

Errasti, A., Bretos, I., & Nunez, A. (2017). The viability of cooperatives: The fall of the Mondragon cooperative Fagor. *Review of Radical Political Economics*, *49*(2), 181–197. https://doi.org/10.1177/0486613416666533

Erskine, M. (2022, September 9). Yvon Chouinard and the Patagonia purpose trust— What is it and will it work? *Forbes*. https://www.forbes.com/sites/matthewerskine/2022/09/16/yvon-chouinard-and-the-patagonia-purpose-trust-what-is-it-and-will-it-work/?sh=da9eeb32deb4

Eum, H.-S. (2017). *Cooperatives and employment: Second global report*. CICOPA. https://www.cicopa.coop/wp-content/uploads/2018/01/Cooperatives-and-Employment-Second-Global-Report-2017.pdf

Ewing, E. (2008, April 3). Cuba's organic gardens. *The Guardian*. https://www.theguardian.com/environment/2008/apr/04/organics.food

Extinction Rebellion. (2019). *This is not a drill*. Penguin.

Ezorsky, G. (2007). *Freedom in the workplace?* Cornell University Press.

Fair Trade Schools. (n.d.). *The problem cocoa tree – A lesson plan for secondary schools*. Fair Trade Foundation. https://schools.fairtrade.org.uk/teaching-resources/the-problem-cocoa-tree-a-lesson-plan-for-secondary-schools/

femProcomuns. (2022). *Commons sustainability model*. https://femprocomuns.coop/commons-sustainability-model/?lang=en

Ferdinand, T. (1887). *Community and society*. Transaction Publishers.

Ferreras, I. (2017). *Firms as political entities; Saving democracy through economic bicameralism*. Cambridge University Press.

Flanagan, J. (1954). The critical incident technique. *Psychological Bulletin, 51*(4), 327.

Food and Agriculture Organization of the United Nations. (n.d.). *Declaration of Nyéléni*. https://www.fao.org/agroecology/database/detail/en/c/1253617/

Foucault, M. (1984). *The Foucault reader* (P. Rabinow, Ed.). Pantheon.

Fourier, C. (1836). *La fausse industrie morcelée, répugnante, mensongère, et l'industrie naturelle, combinée*. Bossange. Internet Archive. https://archive.org/details/lafausseindustr01fourgoog/

Fox, M. (2006). *CECOSESOLA: Four decades of independent struggle for a Venezuelan cooperative*. Voltaire Network. https://www.voltairenet.org/article141230.html

Frankena, W. K. (1973). *Ethics* (2nd ed.). Prentice-Hall.

Freeman, J. (1972). The tyranny of structurelessness. *Berkeley Journal of Sociology, 17*(1), 151–164.

Freeman, R., Harrison, J., Wicks, A., Parmar, B., & de Colle, S. (2010). *Stakeholder theory: The state of the art.* Cambridge University Press.

Freeman, R., & Rogers, J. (1999). *What workers want.* Cornell University Press.

Freire, P. (2018). *Pedagogy of the oppressed.* Bloomsbury Academic.

Freundlich, F., & Arnáez, N. (2014). *Elena, Isabel, y la bici. Cuentos de trabajo y capital: Los cimientos del cooperativismo de trabajo.* CIRIEC. http://ciriec.es/wp-content/uploads/2014/11/comun170.pdf

Friedman, E. (2016). *China on strike narratives of workers' resistance.* Haymarket Books.

Fulton, M., & Girard, J.-P. (2015). *Demutualization of co-operatives and mutuals.* Co-operatives and Mutuals Canada. http://canada.coop/en/demutualization

Garcia, J. (2010). La economía solidaria no está en paro. *Papeles de relaciones ecosociales y cambio global, 110,* 53–65.

Gaztambide-Fernández, R. (2020, April 13). *What is solidarity? During coronavirus and always, it's more than 'we're all in this together'.* University of Toronto: Ontario Institute for Studies in Education. https://www.oise.utoronto.ca/oise/News/2020/What_is_solidarity_during_coronavirus.html

GEO Collective. (2019). *Driving our movement with P2P learning.* Grassroots Economic Organizing. https://geo.coop/articles/driving-our-movement-p2p-learning

GEO Collective. (2020). *Health autonomy beyond the pandemic* [Webinar]. Grassroots Economic Organizing.

https://geo.coop/articles/health-autonomy-beyond-pandemic-webinar

GEO Collective. (2021). *How to strengthen the cooperative community: An interview with E.G. Nadeau.* Grassroots Economic Organizing. https://geo.coop/articles/how-strengthen-cooperative-community

George, H. (1879). *Progress and poverty: An inquiry into the cause of industrial depressions and of increase of want with increase of wealth. The remedy.* Doubleday.

Gibson-Graham, K., Cameron, J., & Healy, S. (2013). *Take back the economy: An ethical guide for transforming our communities.* University of Minnesota Press.

Gills, B. (2020). *Deep restoration: From the great implosion to the great awakening.* Globalizations. https://doi.org/10.1080/14747731.2020.1748364

Girard, J. P. (2008). Les cooperatives de solidarité: Une forme organisationnelle pour renforcer la cohesion sociale? *Synthèse d'une recherche.* ARUC-ÉS. http://www.aruc-es.uqam.ca/Portals/0/cahiers/C-04-2008.pdf

Giroux, H. (2022). *Pedagogy of resistance: Against manufactured ignorance.* Bloomsbury.

Gitlin, T. (2012). *Occupy nation.* It Books.

Godin, B., & Lucier, P. (2014). *Innovo: On the vicissitudes and variations of a concept.* (Project on the Intellectual History of Innovation Working Paper No. 19). INRS. http://www.csiic.ca/PDF/Romans.pdf

Goll, I. (1991). Environment, corporate ideology, and employee involvement programs. *Industrial Relations, 30*(1), 138–149.

Gomes, F., & Reis, J. (2016). *Freedom by a thread*. Diasporic Africa Press.

Gonzales, V. (2010). Italian social cooperatives and the development of civic capacity: A case of cooperative renewal? *Affinities: A Journal of Radical Theory, Culture, and Action*, 4(1), 225–251.

Gordon Nembhard, J. (2014). *Collective courage: A history of African American cooperative economic thought and practice*. Penn State University Press.

Graeber, D. (2012, March). Of flying cars and the falling rate of profit. *The Baffler*. https://thebaffler.com/salvos/of-flying-cars-and-the-declining-rate-of-profit

Graeber, D., & Wengrow, D. (2021). *The dawn of everything: A new history of humanity*. Penguin.

Granovetter, M. S. (1973). The strength of weak ties. *American Journal of Sociology*, 78(6), 1360–1380.

Gray, B., & Purdy, J. (2018). *Collaborating for our future: Multistakeholder partnerships for solving complex problems*. Oxford University Press.

Greenberg, E. (1986). *Workplace democracy: The political effects of participation*. Cornell University Press.

Greenhouse, S. (2019). *Beaten down, worked up: The past, present, and future of American Labor*. Penguin Random House.

Gudynas, E. (2020). El pegajoso mito del crecimiento económico y la crítica al desarrollo. *Revista nuestrAmérica*, 8(16), 1–22. https://doi.org/10.5281/zenodo.6481748

Guggenheim, D. (Director). (2006). *An inconvenient truth* [Film]. Paramount.

Gusfield, J. R. (1978). *Community: A critical response.* Harper & Row.

Habermas, J. (1979). *Communication and the evolution of society.* Beacon Press.

Hamilton, C. (2003). *Growth fetish.* Pluto Press.

Hammonds, C., Kerrissey, J., & Tomaskovic-Devey, D. (2020). *Stressed, unsafe, and insecure: Essential workers need a new, New Deal.* University of Massachusetts Amherst Center for Employment Equity. https://www.umass.edu/employmentequity/stressed-unsafe-and-insecure-essential-workers-need-new-new-deal

Hamper, B. (1986). *Rivethead: Tales from the assembly line.* Warner Books.

Handelsman, J. (1987, April 5). We can't come to an agreement about how to fix your car, Mr. Simons. Sometimes that's the way things happen in a democracy [Cartoon]. *The New Yorker.*

Hawken, P. (2017). *Drawdown.* Penguin.

Heinberg, R. (2021). *Power: Limits and prospects for human survival.* New Society Publishers.

Helfrich, S. (2016). El buen vivir and the commons. *Countercurrents.* https://countercurrents.org/2016/09/el-buen-vivir-and-the-commons/

Heller, F., Pusic, E., Strauss, G., & Wilpert, B. (1998). *Organizational participation: Myth and reality.* Oxford University Press.

Hirota, M. Y. (2020). *Solidarity economy in Barcelona.* Grassroots Economic Organizing. https://geo.coop/articles/solidarity-economy-barcelona-en-es-fr-jp

Hodder, A. (2020). New technology, work and employment in the era of COVID-19: Reflecting on the legacies of research. *New Technology, Work and Employment, 35*(3), 262–275. https://doi.org/10.1111/ntwe.12173

Hodson, R. (2001). *Dignity at work*. Cambridge University Press.

Hopkins, R. (2009). *The transition handbook*. Green Books.

Hossein, C. S. (2015). Black women as cooperators: Rotating savings and credit associations (ROSCAs) in the Caribbean and Canada. *Journal of Co-operative Studies, 48*(3, Winter), 6–17.

Houtart, F. (2011). El concepto de sumak kawsay (buen vivir) y su correspondencia con el bien común de la humanidad. *Revista de filosofía, 29*(69), 7–33.

Huizinga, J. (2016). *Homo ludens: A study of the play element in culture*. Angelico Press.

Hwang, D.-H. (2021). *Squid game* [TV Series]. Siren Pictures.

Iannello, K. (2013). *Decisions without hierarchy: Feminist interventions in organization theory and practice*. Routledge. https://doi.org/10.4324/9781315021225

Illich, I. (1970). *Deschooling society*. Marion Boyers.

Illich, I. (2005). *The rivers north of the future: The testament of Ivan Illich*. House of Anansi.

IMAGINE2012. (2012). *IMAGINE2012 contribution to the ICA declaration*.

Imaz, O., Freundlich, F., & Kanpandegi, A. (2022). The governance of multi-stakeholder cooperatives in Mondragon: The evolving relationship among purpose, structure and process. In S. Novkovic, K. Miner, & C. McMahon (Eds.),

Humanistic governance in democratic organizations: The cooperative difference. Palgrave Macmillan.

International Cooperative Alliance. (n.d.). *Cooperative identity, values & principles.* https://www.ica.coop/en/cooperatives/cooperative-identity

International Cooperative Alliance. (2015). *Guidance notes on the cooperative principles.* https://www.ica.coop/en/media/library/research-and-reviews/the-guidance-notes-on-the-co-operative-principles

International Cooperative Alliance Global Youth Network. (2021). *Cooperative spring: A co-op youth toolkit.* https://globalyouth.coop/en/coopspring/introduction-what-it-how-use-it

International Labour Organization. (2018). World employment and social outlook 2018: Greening with jobs. https://www.ilo.org/wcmsp5/groups/public/--dgreports/--dcomm/--publ/documents/publication/wcms_628654.pdf

Ishay, M. (2004). *A history of human rights.* University of California Press.

Ishiguro, K. (2021). *Klara and the sun.* Knopf.

Jackson, T. (2017). *Prosperity without growth: Foundations for the economy of tomorrow.* Routledge.

Jacques, R. (1996). *Manufacturing the employee: Management knowledge from the 19th to 21st Centuries.* Sage.

Ji, M., & Robinson, T. (2012). *Immigrant worker owned cooperatives: A user's manual.* The Cooperative Foundation. https://community-wealth.org/sites/clone.community-wealth.org/files/downloads/WrkrCoopManual%205-31-12.pdf

Kallis, G., Kostakis, C., Lange, S., Muraca, B., Paulson, S., & Schmelzer, M. (2018). Research on degrowth. *Annual Review of Environmental Resources*, *43*(4), 1–26. https://doi.org/10.1146/annurev-environ-102017-025941

Kantor, J., Weise, K., & Ashford, G. (2021, June 15). The Amazon that customers don't see. *New York Times*. https://www.nytimes.com/interactive/2021/06/15/us/amazon-workers.html

Kaswan, M. (2014). *Happiness, democracy and the cooperative movement*. State University of New York Press.

Kendall, B., Gill, R., & Cheney, G. (2007). Consumer activism and corporate social responsibility: How strong a connection. In S. May, G. Cheney, & J. Roper (Eds.), *The debate over corporate social responsibility* (pp. 241–264). Oxford University Press.

Kerin, D. (2021, November 29). The legacy of Arizmendiarrieta: A system of cooperatives as a means: Climate emergency, species extinction and war. Arizmendi International Gathering 2021. https://arizmendigathering.files.wordpress.com/2021/11/paper-what-arizendis-legacy-holds-for-our-australian-and-global-future-paper-for-november-2021.pdf

Kerswell, T., & Pratap, S. (2019). *Worker cooperatives in India*. Palgrave Macmillan. https://doi.org/10.1007/978-981-13-0384-5

Klein, N. (2007). *The shock doctrine: The rise of disaster capitalism*. Knopf Canada.

Klein, J.-L. (2013). Introduction: Social innovation at the crossroads between science, economy, and society. In F. Moulaert, D. MacCallum, A. Mehmood, & A. Hamdouch

(Eds.), *The international handbook on social innovation* (pp. 9–12). Edward Elgar. https://doi.org/10.3935/rsp.v21i3.1225

Klein, N. (2014). *This changes everything: Capitalism vs. the climate*. Simon & Schuster.

Kohn, A. (1992). *No contest: The case against competition* (20th Anniversary ed.). Houghton Mifflin.

Kolbert, E. (2014). *The sixth extinction: An unnatural history*. A&C Black.

Koo, H. (2001). *Korean workers: The culture and politics of class formation*. Cornell ILR.

Koont, S. (2011). *Sustainable urban agriculture in Cuba*. University Press of Florida.

Kopaneva, I., & Cheney, G. (2019). Organizational identity formation in alternative organizations: A study of three benefit corporations. *Management Communication Quarterly*, *33*(4), 484–511. https://doi.org/10.1177/0893318919858684

Korten, D. (2007). *The great turning: From empire to Earth*. Berrett-Koehler.

Kremer, M. (1997, July). *Why are workers' cooperatives so rare?* (NBER Working Paper No. 6118). National Bureau of Economic Research. https://www.nber.org/papers/w6118

Kumakura, Y., & Noyes, M. (2015, July 15–18). Participatory education for cooperative regeneration: Japanese research and Basque practice. [Conference Presentation]. 5th CIRIEC International Research Conference on Social Economy, Lisbon, Portugal.

Kuokkanen, R. (2011). Indigenous economies, theories of subsistence, and women: Exploring the social economy model for Indigenous governance. *The American Indian Quarterly*, 35(2), 215–240. Spring.

Kurosawa, A. (1983). *Something like an autobiography.* Vintage.

Kyanzaire, L. (2022). *Rwanda's cooperatives of trust.* Grassroots Economic Organizing. https://geo.coop/articles/rwandas-cooperatives-trust

Landemore, H. (2020). *Open democracy: Reinventing popular rule for the twenty-first century.* Princeton University Press.

Lapavitsas, C., Ramachandran, M., & Bougiatiotis, Y. (2022, April 15). The Amazon union success shows why the Left needs to focus on Labor. *Jacobin.* https://www.jacobinmag.com/2022/04/amazon-union-staten-island-left-chris-smalls-alu

Larrabure, M., Vieta, M., & Schugurensky, D. (2011). The "new cooperativism" in Latin America: Worker-recuperated enterprises and socialist production units. *Studies in the Education of Adults*, 43(2), 181–196. https://doi.org/10.1080/02660830.2011.11661612

Lawrence, K. (2022, March 28). Amy's Kitchen labor dispute at Santa Rosa plant leads some co-ops to boycott products. *The Press Democrat.*

Lepore, J. (2021, January 11). What's wrong with the way we work. *The New Yorker.* https://www.newyorker.com/magazine/2021/01/18/whats-wrong-with-the-way-we-work

Lerner, J. (2014). *Making democracy fun: How game design can empower citizens and transform politics.* MIT Press.

Levitin, M. (2021). *Generation occupy.* Counterpoint Press.

Levitsky, S., & Ziblatt, D. (2018). *How democracies die.* Crown Publishing Group.

Lichtenstein, N. (2013). *State of the union: A century of American labor.* Princeton University Press. https://doi.org/10.1515/9781400848140

Lindenfeld, F., & Rothschild-Whitt, J. (1982). *Workplace democracy and social change.* Porter Sargent.

Linhart, R. (1981). *L'Établi.* Les Éditions de Minuit.

Logue, D. (2019). *Theories of social innovation.* Edward Elgar.

Logue, J., & Yates, J. (2005). *Productivity in cooperatives and worker-owned enterprises: Ownership and participation make a difference!* International Labour Organization. http://www.oit.org/wcmsp5/groups/public/--ed_emp/--emp_ent/--coop/documents/publication/wcms_746781.pdf

Lucassen, J. (2021). *The story of work: A new history of humankind.* Yale University Press.

Lukes, S. (1974). *Power: A radical view.* Macmillan.

Lund, M., & Novkovic, S. (in press). Multistakeholder cooperatives. In M. Eliott & M. Boland (Eds.), *Edward Elgar handbook on cooperative and mutual enterprise.* Edward Elgar.

Luxembourg, R. (1986). *The mass strike, the political party, and the trade unions.* Bookmarks.

Luzárraga, J., Aranzadi, D., & Irizar, I. (2007, October 22–25). Understanding Mondragon globalization process: Local job creation through multi-localization: Facing globalization threats to community stability. [Paper presentation]. 1st CIRIEC International

Research Conference on the Social Economy, Victoria, British Columbia, Canada.

Lyderson, K. (2009). *Revolt on Goose Island: The Chicago factory takeover and what it says about the economic crisis*. Melville House.

Machado, A. (1982). *Proverbs and song-verse, selected poems* [A. Trueblood, Trans]. Harvard.

Mamouni, E., Mazzarol, T., Soutar, G. N., & Siddique, K. H. (2018). The member wears four hats: A member identification framework for co-operative enterprises. *Journal of Co-Operative Organization and Management*, 6(1), 20–33. https://doi.org/10.1016/j.jcom.2018.03.003

Mangan, A., & Byrne, A. (2018). Marginalising co-operation? A discursive analysis of media reporting on the Co-operative Bank. *Organization*, 25(6), 794–811. https://doi.org/10.1177/1350508418763276

Mansbridge, J. (1983). *Beyond adversary democracy*. University of Chicago Press.

Mantoux, P. (1929). *The Industrial revolution in the eighteenth century: An outline of the beginnings of the modern factory system in England* [M. Vernon, Trans.]. Jonathan Cape.

Marks, G. (2022, May 22). Why giving employees a piece of the pie could boost your business. *The Guardian, US Edition*. https://www.theguardian.com/business/2022/may/22/employee-shares-stocks-us-small-business

Marmot, M. (2015). *The health gap: The challenge of an unequal world*. Bloomsbury Press.

Marx, K. (1844). Critical notes on the article: "The King of Prussia and social reform. By a Prussian". *Vorwarts! 63*.

https://www.marxists.org/archive/marx/works/1844/08/07.htm

Marx, K. (1976). *Capital: Volume I*. Penguin. (Original work published 1867).

Marx, K. (1981). *Capital: Volume III*. Penguin. (Original work published 1894).

Max-Neef, M. (2010). The world on a collision course and the need for a new economy. *AMBIO: A Journal of the Human Environment*, *39*(3), 200–210.

May, S., Cheney, G., & Roper, J. (2007). *The debate over corporate social responsibility*. Oxford University Press.

McKibben, B. (2021, August 25). Slow-walking the climate crisis. *The New Yorker*. https://www.newyorker.com/news/annals-of-a-warming-planet/slow-walking-the-climate-crisis

McNamara, T. (2018). Urban farm-fed cities: Lessons from Cuba's organopónicos. *Sage Magazine*. https://sagemagazine.org/urban-farm-fed-cities-lessons-from-cubas-organoponicos/

Michaud, M., & Audebrand, L. K. (2019). Inside out, outside in: "Supporting members" in multi-stakeholder cooperatives. *Management Decision*, *57*(6), 1382–1398. https://doi-org.myaccess.library.utoronto.ca/10.1108/MD-01-2017-0042

Michels, R., Lipset, S. M., Paul, E., & Paul, C. (2017). *Political parties: A sociological study of the oligarchical tendencies of modern democracy*. Routledge.

Mies, M. (2014). *Patriarchy and accumulation on a world scale: Women in the international division of labour*. Bloomsbury Publishing.

Miles, S. (2005). *Consumerism as a way of life*. Sage.

Mindell, A. (1995). *Sitting in the fire: Large group transformation using conflict and diversity*. Deep Democracy Exchange.

Miner, K., & Novkovic, S. (2020). Diversity in governance: A cooperative model for deeper, more meaningful impact. *The Cooperative Business Journal*. https://ncbaclusa.coop/journal/2020/fall-2020/diversity-in-governance/

Mitchell, B., Head, C., Winfrey, J., Honderd, R., & Michel, C. (2021, October 15). Land, legacy, and concern for community [Webinar]. National Farmers Union. https://www.youtube.com/watch?v=RY4YuPsjN4U

Molina, F. (2005). *José María Arrizmendiarrieta 1915–1976*. Caja Laboral-Euskadiko Kutxa.

Molla, R. (2022, April 8). How a bunch of Starbucks baristas built a labor movement: Inside Starbucks's successful 21st-century union drive. Vox. https://www.vox.com/recode/22993509/starbucks-successful-union-drive

Mollel, T. M. (n.d.). *African theatre and the colonial legacy: A review of the East African scene*. Michigan State University. https://pdfproc.lib.msu.edu/?file=/DMC/African%20Journals/pdfs/Utafiti/vol7no1/aejp007001004.pdf

Monbiot, G. (2022, April 7). 'Learning to live with it'? From Covid to climate breakdown, it's the new way of failing. *The Guardian, US Edition*. https://www.theguardian.com/commentisfree/2022/apr/07/learning-live-covid-climate-breakdown-failing-government-flooding

Monbiot, G. (2022, January 26). Carbon offsetting is not warding off environmental collapse–It's accelerating it. *The Guardian, US Edition*. https://www.theguardian.com/commentisfree/2022/jan/26/carbon-offsetting-environmental-collapse-carbon-land-grab

Mondragón. (1987). Principios básicos de la experiencia cooperativa de Mondragón. *TULankide, 307*(9). https://www.tulankide.com/es/revista/octubre-1987

Mondragon Team Academy. (2014). The art of reading. Glow Junior Cooperative. https://issuu.com/glowjcoop/docs/aathe_art_of_reading_2013_2014__set

Moody, K. (2017). *On new terrain: How capital is reshaping the battleground of class war.* Haymarket Books.

Moore, J. W. (2015). *Capitalism in the web of life: Ecology and the accumulation of capital.* Verso Books.

Morgan, G. (1988). *Creative organization theory: A sourcebook.* Sage.

Morgan, G. (1996). *Images of organization* (2nd ed.). Sage.

Mori, P. A. (2017). Community co-operatives and co-operatives providing public services. In J. Michie, J. Blasi, & C. Borzaga (Eds.), *The Oxford handbook of mutual, co-operative, and co-owned business* (pp. 184–194). Oxford University Press.

Moser, S., & Kleinhückelkotten, S. (2018). Good intents, but low impacts: Diverging importance of motivational and socioeconomic determinants explaining pro-environmental behavior, energy use, and carbon footprint. *Environment and Behavior, 50*(6), 626–656. https://doi.org/10.1177/0013916517710685

Mulder, C. P. (2015). New Era Windows Cooperative: From a sit-down strike to a worker cooperative. In *Transcending Capitalism through cooperative practices* (pp. 69–85). Palgrave Macmillan.

Munshi, D., Cretney, R., Krian, P., Morrison, S. L., & Edwards, A. (2022, November 15). Culture and politics in overlapping frames for the future: Multi-dimensional activist organizing in Aotearoa New Zealand. *Organization*, 1–19. https://doi.org/10.1177/13505084221131641

Murray, R., Caulier-Grice, J., & Mulgan, G. (2010). *Open book of social innovation*. Young Foundation/NESTA.

NCBA-CLUSA. (2018). *The ABCs of cooperative impact*. https://ncbaclusa.coop/resources/abcs-of-cooperative-impact/

NCBA-CLUSA. (2020, June 9). *At Equal Exchange, democratizing the food system is a job for worker-owners, farmers and consumers*. https://ncbaclusa.coop/blog/at-equal-exchange-democratizing-the-food-system-is-a-job-for-worker-owners-farmers-and-consumers/

Nelson, J. A., & Power, M. (2018). Ecology, sustainability, and care: Developments in the field. *Feminist Economics*, 24(3), 80–88. https://doi.org/10.1080/13545701.2018.147391

Neufeld, D. (2021). *Long waves: The history of innovation cycles*. Visual Capitalist. https://www.visualcapitalist.com/the-history-of-innovation-cycles/

Newman, C. (2019, July 25). *Small family farms aren't the answer*. The Medium. https://heated.medium.com/small-family-farms-arent-the-answer-742b6684857e

Ngugi, W. T. (1991). *Decolonising the mind: The politics of language in African literature*. Heinemann.

Nicholls, A., & Murdoch, A. (Eds.). (2012). *Social innovation: Blurring boundaries to reconfigure markets*. Routledge.

Noack, R., & Mehl, S. (2021, June 24). 'This is a food bank now': Workers seized a McDonald's in France. *The Washington Post*. https://www.washingtonpost.com/world/interactive/2021/mcdonalds-marseille-food-bank/

NoBAWC. (n.d.). About NoBAWC. https://nobawc.org/

Nonaka, I., & Takeuchi, H. (1995). *The knowledge-creating company: How Japanese companies create the dynamics of innovation.* Oxford.

Norgaard, K. M. (2011). *Living in denial: Climate change, emotions, and everyday life.* MIT Press.

Novkovic, S. (2008). Defining the co-operative difference. *The Journal of Socio-Economics, 37*(6), 2168–2177.

Novkovic, S., & Webb, T. (Eds.). (2014). *Co-operatives in a post-growth era.* Zed Books.

Noyes, J. H. (1966). *History of American socialisms.* Dover. (Original work published 1870).

Noyes, M. (2007). *Activity 3.1 the problem tree: The workers' inspiration.* Rollingearth: Movement Education. https://rollingearth.org/node/39

Noyes, M. (2009). The worker education problem: Teaching in New York City University-based worker education centers. Rolling Earth, Movement Education. https://www.rollingearth.org/node/146

Noyes, M. (2017). *We'll see it when we know it: Recognizing emergent solidarity economy.* Grassroots Economic Organizing. https://geo.coop/story/well-see-it-when-we-know-it

Noyes, M. (2020). *Learning from the earth: Permaculture meets cooperation at OrganaGardens.* Grassroots Economic Organizing. https://geo.coop/articles/learning-earth

Obando-Arias, M. (2013). *La pedagogía de los caracoles: Chiapas y el sistema educativo rebelde Zapatista de liberación nacional.* Revista Ensayos Pedagógicos.

Okubasu, D. (2022). Humble life of Kenyan priest who created first ever Sacco. Kenyans.Co.Ke. https://www.kenyans.co.ke/news/73649-humble-life-kenyan-priest-who-created-first-ever-sacco

Ollmann, B. (1977). *Alienation: Marx's conception of man in capitalist society.* Cambridge University Press. https://doi.org/10.1017/CBO9780511611902

Olsen, E. K. (2013). The relative survival of worker cooperatives and barriers to their creation, sharing ownership, profits, and decision-making in the 21st Century. In D. Kruse (Ed.), *Sharing ownership, profits, and decision-making in the 21st century (Advances in the economic analysis of participatory labor-managed firms, volume 14)* (pp. 83–107). Emerald Publishing Limited. https://doi.org/10.1108/S0885-3339(2013)0000014005

Open Minds. (2019, April 30). Nova Leap Health acquires Careforce Home Care Workers Cooperative Limited. Open Minds. https://openminds.com/market-intelligence/bulletins/nova-leap-health-acquires-careforce-home-care-workers-cooperative-limited/

Organisation for Economic Co-operation and Development. (2020). *Making the green recovery work for jobs, income and growth.* https://www.oecd.org/coronavirus/policy-responses/making-the-green-recovery-work-for-jobs-income-and-growth-a505f3e7/

Orlando, G. (2020). Recovering solidarity? Work, struggle, and cooperation among Italian recovered enterprises. *Economic Anthropology, 8,* 74–85. https://doi.org/10.1002/sea2.12186

Ortega, I., & Uriarte, L. (2015). *Retos y dilemas del cooperativismo de Mondragón: Tras la crisis de Fagor Electrodomésticos.* Mondragon University.

Ostrom, E. (1990). *Governing the commons: The evolution of institutions for collective action.* Cambridge University Press.

P2P Foundation. (n.d.). *Value flows.* https://wiki.
p2pfoundation.net/Value_Flows

Palmieri, M., & Cooper, C. (2021). *Building legacies:
Retaining jobs and creating wealth through worker
ownership.* Ohio Employee Ownership Center. https://
uploads-ssl.webflow.com/5cdc97dbfcbd7455a5788315/
61804c206657fc5697fd04fc_Building%20Legacies%20_
Report%20(fn)(new).pdf

Parker, M., Cheney, G., Fournier, V., & Land, C. (Eds.).
(2014). *The companion to alternative organization.*
Routledge.

Parker, K., & Horowitz, J. M. (2022, March 9). *Majority of
workers who quit a job in 2021 cite low pay, no opportunities
for advancement, feeling disrespected.* Pew Research Center.
https://www.pewresearch.org/fact-tank/2022/03/09/majority-
of-workers-who-quit-a-job-in-2021-cite-low-pay-no-
opportunities-for-advancement-feeling-disrespected/

Parker, M., & Slaughter, J. (1988). *Choosing sides: Unions
and the team concept.* South End Press.

Park, R., Kruse, D., & Sesil, J. (2004). Does employee
ownership enhance firm survival? In V. Perotin & A.
Robinson (Eds.), *Employee participation, firm performance
and survival (Advances in the economic analysis of
participatory and labor-managed firms, volume 8)* (pp. 3–33).
Emerald Publishing Limited.

Pateman, C. (1970). *Participation and democratic theory.*
Cambridge University Press.

Paterson, A. (2010). A buzz between rural cooperation and
the online swarm. *Affinities: A Journal of Radical Theory,
Culture, and Action, 4*(1), 83–109.

Patmore, G., & Balknave, N. (2018). *A global history of cooperative business*. Routledge.

Pencavel, J. (2013). *The economics of worker cooperatives*. Elgar Research Collection.

Peredo, A. M., McLean, M., & Tremblay, C. (2019). Indigenous social innovation: What is distinctive? And a research agenda. In G. George, T. Baker, P. Tracey, & H. Joshi (Eds.), *Handbook of inclusive innovation: The role of organizations, markets and communities in social innovation* (pp. 107–128). Edward Elgar.

Pérez, L. M. (2021). On her shoulders: Unpacking domestic work, neo-kinship and social authoritarianism in Peru. *Gender, Place & Culture*, 28(1), 1–21. https://doi.org/10. 1080/0966369X.2019.1708273

Perigo, B. (2022, February 14). Inside Facebook's African sweatshop. *Time*. https://time.com/6147458/facebook-africa-content-moderation-employee-treatment/

Permaculture Research Institute. (2022). What is permaculture? https://www.permaculturenews.org/what-is-permaculture/

Pérotin, V. (2004). Early cooperative survival: The liability of adolescence. In D. Jones, V. Pérotin, & A. Robinson (Eds.), *Employee participation, firm performance and survival (Advances in the economic analysis of participatory and labor-managed firms, volume 8)* (pp. 67–86). Emerald Publishing Limited.

Pérotin, V. (2014). Worker cooperatives: Good, sustainable jobs in the community. *Journal of Entrepreneurial and Organizational Diversity*, 2(2), 34–47. https://papers.ssrn.com/sol3/papers.cfm?abstract_id=2437929

Pérotin, V. (2016). What do we really know about workers' co-operatives? In A. Webster, L. Shaw, & R. Vorberg-Rugh (Eds.), *Mainstreaming cooperation: An alternative for the twenty-first century?* (pp. 239–260). Manchester University Press.

Peters, G. P., Minx, J. C., Weber, C. L., & Edenhofer, O. (2011). Growth in emission transfers via international trade from 1990 to 2008. *Proceedings of the National Academy of Sciences*, *108*(21), 8903–8908. https://doi.org/10.1073/pnas.1006388108

Phills, J. A., Deiglmeier, K., & Miller, D. T. (2008). Rediscovering social innovation. *Stanford Social Innovation Review*, *6*(4), 34–43. https://ssir.org/articles/entry/rediscovering_social_innovation

Pieck, E., Vicente, M., & Yomol A'tel, C. de. (2019). *Voces de Yomol A'tel una experiencia de economía social y solidaria*. Universidad Ibero Americana.

Piketty, T., & Saez, E. (2003). Income inequality in the United States, 1913–1998. *Quarterly Journal of Economics*, *118*(1), 1–41. https://doi.org/10.1162/00335530360535135

Polanyi, K. (1944). *The great transformation*. Beacon Press.

Poole, M. S., & Van de Ven, A. (2021). *The handbook of organizational change and innovation*. Oxford University Press.

Potter, B. (1893). *The co-operative movement in Great Britain* (2nd ed.). Swann Sonnenschein & Co.

Poydock, M., Mangundayao, I., McNicholas, C., & Schmitt, J. (2022, February 23). *Data show major strike activity increased in 2021 but remains below pre-pandemic levels: Many worker actions were not captured in the data*. Economic

Policy Institute. https://www.epi.org/publication/2021-work-stoppages/

Preston City Council. (n.d.). *What is the Preston Model?* https://www.preston.gov.uk/article/1339/What-is-Preston-Model

Putnam, R. D. (2000). *Bowling alone: The collapse and revival of American community.* Simon & Schuster.

Pyles, L. (2013). *Progressive community organizing: Reflective practice in a globalizing world.* Taylor & Francis.

Quammen, D. (2013). *Spillover.* Norton.

Rancière, J. (1991). *The ignorant schoolmaster: Five lessons in intellectual emancipation* [K. Ross, Trans.]. Stanford University Press.

Rancière, J. (2006). *Hatred of democracy.* Verso.

Ranis, P. (2016). *Cooperatives confront capitalism: Challenging the neoliberal economy.* Zed Books.

Raupp, J. (2014). The concept of stakeholders and its relevance for corporate social responsibility communication. In O. Ihlen, J. Bartlett, & S. May (Eds.), *The handbook of communication and corporate social responsibility* (pp. 276–294). Wiley.

Raworth, K. (2017). *Doughnut economics: Seven ways to think like a 21st-century economist.* Chelsea Green Publishing.

Razeto, L. (2017). *Empresas cooperativas y economía de mercado.* Universitas Nueva Civilización.

Razeto, L. (2019). *Solidarity economy roads.* Grassroots Economic Organizing. https://geo.coop/story/solidarity-economy-roads-chapter-1

Razeto, L. (2020). *How to create a solidarity enterprise.* Grassroots Economic Organizing. https://geo.coop/articles/how-create-solidarity-enterprise

Reuten, G. (2021). The employment performance of the Mondragon worker cooperatives 1983–2019. (Euricse Working Papers No. 118). European Research Institute on Cooperative and Social Enterprises. http://doi.org/10.2139/ssrn.3992304

Rhodes, R. (2012). *Empire and cooperation: How the British Empire used cooperatives in its development strategies 1900–1970* (2nd ed.). Birlinn Ltd.

Ridley-Duff, R. (2015). *The case for fair shares.* FairShares Association.

Ridley-Duff, R. (2021). New co-operativism as social innovation: Progress or regress? *Journal of Co-operative Studies, 53*(3), 5–24. http://shura.shu.ac.uk/28595/

Robinson, K. S. (2012). *2312.* Orbit Books.

Rockoff, J. D. (2015, December 17). Martin Shkreli: From biotech entrepreneur to accused criminal. *Wall Street Journal.* https://www.wsj.com/articles/martin-shkreli-from-biotech-entrepreneur-to-accused-criminal-1450389335

Rodney, W. (2011). *How Europe underdeveloped Africa.* Black Classic Press.

Roediger, D. (1988). Labor in white skin: Race and working class history. In D. Roediger (Ed.), *Towards the abolition of whiteness: Essays on race, politics, and working class history* (pp. 287–308). Verso Books.

Roper, J., & Cheney, G. (2005). The meanings of social entrepreneurship today. *Corporate Governance International*

Journal of Business in Society, 5(3), 95–104. http://doi.org/10. 1108/14720700510604733

Rossiter, N. (2006). *Organized networks: Media theory, creative labour, and new institutions.* NAi Publishers.

Rothschild, J., & Whitt, J. A. (1986). *The cooperative workplace: Potential and dilemmas of organizational democracy and participation.* Cambridge University Press.

Rousell, D., Cutter-Mackenzie, A., & Foster, J. (2017). Children of an earth to come: Speculative fiction, geophilosophy and climate change education research. *Educational Studies, 53*(6), 654–669. https://doi.org/10.1080/ 00131946.2017.1369086

Russell, V. (2020). Keeping warm cookies: Cultural discourses of fun talk in public participation. *Journal of Civil Society, 16*(3), 216–233. https://doi.org/10.1080/17448689.2020. 178824

Salgado, S. (1993). *Workers: An archaeology of the industrial age.* Phaidon.

Salgado, S. (2000). *Migrations: Humanity in transition.* Aperture.

Sampaio, C. A. C., Fernandes, V., Azkarraga, J., & Altuna, L. (2012). Revisitando a experiência de cooperativismo de Mondragón a partir da perspectiva da ecossocioeconomia. *Desenvolvimento e Meio Ambiente, 25*(1), 153–165. http:// dx.doi.org/10.5380/dma.v25i0.25983

Santiago, J. (2021). *Political solidarity economy.* Gatekeeper Press.

Santos-Larrazabal, J., & Basterretxea, I. (2021). Intercooperation, flexicurity and their impact on workers: The case of Fagor Electrodomésticos. *Annals of Public and*

Cooperative Economics, 93(3), 1–29. https://doi.org/10.1111/apce.12329

Sayer, D. (1990). *Capitalism and modernity: An excursus on Marx and Weber*. Routledge.

Saz-Gil, I., Bretos, I., & Díaz-Foncea, M. (2021). Cooperatives and social capital: A narrative literature review and directions for future research. *Sustainability*, *13*(2), 534–552. https://doi.org/10.3390/su13020534

Scanlan, M. K. (2021). *Prosperity in the fossil-free economy: Cooperatives and the design of sustainable businesses*. Yale University Press.

Schneider, N. (2018). *Everything for everyone: The radical tradition that is shaping the next economy*. Nation Books.

Schneider, N., & Scholz, T. (2017). *Ours to hack and to own: The rise of platform cooperativism, a new vision for the future of work and a fairer Internet*. OR Books.

Schoeniger, G. G., & Taulbert, C. L. (2010). *Who owns the ice house? Eight life lessons from an unlikely entrepreneur*. Eli Press.

Schoening, J. (2010). The rise and fall of Burley Design Cooperative. *Oregon Historical Quarterly*, *111*(3), 312–341.

Schuman, M. H. (2020, April 2). Comparative resilience: 8 principles for Post-COVID reconstruction. Commentary on Community Economics. https://michaelhshuman.com/comparative-resilience-8-principles-for-post-covid-reconstruction/

Schumpeter, J. (2008). *Capitalism, socialism, and democracy*. Harper Perennial Modern Classics.

Scott, S. M. (2021). *Languages of economic crises*. Routledge.

Senge, P. (2006). *The fifth discipline: The art and practice of the learning organization.* Random House.

Sennett, R. (2012). *Together: The rituals, pleasures and politics of cooperation.* Yale University Press.

Sethi, S. P. (1977). *Advocacy advertising and large corporations.* Lexington Books.

Shaikh, A. (2016). *Capitalism: Competition, conflict, crises.* Oxford University Press.

Shaviro, S. (2014). *The universe of things: On speculative realism.* University of Minnesota Press.

Shell Oil. (2019). *Nature based solutions.* https://reports.shell.com/sustainability-report/2019/special-reports/nature-based-solutions.html

Shipper, F., Manz, C., Manz, K., & Harri, B. (2013). Collaboration that goes beyond co-operation: It's not just "if" but "how" sharing occurs that makes the difference. *Organizational Dynamics, 42*(2), 100–109. http://doi.org/10.1016/j.orgdyn.2013.03.003

Shor, I. (1987). *Critical teaching and everyday life.* University of Chicago Press.

Silverman, J. (2021, July 9). The billionaire space race is a tragically wasteful ego contest. *The New Republic.* https://newrepublic.com/article/162928/richard-branson-jeff-bezos-space-blue-origin

Sitrin, M. (2012). *Everyday revolutions: Horizontalism and autonomy in Argentina.* Bloomsbury Publishing.

Sitrin, M., & Sembrar, C. (2020). *Pandemic solidarity: Mutual aid during the Covid-19 crisis.* Pluto Press.

Slaughter, J. (2013, April 4). Can worker-owners make a big factory run? Counterpunch. https://www.counterpunch.org/2013/04/04/can-worker-owners-make-a-big-factory-run/.

Smart, B. (2010). *Consumer society: Critical issues and environmental consequences.* Sage.

Smit, S., Hirt, M., Greenberg, E., Lund, S., & Buehler, K. (2021, June 14). Looking beyond the pandemic: Could the world economy gain more than it lost to COVID-19? McKinsey & Company. https://www.mckinsey.com/business-functions/strategy-and-corporate-finance/our-insights/looking-beyond-the-pandemic-could-the-world-economy-gain-more-than-it-lost-to-covid-19

Smith, S. C., & Rothbaum, J. (2014). Co-operatives in a global economy: Key issues, recent trends and potential for development. In S. Novkovic & T. Webb (Eds.), *Co-operatives in a post-growth era* (pp. 221–241). Zed Books.

Sociocracy for All. (2021). Sociocracy for All governance agreement. https://www.sociocracyforall.org/sociocracy-for-all-governance-agreement/

Solidarity NYC. (2013). *Growing a resilient city: Possibilities for collaboration in NYC's solidarity economy.* http://solidaritynyc.org/wp-content/uploads/2013/02/Growing-A-Resilient-City-SolidarityNYC-Report.pdf

Solnit, R. (2009). *A paradise built in hell: The extraordinary communities that arise in disaster.* Penguin.

Spade, D. (2020). *Mutual aid: Building solidarity during this crisis (and the next).* Verso Books.

Spear, R. (2009). Social entrepreneurship in co-operatives. In I. McPherson & E. McLauglin-Jenkins (Eds.), *Integrating diversities with a complex heritage: Essays in the field of co-operative studies*. New Rochdale Press.

Spear, R. (2019). Collective social entrepreneurship. In A. de Bruin & S. Teasdale (Eds.), *A research agenda for social entrepreneurship* (pp. 82–93). Edward Elgar. https://doi.org/ 10.4337/9781788972321.00012

Spector, P. E. (2002). Employee control and occupational stress. *Current Directions in Psychological Science, 11*(4), 133–136. https://doi.org/10.1111/1467-8721.00185

Srnicek, N. (2016). *Platform capitalism*. Wiley.

Standing, G. (2018, October 25). The precariat: Today's transformative class? *Resilience*. https://www.resilience.org/ stories/2018-10-25/the-precariat-todays-transformative-class/

Steinbeck, J. (1966). *America and Americans*. Viking.

Stohl, C. (1995). *Organizational communication: Connectedness in action*. Sage.

Stohl, C., & Cheney, G. (2001). Participatory processes/ paradoxical practices: Communication and the dilemmas of organizational democracy. *Management Communication Quarterly, 14*, 349–407.

Stuchtey, M., Enkvist, P.-A., & Zumwinkel, K. (2016). *A good disruption: Redefining growth in the twenty-first century*. Bloomsbury Press.

Sustainable Economies Law Center. (2015, June 2). *Worker self-directed nonprofits: Workplace democracy in nonprofit organizations* [Webinar]. YouTube. https://youtu.be/ uU1w9uXGGLY

Sustainable Solutions Group. (2014). *A cooperative solution to climate change*. International Cooperative Alliance.

Taalbi, J. (2019). Origins and pathways of innovation in the third industrial revolution. *Industrial and Corporate Change*, *28*(5), 1125–1148. https://doi.org/10.1093/icc/dty053

Taylor, A. (2019). *Democracy may not exist, but we'll miss it when it's gone.* Metropolitan Books.

Terkel, S. (1974). *Working: People talk about what they do all day and how they feel about what they do.* The New Press.

TESA Collective. (2017). *Co-opoly: The game of cooperatives* [Board game].

Thompson, D. (2012). *Weavers of dreams.* Twin Pines Press.

Thunberg, G. (2021, October 21). There are no real climate leaders yet – Who will step up at Cop26? *The Guardian.* https://www.theguardian.com/commentisfree/2021/oct/21/climate-leaders-cop26-uk-climate-crisis-glasgow

Tompkins, P. K. (1962). *An analysis of communication between selected units of a national labor union* [Doctoral dissertation]. Purdue University.

Tönnies, F. (1957). *Community and society.* Dover. (Original work published 1887).

Trentmann, F. (2016). *Empire of things: How we became a world of consumers, from the fifteenth century to the twenty-first.* Harper Collins.

Tsing, A. (2015). *The mushroom at the end of the world: On the possibility of life in capitalist ruins.* Princeton University Press.

Unicorn Grocery. (n.d.). *Co-op values.* https://www.unicorn-grocery.coop/our-co-op/our-values/

University of Wisconsin Center for Cooperatives. (2021). *Latinx cooperative research.* https://uwcc.wisc.edu/research/latinx-cooperative-research/

Vargas, L., & Bustillos, G. (1988). *Técnicas participativas para la educación popular*. Alforja.

Vázquez, A. (2001). Falacias de la participación, *La empresa participativa: una visión sobre el papel de las personas en las organizaciones*. Cluster del Conocimiento.

Velasquez, B. (2021, November 17–18). Address to the Rocky Mountain Farmers Union Conference, Denver, Colorado, United States.

Verbos, A. K., Henry, E., & Peredo, A. M. (2017). *Indigenous aspirations and rights: The case for responsible business management*. Routledge.

Vieta, M. (2010). The new cooperativism. *Affinities: A Journal of Radical Theory, Culture, and Action, 4*(1), 1–11.

Vieta, M. (2014). Learning in struggle: Argentina's new worker cooperatives as transformative learning organizations. *Relations Industrielles/Industrial Relations, 69*(1), 186–218. https://doi.org/10.7202/1024212ar

Vieta, M. (2016). Autogestión: Prefiguring the "new cooperativism" and "the labour commons". In C. DuRand (Ed.), *Moving beyond capitalism* (pp. 55–63). Routledge.

Vieta, M. (2018). The new cooperativism in Latin America: Implications for Cuba. In S. Novkovic & H. Veltmeyer (Eds.), *Cooperativism and local development in Cuba: An agenda for democratic social change* (pp. 51–81). Brill Academic Publishers.

Vieta, M. (2019). Recuperating and (re)learning the language of autogestión in Argentina's empresas recuperadas worker cooperatives. *Journal of Cultural Economy, 12*(5), 401–422. https://doi.org/10.1080/17530350.2018.1544164

Vieta, M. (2020). *Workers' self-management in Argentina: Contesting neo-liberalism by occupying companies, creating cooperatives, and recuperating autogestión.* Brill Academic Publishers and Haymarket Books.

Vieta, M., Depedri, S., & Carrano, A. (2017). *The Italian road to recuperating enterprises and the legge marcora framework: Italy's worker buyouts in times of crisis.* European Research Institute on Cooperative and Social Enterprises. https://doi.org/10.13140/rg.2.2.34448.81923

Vieta, M., & Duguid, F. (2020, April 20). Canada's co-operatives: Helping communities during and after the coronavirus. *The Conversation Canada.*

Vieta, M., & Lionais, D. (2022). The new cooperativism, the commons, and the post capitalist imaginary. *Journal of Co-operative Studies.* (Forthcoming).

Vieta, M., Quarter, J., Spear, R., & Moskovskaya, A. (2016). Participation in worker co-operatives. In D. Horton Smith, R. A. Stebbins, & J. Grotz (Eds.), *Palgrave handbook of volunteering, civic participation, and nonprofit associations* (pp. 436–453). Palgrave Macmillan.

Visser, W., & Tolhurst, N. (2017). *The world guide to CSR: A country-by-country analysis of corporate sustainability and responsibility.* Routledge.

Waring, M. (1990). *If women counted. A new feminist economics.* Harper Collins.

Watson, M. (2014). Freedom schools then and now: A transformative approach to learning. *Journal for Critical Education Policy Studies, 14*(1), 170–190.

Weaver, J. (2010). *Educating the posthuman.* Sense Publishing.

Webb, T., & Cheney, G. (2014). Worker-owned-and-governed cooperatives and the wider cooperative movement: Challenges and opportunities within and beyond the global economic crisis. In M. Parker, G. Cheney, V. Fournier, & C. Land (Eds.), *The Routledge companion to alternative organization* (pp. 64–88). Routledge.

Weber, M. (1978). *Economy and society: An outline of interpretive sociology, two vols* (G. Roth & C. Wittich, Trans.). University of California Press. (Original work published 1922).

West, E., & Gordon Nembhard, J. (2020). *Latinx co-op power in the US*. University of Wisconsin Center for Cooperatives. https://resources.uwcc.wisc.edu/Research/Latinx_Report_092020.pdf

Whitman, J. (2011). *The worker cooperative life cycle.* Babson-Equal Exchange Cooperative Curriculum.

Whyte, W. F., & Whyte, K. K. (1991). *Making Mondragon: The growth and dynamics of the worker cooperative complex* (2nd ed.). Cornell University Press.

Williams, R. (1976). Developments in the sociology of culture. *Sociology, 10*(3), 497–506. https://doi.org/10.1177/003803857601000306

Williams, R. (1985). *Keywords, A vocabulary of culture and society* (revised ed.). Oxford University Press.

Williams, T. T. (2004). *The open space of democracy.* Wipf & Stock.

Williams, R. C. (2007). *The cooperative movement: Globalization from below.* Ashgate.

Witherell, R., Cooper, C., & Peck, M. (2012). *Sustainable jobs, sustainable communities: The union co-op model.* United Steelworkers Union.

Wolff, R. (2021). The next system: Workers direct themselves. In J. G. Speth & K. Courrier (Eds.), *The new system reader: Alternatives to a failed economy* (pp. 202–205). Routledge.

Woodcock, J., & Graham, M. (2019). *The gig economy: A critical introduction*. Polity.

Worcester Youth Co-ops. (n.d.). *Our origin*. https://worcesteryouthcoops.org/about/our-beginnings/

Wright, C. (2014). *Worker cooperatives and revolution: History and possibilities in the United States*. BookLocker.

Wynne, J. T. (2016). Strong people don't need strong leaders. In A. H. Normore & J. S. Brooks (Eds.), *The dark side of leadership: Identifying and overcoming unethical practice in organizations (Advances in educational administration, Vol. 26)* (pp. 95–112). Emerald Publishing Limited. https://doi.org/10.1108/S1479-366020160000026006

Yang, S., Keller, F. B., & Zheng, L. (2017). *Social network analysis: Methods and examples*. Sage.

Zamagni, S. (2014). Choices, incentives and co-operative organization. In S. Novkovic & T. Webb (Eds.), *Co-operatives in a post-growth era: Creating co-operative economics* (pp. 157–175). Zed Books.

Zamagni, S., & Zamagni, V. (2010). *Cooperative enterprise: Facing the challenge of globalization*. Edward Elgar.

Zemos98. (2021). *Commonspoly* [Board game].

Zevi, A., Zanotti, A., Soulage, F., & Zelaia, A. (2011). *Beyond the crisis: Cooperatives, work, finance. Generating wealth for the long term*. CECOP Publications.

Zorn, T. E., Jr., Christensen, L. T., & Cheney, G. (1999). *Do we really want constant change?* Berrett-Koehler.

Zuboff, S. (2019). *The age of surveillance capitalism: The fight for a human future at the new frontier of power*. Profile Books.

INDEX

255